Risk Terrain Modeling Compendium

MW01537266

Edited By
Joel M. Caplan, Ph.D.
Leslie W. Kennedy, Ph.D.

RUTGERS
Center on Public Security

*Wojciech & John —
To our partners in crime—
mapping.*

Joel Caplan

Newark
New Jersey
USA

This entire book is available to anyone for free download at www.riskterrainmodeling.com

Suggested Citation:
Caplan, J. M. & Kennedy, L. W. (Eds.) 2011. *Risk Terrain Modeling Compendium*. Newark, NJ: Rutgers Center on Public Security.

Produced by Rutgers Center on Public Security:
Based at the Rutgers University School of Criminal Justice, the Rutgers Center on Public Security (RCPS) offers a multidisciplinary approach to the academic study and practical application of ways in which democratic societies can effectively address crime, terrorism and other threats to public security. This involves the prevention of, protection from and response to natural or human-made events that could endanger the safety or security of people or property in a given area. RCPS engages in innovative data analysis and information dissemination, including the use of GIS, for strategic decision-making and tactical action. Visit RCPS online for current research projects, reports and publications: www.rutgerscps.org

Acknowledgements

The opinions expressed in each chapter of this document are the views of the chapter's author(s) and do not necessarily reflect the views and opinions of the editors, the authors of other chapters, the Rutgers Center on Public Security, Rutgers University, or the School of Criminal Justice.

All U.S. Census Bureau materials, regardless of the media, are entirely in the public domain. There are no user fees, site licenses or any special agreements, etc., for the public or private use, and/or reuse of any census title. As a tax funded product, it is all in the public record.

Companies, products or websites mentioned herein are trademarks, registered trademarks, or service marks of their respective owners and are the property of their respective owners.

Table of Contents::

Preface::

By Joel M. Caplan and Leslie W. Kennedy | Rutgers University

*R*isk terrain modeling (RTM) is an approach to risk assessment in which separate map layers representing the influence and intensity of a crime risk factor at every place throughout a geography is created in a geographic information system (GIS). Then all map layers are combined to produce a composite "risk terrain" map with values that account for all risk factors at every place throughout the geography. RTM builds upon principles of hotspot mapping, environmental criminology, and problem-oriented policing to produce maps that show where conditions are ideal or conducive for crimes to occur in the future given the existing environmental contexts. It offers a new and statistically valid way to articulate and communicate crime-prone areas at the micro-level according to the spatial influence of criminogenic features.

The *Risk Terrain Modeling (RTM) Manual* (free eBook at www.riskterrainmodeling.com) presented the theoretical framework and complete steps of RTM, as summarized below. The *Risk Terrain Modeling Compendium* presents concepts and techniques for improving and applying risk terrain models that were not already discussed at length in the *RTM Manual*. Part 1 offers an overview of risk terrain modeling, explains the origin of its development, and discusses the important concept of "operationalizing spatial influence". Part 2 is a series of literature reviews with risk factors that are known to be related to a variety of crime types. The literature reviews follow a standard format: They begin with an operational definition of the crime under study, continue with an annotated list of empirically-supported risk factors for crime, and then discuss the settings and times in which these crimes are most likely to occur. This information is valuable for risk terrain modeling to help set the context in which one would expect to see these crimes occur, to determine analytical extents (e.g. local or global), to define data needs, and to produce risk map layers accordingly. Part 3 demonstrates how RTM can be applied to different crime types and settings, and how it can be used for a variety of practical endeavors. Part 4 concludes the book with thought pieces about RTM's future potential applications to research, technology, and activities related to public safety and security.

Steps of Risk Terrain Modeling

1. Select an outcome event of particular interest
2. Choose a study area
3. Choose a time period
4. Obtain base maps of your study area
5. Identify aggravating and mitigating factors related to the outcome event
6. Select particular factors to include in the RTM
7. Operationalize the spatial influence of factors to risk map layers
8. Weight risk map layers relative to one another
9. Combine risk map layers to form a composite map
10. Finalize the risk terrain map to communicate meaningful and actionable information

Risk Terrain Modeling Compendium | 2011 | Caplan and Kennedy

Part 1

Cartographic Models of Environmental Contexts

Presents an overview of risk terrain modeling and an explanation of its origin. Also includes a detailed discussion of "spatial influence", a key concept of RTM.

Contributing Authors:
Caplan, J. M.
Kennedy, L. W.

Chapter 1::
Risk Terrain Modeling Overview

By Joel M. Caplan and Leslie W. Kennedy | Rutgers University

With the growing utilization of intelligence-led operations in the public safety and security community, risk assessments for crime and other hazards are especially important for tactical actions, resource allocations, and short- and long-term planning. Risk terrain modeling (RTM) is an approach to spatial risk assessment that utilizes a geographic information system (GIS) to attribute qualities of the real world to places on a digitized map. It operationalizes the spatial influence of crime factors to common geographic units, then combines separate map layers together to produce risk terrain maps showing the compounded presence, absence, or intensity of all factors at every location throughout the landscape. Risk terrain maps show places where conditions are conducive for certain events to occur in the future based on the environmental context for criminogenesis. RTM builds upon underlying principles of hotspot mapping, environmental criminology, and problem-oriented policing, and offers a statistically valid way to articulate and communicate criminogenic and vulnerable areas at the micro-level. It "paints a picture" of place-based environmental context.

Risk terrain modeling comprises three concepts. <u>Risk</u> suggests the likelihood of an event occurring given what is known about the correlates of that event, and it can be quantified with positive, negative, low or high ordinal values. The measures are ordinal because we do not necessarily know that a risk value of 10 is twice as risky as a value of 5, but we know it is higher. Using risk as a metric, it is possible to model how risk evolves spatially and temporally, accounting for the different stages of a crime event[1]. A <u>terrain</u> is a map of the study area that represent a continuous surface of places where values of risk exist. Raster maps are often used to represent terrains in RTM because of their ability to model continuous surfaces. <u>Modeling</u> broadly refers to the abstraction of the real world at certain places. Specifically within the context of RTM, modeling refers to the process of attributing qualities of the real world to micro-level places within a terrain, and combining multiple terrains together to produce a single composite map where the newly derived value of each place represents the compounded criminogenic risk of that place.

Crime explanations can be accounted for in a risk terrain model by different factors that tie different components of risk together to explain individual, group, and institutional influences and impacts on crime events. Clustering of illegal activity in particular areas is explained in a risk terrain model by the unique combination of criminogenic factors that make these areas opportune locations for crime. This occurs where the potential for, or risk of, crime comes as a result of all the attributes found at these places. Attributes of places themselves do not create crime. They simply point to locations where, if the conditions are right, the risk of crime or victimization will be high. For example, the attributes of open space, presence of children, and proximity to schools may indicate a playground. These attributes combined can be used to anticipate the types of behavior that would be expected in a playground—reducing the uncertainty that forecasts about what would transpire there are wrong. In this way, RTM uses the spatial influence of environmental features as a means of assigning likelihood (or risk) that certain events will happen at particular places. Outcomes may be benign (e.g. children playing) or they may take on a more sinister character where a combination of certain types of factors related to crime creates a context in which the risk of crime events can occur.

Spatial influence refers to the way in which crime correlates, as features of a landscape, affect places throughout the landscape. For instance, empirical knowledge that bars correlate with locations of shootings can be mapped in several ways to show more or less crime-prone places, such as places with bars, places within certain distances from bars, or places with higher concentrations of bars. Rather than just a feature's presence, its influence on space is important because context affects criminal behavior. A key component of risk terrain modeling is to operationalize the spatial influence of crime factors, as discussed in detail in Chapter 3. The objective in doing this is to create separate maps of the study area, each representing the criminogenic influence of a risk factor throughout the landscape. At least one raster map is created for each risk factor to represent the intensity of its criminogenic influence at every micro-level place throughout the study area.

Cells within a raster map are usually the unit of analysis for RTM. Figure 1-1 presents a risk terrain map for shootings in Irvington, NJ. It was produced according to the steps outlined in the *Risk Terrain Modeling Manual* (available at www.riskterrainmodeling.com) and includes four risk factors that previous empirical research found to be correlated with shooting incidents: Gang member residences, bus stops, schools, and facilities of bars, clubs, fast food restaurants, and liquor stores. Data on gang members was comprised of addresses of all known gang members' residences[2], and was operationalized as a density map because the spatial influence of these features was understood as "areas with greater concentrations of gang members residing will increase the risk of those places having shootings." Addresses of all public bus stops were obtained from NJ Transit (New Jersey's public transportation corporation) and operationalized as a distance map up to 555 feet away because the spatial influence of these features was understood as "up to one and a half blocks away from bus stops--transportation resources that motivated offenders and targeted victims frequent and use regularly--are at greater risk for shootings because targeted victims are most vulnerable when they arrive at or leave these destinations"[3]. Addresses of all public and private school buildings were obtained from the NJ Department of Education through the New Jersey Geographic

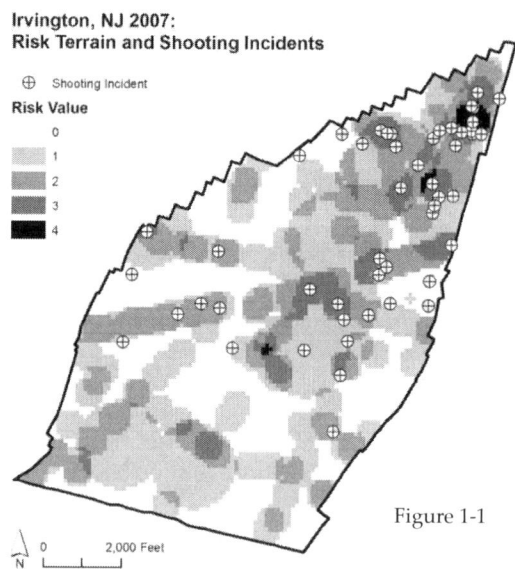

Irvington, NJ 2007:
Risk Terrain and Shooting Incidents

⊕ Shooting Incident

Risk Value
0
1
2
3
4

0   2,000 Feet

Figure 1-1

Information Network and operationalized as "distances up to three blocks (up to 1,110ft) are at the greatest risk for shootings"[4]. Bars, clubs, fast food restaurants, and liquor establishments were operationalized as "distances within 370ft (about 1 block) from any of these establishments are at the greatest risk for shootings.

Table 1-1: Logistic Regressions for Period 1 Risk Value on Period 2 Shooting

	B	S.E.	Wald	df	Sig.	Exp(B)	95% C.I. for Exp(B)	
							Lower	Upper
Risk Value	.888	.145	37.606	1	<.001	2.431	1.830	3.230
Nagelkerke R Square = .081								

The risk terrain model (Figure 1-1) of places in Irvington that share the locations and/or spatial influences of all aforementioned shooting risk factors has high predictive validity. Logistic regression results presented in Table 1-1 suggest that for every increased unit of risk, the likelihood of a shooting more than doubles (Exp(B) = 2.43, p< 0.01). Stated another way, the likelihood of a shooting happening at particular 100ftx100ft places in Irvington during 2007 increases by 143% as each additional risk factor affects that place.

Looked at in a different way, as shown in Table 1-2, more than 42% of all shooting incidents occurred in the top 10% of the highest risk places during calendar year 2007 (Pearson Chi-Square=55.897; df=1; p<0.01). The highest risk places were designated as such with a first-tier sorting of the risk values of all cells (N=3,975) in descending order and then a second-tier sorting by random number to randomize the sorting of cells with the same risk values[5]. Then the first 398 cells were defined as "highest risk" and all other cells were designated as "not highest risk".

Table 1-2

Place Designated as Top 10% of Highest Risk? (N=3,975)	Any Shootings Present During 2007 (Yes %, n=47)
No	57.4%
Yes	42.6%
Pearson Chi-Square=55.897; df=1; p<0.01	

In sum, this risk terrain map produced with thoughtfully operationalized criminogenic features yielded a valid and reliable model of place-based criminogenic context that was empirically and theoretically grounded. The criminogenic features were selected according to findings from previous empirical research, and they were included in the model in a manner that accounted for their spatial influence at all nearby and faraway places throughout the environment. The resulting risk terrain map articulates environmental contexts of places that are most likely to attract, enable and/or generate criminal shooting incidents as a function of the combined spatial influences of criminogenic features within the study area. This means that the technique for operationalizing spatial influences of criminogenic features is very important, and can ultimately effect the validity and reliability of risk terrain maps. Chapter 3 is devoted to this topic and explains the three primary cartographic operationalization techniques in detail. First, though, Chapter 2 discusses the historical development of RTM in detail.

Chapter 2::
The Origin of Risk Terrain Modeling

By Joel M. Caplan and Leslie W. Kennedy | Rutgers University

This chapter explains the history of the risk terrain modeling method's development, which started while studying shootings in a high crime community: Irvington, NJ. In this inaugural work, we considered attributes that would address the risks that appear for victims, considering the presence of offenders and the actions of law enforcement. We also addressed the physical attributes of the community as it related to creating context for crime. This example includes, as well, an important aspect in the consideration of crime emergence; that is, the temporal changes that take place in an environment as a result of the interactions that are documented in the risk terrain maps at different time periods.

The First Study Area

Irvington is a township in New Jersey that has been a particular concern of local and state law enforcement over the last six years. Murder rates for 2007 were 38.7 compared to a national average for similar size cities across the country of 4.9 per 100,000 (UCR, 2007). The township is relatively small, sandwiched between a slightly bigger suburban township to the north and the larger city of Newark to the south. The community had drawn a considerable amount of attention for extreme violence as it was the location of a large number of shootings and other violent crimes. This is partly due to the fact that it contains a large, vibrant drug market. In addition, it contains a large number of gang members living in the town. The combination of these factors and the growth of violence encouraged the State Police to set up a special task force to police in this area as a supplement to the smaller and overtaxed township police.

The task force consists of uniformed troopers who patrol targeted areas defined on the basis of where prior acts of violence occurred. A shooting response team investigates all shootings where a victim was actually injured by gunfire. The task force may act in a highly visible saturation capacity or in aggressive patrols focusing on the suppression of open air drug markets. The shooting response team conducts shooting investigations and works with the patrol troopers and undercover operatives by pointing them towards areas of potential violence, such as, gang-related retaliatory shootings. The task force is a unique organization within the state police agency as troopers and detectives work out of a station house in the center of the city and are assigned fulltime to this detail, often for a period of several years.

As a result of task force operations, there has been an increase in drug arrests and a reduction of shootings in this area. This reduction in violence was dramatic at the onset of the operation, but has since leveled off and remained fairly constant. In discussions with the authors, State Police executives were looking for more robust analysis of the data they were collecting about their operations and the crime in their patrol areas, specifically to increase their ability to use forecasting to direct police operations. In particular, they were interested in knowing where the next shootings would occur. At the onset, we were given four sets of data: Known gang residences: Drug arrests: Infrastructure; and Shootings. The project began with mapping individual layers, creating point maps, and looking for relationships among these data with other spatial information—such as census data.

Known gang residences were layered with drug arrest locations and sure enough, there appeared to be a spatial relationship. As shown in Figure 2-1, drug arrests (which can be considered a proxy measure of drug sales, or even police activity), cluster in areas where large numbers of gang members live. Shootings also appeared to occur in areas where gang members lived--as shown in Figure 2-2, and where certain business/retail infrastructure were located--as shown in Figure 2-3. Liquor stores, bars, strip clubs & fast food restaurants help to explain shooting locations in addition to highly concentrated gang and drug areas.

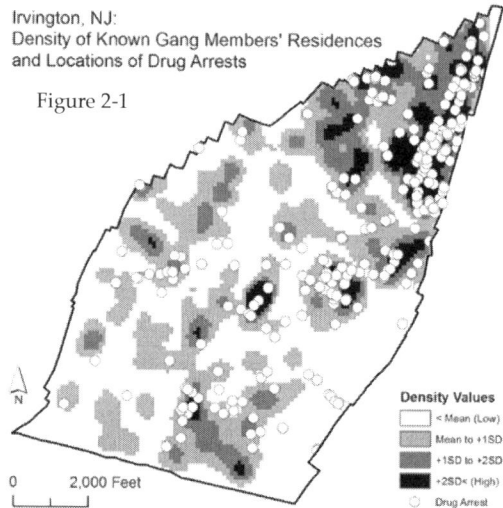

Irvington, NJ:
Density of Known Gang Members' Residences
and Locations of Drug Arrests

Figure 2-1

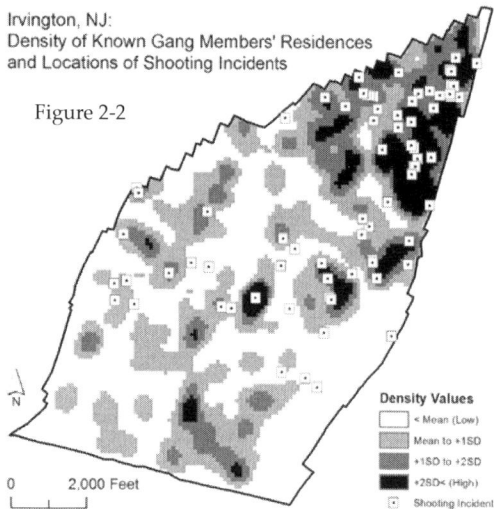

Irvington, NJ:
Density of Known Gang Members' Residences
and Locations of Shooting Incidents

Figure 2-2

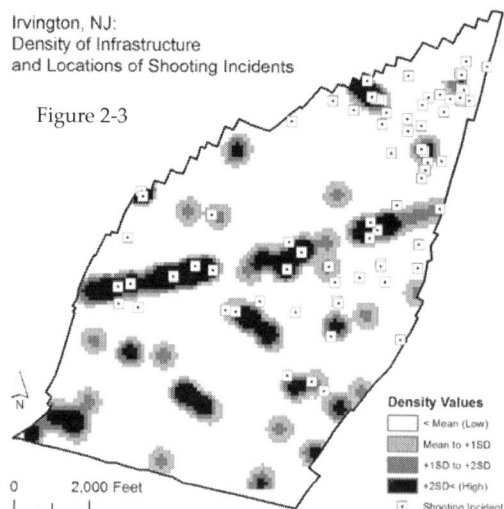

Irvington, NJ:
Density of Infrastructure
and Locations of Shooting Incidents

Figure 2-3

It was reasoned that if each individual factor was spatially related to shootings, then all factors together must be even more related. So a methodology was developed (i.e., what later became risk terrain modeling) to create a single composite map. Steps of risk terrain modeling (RTM) produce (composite) risk terrain maps that forecast areas with the greatest potential for shootings to occur in the future, not just because police statistics show that shootings occurred there yesterday, but because the social and environmental conditions are ripe for shootings to occur there tomorrow.

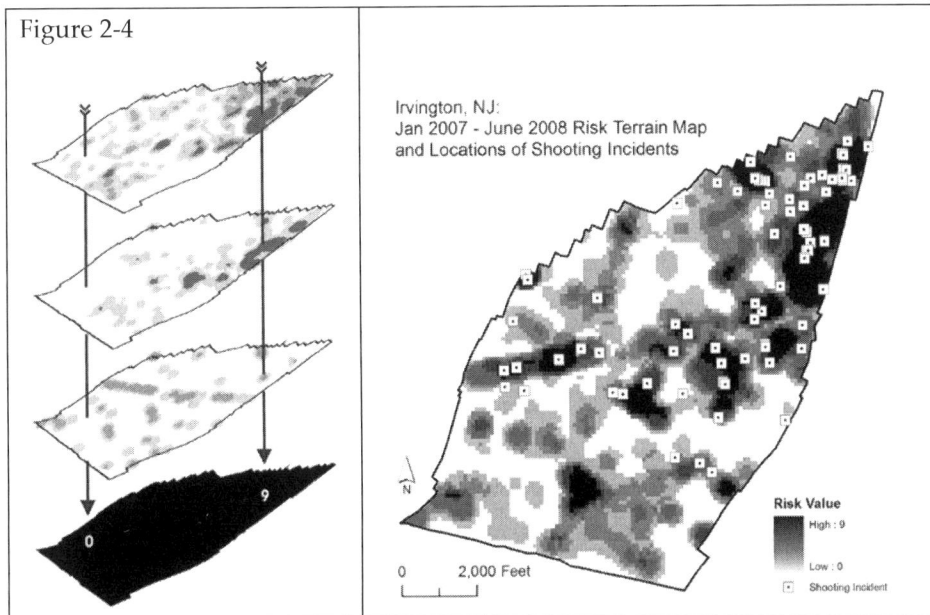

Figure 2-4

Irvington, NJ:
Jan 2007 - June 2008 Risk Terrain Map and Locations of Shooting Incidents

Risk Value
High : 9
Low : 0
Shooting Incident

0   2,000 Feet

As shown in Figure 2-4, the new composite "risk terrain" map closely matches locations of actual shootings over an 18 month period for which gang, drug and infrastructure data were used. This is intriguing since it suggests that certain qualities of space coincide with locations of shooting incidents. But it was not yet obviously more informative than knowing where past shootings were in order to forecast future shooting locations, that is, until time was incorporated into the risk terrain model.

When risk terrain maps were produced for separate six-month time periods, clusters of high risk apparent in earlier risk terrain maps appeared to forecast the locations of shootings during the subsequent time period. In Row 1 of Figure 2-5, notice how shooting incidents dispersed South, and then to the West—as "forecast" by the risk terrain maps from the previous time periods. Although this pattern is (visibly) slight, Row 2 in Figure 2-5 helps to explain why this movement was happening. Consistent with the operationalization of the "drug arrest" data within the risk terrain model, drug arrests--as a proxy for police activity, were expected to attract violence due to conflict over "new turf" that was created with the arrest of a drug seller. As part of the State Police Taskforce, drug arrests were targeted at different locations over time. As the map in Figure 2-5 at Row 2 Column A shows, police activity was strong and focused consistently in the Northeast over time. However, noticeably more arrests were made in the Southeast and then in the Southwest during the next two time periods--as highlighted by the arrows in the maps at Row 2 Columns B and C, respectively. This shift in police activity from the Northeast to the south and then to the west, roughly matches the movement of shootings, and is consistent with the periodic risk terrain maps. Given that drug activity was the most dynamic factor of these

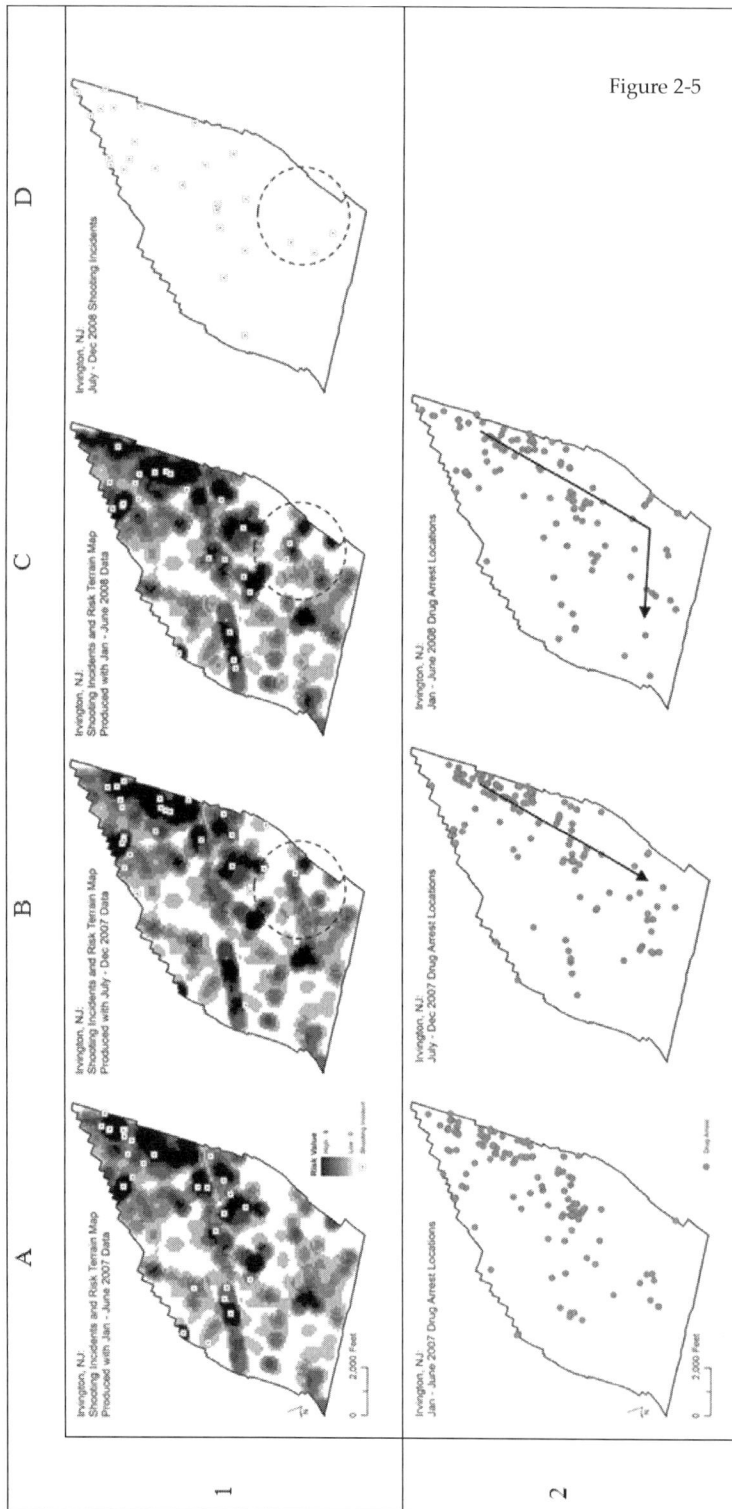

Figure 2-5

inaugural risk terrain maps, this risk terrain model served as an evaluation of the impact of police activities, while "controlling" for other environmental contexts (i.e. gang residences and infrastructure). It is also apparent from the maps in Row 1 of Figure 2-5 that shootings did not always occur in the future at places where they mostly occurred in the past--suggesting that a sole reliance on conventional hotspot mapping to predict future shooting locations would have been less than effective (this is a hypothesis derived from these maps that was subsequently tested and is discussed later in this chapter).

$\mathcal{F}$or this inaugural risk terrain model, data layers representing the qualities of space was determined rather simply by what the police had access to and that they maintain, validate, and update regularly to support internal crime analysis and police investigations. So, a density map was created from the points of gang members' residences to become one of the three risk map layers. The spatial influence of "gang members' residences" was operationalized as: "Areas with greater concentrations of gang members residing will increase the risk of those places having shootings." The spatial influence of "infrastructure" was operationalized as: "High concentrations of bars, strip clubs, bus stops, check cashing outlets, pawn shops, fast food restaurants, and liquor stores will increase the risk of those dense places having shootings." The spatial influence of "drug arrests" was operationalized as: "Areas with high concentrations of drug arrests will be at a greater risk for shootings because these arrests create new 'open turf' that other drug dealers fight over to control." So, a density map was created from the points of drug arrests to become the last of the three risk map layers. The specific parameters for each of the three density maps were a bandwidth of 1,000 feet and a cell size of 100 feet. A 1,000 foot bandwidth was selected because it seemed a reasonable sphere of influence for shooters[6]—the average block face is approximately 350 feet. 100x100 foot cells were the smallest area that our computers could process reasonably fast and, for the purposes of this risk terrain model, if a risk terrain map could assess the risk of shootings at small (but reasonable) geographic units (e.g. 2 inches would be unreasonable since a person cannot even fit in that space), it would provide the most utility for operational policing compared to larger, less specific, units of analysis.

So, what is happening to the Irvington environment that makes shootings likely to emerge in certain micro-level places? The environment changes, in this example, primarily because of police interventions that target certain areas for drug arrests at different times throughout the year. While infrastructure and known gang member residences may vary slightly bi-annually, drug arrests are the most dynamic feature of this risk terrain model. Therefore, shooting activity is likely moving in response to increased police presence in certain areas (see Chapter 23). Empirical tests of predictive validity found that these risk terrain maps accurately forecast future shooting locations. But the series of maps--and visible changes--alone communicate the profound impact that police interventions had on the places that were targeted. The six-month spatial lag inherent in this risk terrain model suggests that targeted police presence and a saturation of drug arrests in certain areas (particularly areas near high concentrations of bars, strip clubs, bus stops, check cashing outlets, pawn shops, fast food restaurants, liquor stores, and gang members' residences) will attract shootings during the subsequent six-month time period. Risk terrain modeling makes it clear that understanding the spatial-temporal interaction effects of certain qualities of space is key to assessing emergent criminogenic risks.

Criminological research has identified a variety of independent variables that have been found to correlate significantly with particular crime outcomes. Risk terrain modeling simultaneously applies all of these empirical findings to practice. The intent of RTM is to return to the principle that we can understand crime not just on the basis of knowing what occurred prior to the incident that we are interested in but also that we understand the social and physical contexts in which crime can occur. This approach is consistent with efforts over the years to examine crime in terms of spatial factors that precede, interact with, and follow the incident's emergence.

$\mathcal{T}$he identification of crime hotspots through mapping, and the targeting of police activity to these places, has been recognized in high-quality evaluation research as an effective crime-fighting technique. Despite the evident success of this technology in operational policing, there is often a disconnect between the conventional practice of density mapping and the demands by police agencies to be responsive to the dynamic nature and needs of the communities they serve. In the past, crime mapping has been restricted to fairly simple density maps based on the retrospective analysis of crime data[7]. This reactive approach makes analysts less attuned to the idea of crime risk or potential and it essentially assumes that crime will most likely always occur precisely where it did in the past—even if police intervene[8]. RTM builds upon underlying principles of hotspot mapping and near repeat analysis, but offers a new and statistically valid way to articulate and manage criminogenic areas.

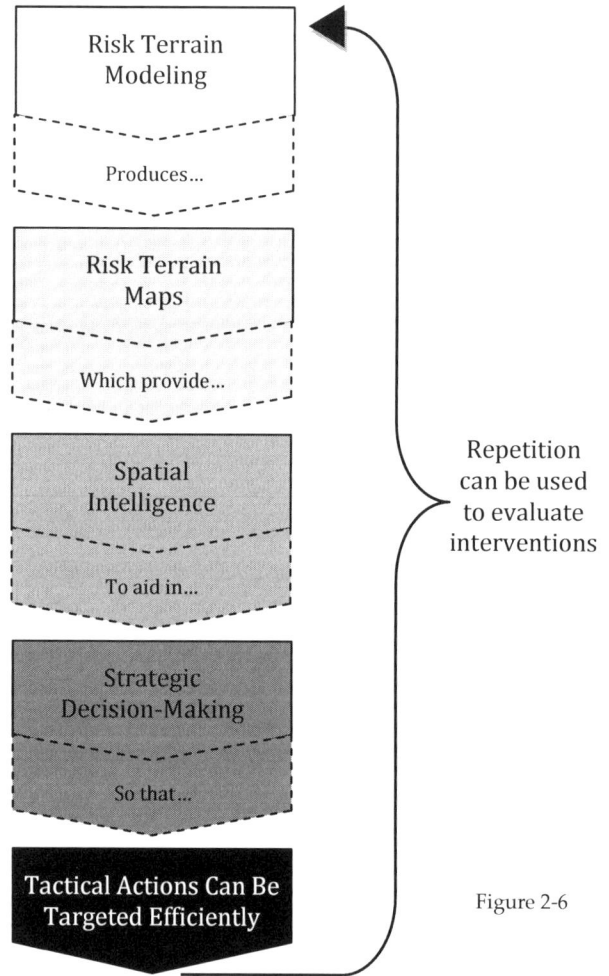

Risk Terrain
Modeling

Produces...

Risk Terrain
Maps

Which provide...

Spatial
Intelligence

To aid in...

Strategic
Decision-Making

So that...

**Tactical Actions Can Be
Targeted Efficiently**

Repetition
can be used
to evaluate
interventions

Figure 2-6

Chapter 3::
Operationalizing the Spatial Influence of Criminogenic Features

By Joel M. Caplan | Rutgers University

*I*magine you are an unfamiliar visitor to an American city. As you stand on the sidewalk, you call a local friend on the cell phone in order to meet; he asks where you are. There are no street signs nearby. As you walk to the street corner to figure out the specifics of your location, you nonchalantly describe the area as the "bar district" in order to break the silence over the phone and in the hopes that your friend knows where you are talking about. You are not in a bar and you may not even be directly in front of a bar. Why, then, would you describe this part of the city as the bar district? The simple answer, perhaps, is because you observed a high concentration of bars within the area and you define that quality of the environment to be a "bar district." From a criminological perspective, bars and other liquor establishments are known to correlate with robberies[9]. You might be at even greater risk of being robbed if you are within one block from a bar as opposed to farther away[10]. Therefore, it could be argued with empirical support that you are at greater risk of robbery where you stand talking on the phone compared to elsewhere in the city where there is a lower concentration of bars and you would not be near any of them. Risk is defined by Kennedy and Van Brunschot[11] as "a consideration of the probabilities of particular outcomes". In this example, your risk of robbery is not only a function of the criminogenic features (i.e., bars) themselves, but also the distribution of those features throughout the environment, your proximity to them, and the distal limits of the influences those features have-- both individually and combined--on the attraction of potential offenders, suitable victims, and crime.

For many decades, criminologists have identified features of places that help to explain occurrences and distributions of criminal behavior and reported crime incidents. Yet, it is not the mere presence or absence of the features that attract or generate crime[12]. It is the spatial influence of these criminogenic features on their environments that enable motivated offenders and increase the likelihood of illegal activity at certain places. For example, as was presented above, the spatial influence of bars as a risk factor for robbery could be described as "being within a certain distance from a single bar heightens your risk of victimization;" or, "being at a place with a high nearby concentration of bars heightens your risk of victimization." Both of these situations could be true at the same time, or only one or neither could be true depending on where you are located within the city. Notice, though, that at the micro-level unit of "the place where you are standing," your risk of being robbed could vary according to the spatial influences that bars have on their environments.

With the growing utilization of spatial risk assessments and predictive analytics in the criminal justice community[13] operationalizing the spatial influence of crime factors to geographic units throughout a terrain is an important task that requires special consideration and tools[14]. In particular, a geographic information system (GIS) allows analysts to create visual narratives of how environmental settings become conducive to crime. GIS allows us to explore spatial influence, which refers to the way in which features of an environment affect places throughout the environment. There are many types of environments to which this concept can apply, including small and large extents (e.g. local or global), and rural, suburban, and urban areas. This chapter explores ways in which correlates of crime (i.e. criminogenic features) can be operationalized to maps, using GIS, to represent their impacts on the environments of which they are a part. Attending to this detail of map making is particularly important and necessary for maximizing the reliability and validity of assessments of the likelihood of crime to occur at certain places within a study area.

$\mathcal{M}$otivated offenders will commit crime against suitable targets at certain places according to the environmental characteristics of those places that make it easier to complete the crime successfully and reap the rewards without punishment (e.g., getting caught)[15]. Event-dependent theories and approaches to crime analysis require police to focus on events that have not occurred yet by anticipating and controlling the behavior of individuals no matter where they are or where they are traveling to or from. This is a very difficult endeavor. What is more manageable for police agencies is to allocate resources to places that are most attractive to motivated offenders and to where crime is most likely to occur given certain characteristics of the environment[16]. These are the places with the greatest risk of crime to occur. In the long-standing debate in criminology concerning what promotes crime, it is not enough to say that risk of crime increases when the numbers of criminals increase. What is more likely is that the risk of crime at places that have criminogenic attributes is higher than other places because these locations attract motivated offenders (or more likely concentrate them in close locations) and are conducive to allowing certain events to occur.

Paul and Patricia Brantingham provided important conceptual tools for understanding relationships between places and crimes. They referred to the "environmental backcloth" that emerges from the confluence of routine activities and physical structures overlaying areas[17]. This backcloth is dynamic and can be influenced by the forces of "crime attractors" and "crime generators" which contribute to the existence of crime hotspots[18]. Attractors are those specific things that attract offenders to places in order to commit crime. Generators refer to the greater opportunities for crime that emerge from increased volume of interaction occurring at these areas. The concentration of crime at specific places or "hotspots" is consistent with the idea of an environmental backcloth, is well supported by research[19], and comports with the daily findings of crime analysts in law enforcement agencies around the world[20]. Crime hotspots tells where behavior is clustered. Connecting criminal behavior to precursory environmental context is more challenging, but important for comprehensive crime analysis and forecasting efforts. As Abbott[21] states about the central tenets of the human ecologists who were the first to systematically study crime in space, "the Chicago School thought that no social fact makes any sense abstracted from its context in social (and often geographic) space and social time. ...Every social fact is situated, surrounded by other contextual facts and brought into being by a process relating it to past contexts."

Operationalizing the spatial influence of a crime factor tells a story, so to speak, about how that feature of the environment affects behaviors and attracts or enables crime occurrence at places nearby to and far away from the feature itself[22]. Geographic information systems can produce maps that visually articulate these environmental contexts where certain crimes are more or less likely to occur as a result of the combined influence of one or more criminogenic features affecting the same place. In this way, criminal behavior is modeled as less deterministic and more a function of a dynamic interaction that occurs at places.

Risk assessment, defined by Kennedy and Van Brunschot[23] as "a consideration of the probabilities of particular outcomes", provides an efficient way to analyze crime opportunities[24]. However, challenges appear in the operationalization of risk in a GIS. The way that criminogenic features have been modeled in a GIS is often contrary to how people experience and conceptualize their environments[25]. When assessing the risk of crime to occur at conceivably any location throughout a landscape, the use of vector points, lines and polygons in a GIS are poor representations of criminogenic features on a map because they bear no particular relationship to the dynamic environments of which they are a part[26]. "Points, lines, and polygons that define vector objects do not have naturally occurring counterparts in the real world," explained Couclelis[27]. They are approximations of environmental features, but without any theoretical or empirical link to their geographies[28]. The way people conceptualize and operate in space is an important consideration for the mapping of crime risk throughout landscapes. Cartographically modeling these conceptualizations and the spatial influence of criminogenic features in a GIS in a way that reflects the actors' views is an important part of what Freundschuh and Egenhofer[29] describe as "Naïve Geography, a set of theories of how people intuitively or spontaneously conceptualize geographic space and time"[30], and can yield more meaningful and actionable spatial intelligence for use by public safety professionals[31].

The best way to map crime factors for the articulation of criminogenic backcloths[32] is to operationalize the spatial influence of each factor, acting as crime generators, throughout a common landscape rather than atheoretically mapping the factors as points, lines or polygons in a manner that keeps them disconnected from their broader social and environmental contexts. To succeed at this task, one needs to incorporate information about these places that would be expected to increase risks of crime. Fortunately, decades of criminological research have identified a variety of independent variables to be significantly correlated with a range of crime outcomes that can be used to inform such expectations. For example, Caplan, Kennedy and Miller[33] studied gang-related shootings and operationalized the spatial influence of known gang members' residences as "areas with greater concentrations of gang members residing will increase the risk of those places having shootings" and depicted this as a density map created in a GIS from known addresses of gang members' residences. Or, Moreto, Piza and Caplan[34] identified aggravating factors for residential burglary to be related to proximity to known (ex-)burglars' residences, public transportation, pawn shops, and drug markets, and operationalized each factor to affect the surrounding area's risk up to a certain distance away.

$\mathcal{O}$perationalizing the spatial influence of crime risk factors addresses various theoretical and methodological issues concerning the use of GIS for crime forecasting and assessing place-based victimization risk[35]. The most basic utility of this innovation is that it maximizes the validity of cartographic models and empirical measures used for statistical tests. The next few sections exemplify these effects to crime analysis when the same crime correlate is modeled in a GIS according to three primary types of operationalized spatial influences.

Point Pattern Analysis

$\mathcal{F}$igure 3-1 shows point symbols representing the locations of shooting incidents (the crime) and bars, clubs, fast food restaurants and liquor stores (the crime generators) in Irvington, NJ. These crime generators, or criminogenic features of the landscape, are correlated with shooting incidents in several empirical research studies, both in Irvington and other settings[36]. There are 102 features and 60 shooting incidents from 2007 represented on the map in Figure 3-1. Visual inspection of the map suggests that shooting incidents are distributed in a similar way as criminogenic features. However, only one shooting incident was within or at the exact same address as a fast food restaurant.

Given the state of knowledge from existing empirical research, it might be said that Irvington as a whole is at greater risk for shootings compared to other municipalities because it has higher numbers of criminogenic features. However, short of revoking business licenses and forcibly closing all or some of the most problematic establishments, this fact would be less than useful for Irvington's police who must operate at micro-level places within their municipality to suppress and prevent shootings and other violence. Accepting that their city is empirically more crime-prone compared to other cities and doing nothing about it is not an option.

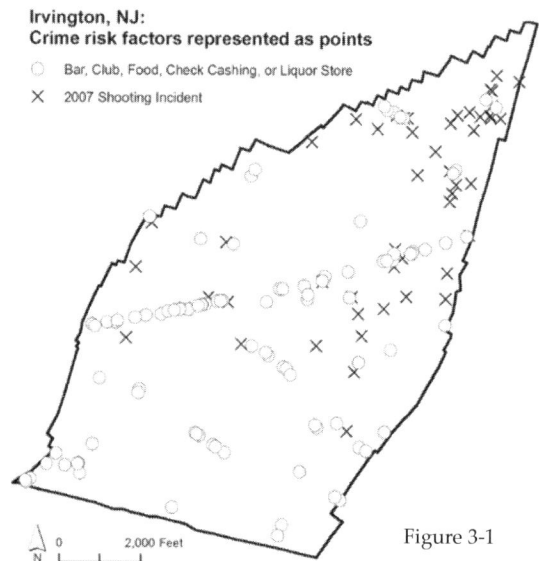

Irvington, NJ:
Crime risk factors represented as points

○ Bar, Club, Food, Check Cashing, or Liquor Store
✕ 2007 Shooting Incident

0   2,000 Feet

Figure 3-1

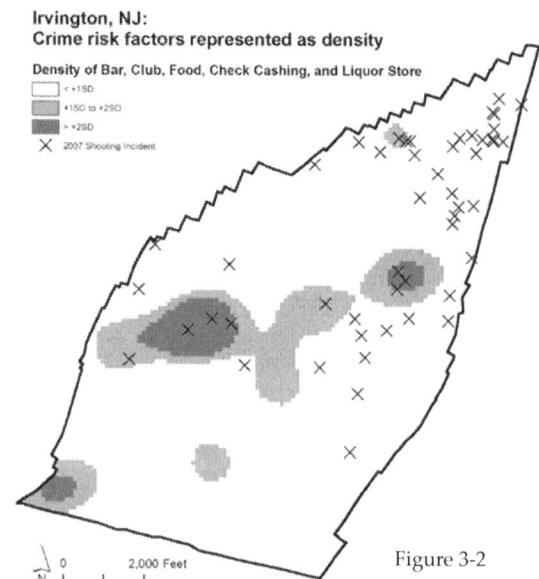

Irvington, NJ:
Crime risk factors represented as density

Density of Bar, Club, Food, Check Cashing, and Liquor Store

0   2,000 Feet

Figure 3-2

24   Risk Terrain Modeling Compendium | 2011 | Caplan and Kennedy

Spatial Concentration

$\mathcal{B}$ars, clubs, fast food restaurants, check cashing outlets and liquor stores are often not the exact locations where associated crimes happen. Rather, shootings occur at places that are in some way defined or influenced by them. As shown in Figure 3-2, the spatial influence of these features on shooting incidents is related to their concentration at places throughout the municipality, and was operationalized as a raster density map. Shooting incidents are cartographically modeled as more likely to happen at places were bars, clubs, fast food restaurants, check cashing outlets, and/or liquor stores are most concentrated. "Places" are defined in the raster map as cells sized 100ftx100ft and the distal limits of nearby features (i.e., the bandwidth, or search radius) used to define the density of each place was set at 1,480 feet (i.e., approximately four blocks; a meaningful sphere of influence for these criminogenic features as attributes of places within the radius). The density map is symbolized according to standard deviational breaks, with all places colored in darker gray having density values greater than +2 standard deviations from the mean density value—which statistically puts these places in the top 5% of the most densely populated with criminogenic features. As shown on the map, places with greater concentrations of criminogenic features appear to be more frequented by shootings than the bars, clubs, fast food restaurants, and liquor stores themselves (compared to Figure 3-1). In fact, 13 out of 60 (22%) shootings during 2007 occurred at places with density values above +1 standard deviations.

Given the state of knowledge from existing empirical literature and the spatial influence of criminogenic features to be operationalized as the concentration of these features throughout the environment, it might be said that places in Irvington with higher concentrations of bars, clubs, fast food restaurants and liquor stores are at greater risk for shootings compared to all other places within the municipality. This fact might encourage Irvington police to prioritize and allocate resources to the most dense places. In this way, police could preemptively target a few high density areas of criminogenic features rather than allocating resources to every individual feature in an effort to control and prevent shootings.

Spatial Proximity

$\mathcal{P}$erhaps bars, clubs, fast food restaurants and liquor stores are the venues where most suitable victims hang out or where the most likely and motivated offenders visit, become intoxicated, or lose self-control[37]. However, due to increased police presence or other capable guardians such as bouncers, witnesses or CCTV cameras, offenders do not shoot their victims inside or directly outside of such facilities. Rather, shootings are more likely to occur at certain distances away. Thought of in this way, the spatial influence of bars, clubs, fast food restaurants and liquor stores on shootings is more a function of distance from the closest feature rather than the presence or absence of the feature at the shooting incident location. Figure 3-3 shows a map that operationalizes this distal spatial influence with a 370 foot buffer (about 1 block) around all features. Although only one shooting out of 60 during 2007 happened exactly at or in a bar, club, fast food restaurant, or liquor store, 31 shootings occurred within one block from these features. The operationalized spatial influence of the highest risk created by these features to be all places within 370 feet—a definition that was grounded in theory and empirical research, identified places with more than half (52%) of all shooting incident locations[38].

It is realized that these results are arguably due to identifying a larger catchment area to which shootings are aggregated. Compared to feature points themselves, this is true. However, the coverage area of places with density values above +1 standard deviations is 0.806 square miles, and the coverage area of places within one block of a criminogenic feature is 0.725 square miles; this is about one quarter of 1% of Irvington's total area. So, more shootings occurred in a smaller area that was deemed affected by nearby criminogenic features in a conceptually meaningful way. While empirical research suggests that bars, clubs, fast food restaurants, and liquor stores are correlated with shootings, the most meaningful cartographic model of places that are at the greatest risk of shootings is one that

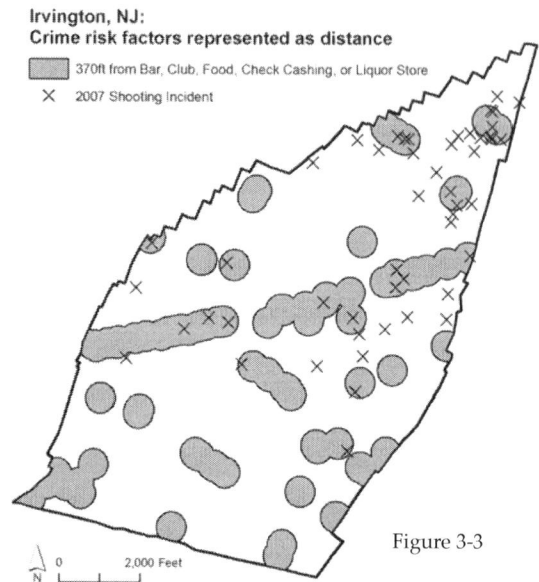

Irvington, NJ:
Crime risk factors represented as distance

370ft from Bar, Club, Food, Check Cashing, or Liquor Store
X   2007 Shooting Incident

Figure 3-3

0   2,000 Feet

operationalizes the spatial influence of these features on shooting incidents to be up to a certain distance away. This might not be the case in other jurisdictions or for other crime types, but it is corroborated by existing research[39] and it reinforces the importance of modeling these criminogenic features in commensurate ways on a map.

There are two lessons learned from this discussion. First, it is reasonable to rely on theory and empirical research to identify crime correlates and to operationalize their spatial influence. Second, there are many ways to operationalize the spatial influence of crime correlates about their environments, but some methods are more appropriate and efficacious than others. These insights reinforce the notion that approaches to crime analysis, spatial risk assessment, and crime forecasting cannot be atheoretical and must be evidence-based. They must be grounded in ways that account for the dynamic interaction of all criminogenic features throughout a landscape. Part 2 of this book presents risk factors for a variety of crime types (ordered alphabetically)—based on extensive literature reviews of empirical research, that you can use to develop your own risk map layers and risk terrain maps in the most reasonable and efficacious way.

Part 2

Criminogenic Features and Crime Correlates

Presents literature reviews with risk factors that are known to be related to a variety of crime types:

Arson
Sexual Assault
Aggravated Assault
Simple Assault
Auto Theft
Residential Burglary
Drug Dealing in Open-Air Markets
Larceny-Theft
Loitering
Murder, Non-Negligent Manslaughter
Street Prostitution
Forcible Rape
Street Robbery
Gun Shootings

Contributing Authors:
Caplan, J. M.
Chowdhury, L.
Drucker, J.
Fujita, S.
Gaziarifoglu, Y.
Kennedy, L. W.
Moreto, W. D.
Rusnak, D. M.

Chapter 4::
Risk Factors of Arson

By Jill Drucker | Rutgers University

Summary of Key Factors: Residential buildings; Outdoor locations; Vacant and abandoned buildings; Buildings in tax arrears; History of previous fires; Education establishments; Places of worship; Proximity to drug dealing areas.

Operational Definition

Arson is defined as any fire of an incendiary or suspicious origin. In the United States, arson is the leading case of fires totaling approximately 267,000 fires each year. Over 2,000 injuries, 475 deaths, and $1.4 billion in property loss occur each year.[40]

Aggravating and Mitigating Risk Factors Based on a Review of Empirical Literature

Residential Buildings: In 2009, 14,693 agencies in the United States reported 51,380 arson fires. Of the 22,867 fires that occurred in structures, 10,859 occurred in single occupancy residential buildings and 3,629 occurred in other types of residential buildings.[41] Arson fires are frequently set in homes in attempts to defraud insurance companies, attempts to be re-housed, due to arguments, to hide evidence of another crime, or due to children playing with matches or lighters.[42]

Outdoor locations: Seventy-five percent of intentional fires occur outside. Outdoor fires are typically set in open areas such as farmlands or fields (36.9%), wild lands or woods (9.0%), highways, parking lots, or streets (8.5%) and other outside areas (31.1%).[43]

Vacant and Abandoned Buildings: Vacant and abandoned buildings are frequent targets for arson.[44] Between 2003 and 2006, an estimated average of 31,000 structure fires occurred in vacant buildings of which 43% were intentionally set.[45]

Buildings in Tax Arrears: Half of all buildings that experience an incident of arson are in tax arrears with the average period being more than one year.[46]

History of Previous Fires: In accordance with broken windows theory, buildings that are boarded up or partially destroyed by fire or are near buildings that are boarded up or partially destroyed by fire are more likely to become targets of arson.[47]

Education Establishments: Schools may be the target of arson due to vandalism or in order to conceal evidence of a burglary. School buildings appear to be accessible, have little perimeter protection, and are vacant during hours of darkness, possibly increasing the risk of arson.[48] Schools also have large numbers of potential offenders in high-risk age groups.[49]

Places of Worship: Churches, temples, mosques and other places of worship are easy targets for arson due to lax security. Arson fires may also cover up evidence of other crimes such as burglary or be set by vagrants who use the places of worship as shelter.[50]

Proximity to Drug Dealing Areas: Drug use and the illegal drug trade impact the crime of arson because sometimes an arsonist is under the influence of drugs or alcohol when he or she commits the crime, techniques involved in processing drugs sometimes cause explosions or fires, and drug dealers may set fires to property as retaliation when drug payments are not delivered or to intimidate rivals.[51]

Setting Effects

Large metropolitan cities have the highest rates of arson. The number of intentional fires in large metropolitan cities with populations over 250,000 is roughly four times the number of intentional fires in small towns with populations of 2,500 to 4,999.[52]

Temporal Differences

Time of Day: The two time periods with the highest percentage of arson fires are 4 p.m. to 8 p.m. and 8 p.m. to midnight.[53]

Day of the Week: Arson fires occur throughout the week, but occur slightly more frequently on Saturdays and Sundays.[54]

Time of the Year: The occurrence of intentionally set fires peaks in March and April, months with low humidity and high winds, and again in July.[55]

Holidays: Peak days for building fires are July 4, July 5, October 31, and January 1.[56]

Arson fires at schools typically occur when schools are unoccupied (before and after school hours, weekends, and vacations)[57]

Chapter 5::
Risk Factors of (Sexual) Assault

By Danielle M. Rusnak | Rutgers University

Summary of Key Factors: Proximity to Bars/Clubs, Schools/Colleges, Parks, Offender's Residence; Distribution of Age, Gender, Wealth, Crime; Time of day, Day of week.

Operational Definition

Sexual assault is "the penetration, no matter how slight, in which physical force or coercion is used or in which the victim is physically or mentally incapacitated".[58] Based on this definition of sexual assault both cases of rape (forcible, date, stranger and acquaintance[59]) and child molestation (male vs. female victim; pedophile vs. hebephile)[60] will be considered in this brief's operational definition. It is important to acknowledge not only the definition used for sexual assault, but that within sexual assault the offender-victim relationship may play a role in the incident.[61]

Sexual assault may involve a variety of serious and minor criminal behaviors. Among these behaviors, the use of force might or might not be the case, coercion and substance use may also be involved. The sole focus on the behavior and personality of an offender in current research produces a dilemma in that when used alone and without spatial or temporal considerations they are insufficient for meaningful prevention activities.

It is important to note that in the spatial analysis of crime, a clear distinction between offenses is imperative as every crime is built on different situational factors and behaviors relative to each event. This is especially important when disaggregating the category of sexual assault to rapists and child molesters, for instance, since definitions become more complicated and risk factors may vary.

Aggravating/Mitigating Risk Factors Based on a Review of Empirical Literature

Spatial Correlates of Sexual Assault

Geographic Proximity to Bars/Clubs: Offenders may prefer to target their victims when they are intoxicated and unable to pay attention to their personal safety. "Approximately 50% of sexual assaults involve alcohol"[62]. It is also important to note that the offender may consume alcohol before a sexual assault; so too may the victim that may consume alcohol.

Geographic Proximity to Schools/Colleges: Sexual assault among college women is about three times that of sexual assault among the general population of women.[63] Most rapes on campuses occur after heavy, or binge, drinking on campuses.[64] Additionally, more than half of the college men (58%) who participated in a recent study reported committing some form of sexual assault.[65]

Geographic Proximity to Parks: About 15% of sexual assaults take place in public locations such as streets or parks.[66] Offenders who victimize adults were found to live significantly closer to schools <u>and</u> parks than those who targeted children.[67] Additionally, there appears to be no difference between proximity of offenders who victimize strangers compared to those who victimize family or acquaintances.[68]

Geographic Proximity to Offender's Residence: Sexual assault offenders are restricted by law to live in certain areas and adhere to zoning restrictions (e.g., not residing within 2,500 ft. of a school). According to routine activities theory, an offender is not likely to travel too far outside of the vicinity of his/her home to commit the crime.[69] To date, no study has directly measured whether residence restrictions, or geographical proximity actually reduce recidivism of sexual offenders, therefore examination of where sex offenders reside (or are registered as residing) may be beneficial if it is observed that many sexual assaults in a particular jurisdiction happen within close proximity to specific known sex offenders or places with high concentrations of known sex offenders residing.

<u>*Non-Spatial Correlates of Sexual Assault*</u>

Distribution of Age: Young women are at greater risk than older women for interpersonal violence.[70] Additionally, most sexual assaults have been noted to occur on college campuses which further indicates a younger population at risk.

Distribution of Gender: Around 95% of sexual assault victims are women.[71] Therefore, highly concentrated areas of females might be at a greater risk of victimization.

Distribution of Wealth: Wealth might not affect initial offending but it may be appropriate to examine for already registered sex offenders with regard to recidivism. Registered sex offenders tend to live in economically deprived areas because of residency restrictions and employment opportunities available to them.[72] Overall, research suggests that economic factors are a good predictor of an offender's choice of residence.[73]

Distribution of Crime (Crime rates/trends): Areas with higher crime rates are often identified as correlates for sexual violence. "Ecological proximity to violence is an important determinant of victimization".[74]

Setting Effects

Offenders, targets and crimes can vary by setting. For example, sexual assaults in a rural setting may not necessarily have public transport as a major correlate of risk since that form of transport is used less frequently than in urban settings. Regarding offender-victim relationships, the parties may be strangers, acquaintances or family, each of which may dictate a different location desirable for a sexual assault; such as outside or in the confines of a building, and dependent upon the victim and/or offender of interest. Keep in mind is that sexual assault may vary by setting since each subtype of sexual assault (rape: forcible, date, stranger and acquaintance; and child molestation: male vs. female victim; pedophile vs. hebephile) may have different correlates associated with it.

Temporal Differences

Different times of day, week or even year (e.g., season) may have different effects on how both offenders and victims behave. Individuals at a bar/club at night are generally intoxicated and may be alone with a diminished concern for personal safety. Night times will provide more suitable targets for sexual assaults that occur in outside settings; a group of potential targets walking home from school during daylight hours is less at risk of sexual assault than an intoxicated individual walking home alone from a bar. Additionally, drinking mostly occurs during the weekends--especially on college campuses. Therefore, weekdays may be considered less risky for sexual assault compared to weekend days. Risk factors such as drinking and staying out late at night may also occur more often on holidays (e.g., St. Patrick's Day, Thanksgiving, New Years Eve, etc.), so a seasonal component to risk assessment for sexual assault is important as well. A potential victim's age may also be a key factor in risk assessment because different age groups congregate at different locations and at different times.

Chapter 6::
Risk Factors of Aggravated Assault
By Jill Drucker | *Rutgers University*

Summary of Key Factors: Bars and nightclubs; Entertainment venues; Gang activity; Drug trade; Drug or alcohol use.

Operational Definition

$\mathcal{F}$or the purpose of this research brief, aggravated assault is defined as an attack or attempted attack with a weapon, regardless of whether or not an injury occurred, as well as an attack without a weapon when serious injury occurred. Serious injury includes broken bones, lost teeth, internal injuries, loss of consciousness, and any other unspecified injury that requires two or more days of hospitalization.[75]

Aggravating/Mitigating Risk Factors Based on a Review of Empirical Literature

Bars and nightclubs: Many assaults occur in and around bars, nightclubs, and similar liquor serving facilities such as pubs or taverns. Alcohol consumption leads to risk taking behavior, less concern over consequences or punishments, high levels of emotion, and poor communication, all which may cause a violent altercation. The physical environment of bars or nightclubs are conducive to altercations as they are often overcrowded and under-regulated. Bars and nightclubs may also cater to prostitution, drug dealing or aggressive entertainment. In addition, if a particular geographical location has many bars and nightclubs, customers from different social groups may encounter one another leading to violence.[76]

Entertainment Venues: Stadiums, arenas, sporting grounds, and concert halls are conducive to aggravated assault because of overcrowding, high level of physical contact, alcohol consumption, high energy levels, and the adversarial nature of competitions.[77]

Gang Activity: According to the FBI, criminal gangs commit as much as 80% of crime in many areas. Such crimes include simple and aggravated assault.[78]

Drug Trade: The presence of drug markets increases the likelihood of violence, including aggravated assault. Violence is common in drug markets as dealers and customers often resort to violence in order to solve disputes and to maintain business.[79]

Drug or Alcohol Use: In 2007, the Criminal Victimization in the United States report indicated that 33.5% of offenders arrested for aggravated assault were perceived to be under the influence of drugs or alcohol.[80]

Demographic Factors

Age: In 2004, 7% of felons convicted of aggravated assault were under the age of 20, 42% were between ages 20 and 29, 27% were between ages 30 and 39, 17% were between ages 40 and 49, 5% were between ages 50 and 59, and 2% were between ages 60 and 69.[81]

Gender: Men are more likely to experience aggravated assault than females.[82]

Race: Blacks are more likely than all other races to be victims of aggravated assault. Hispanics and non-Hispanics are equally likely to experience aggravated assault.[83]

Setting Effects

Of the 806,843 total aggravated assaults committed in 2009 that were analyzed by the FBI, 701,454 (86.9%) occurred in metropolitan areas; 57,750 (7.2%) occurred in cities outside metropolitan areas; and 47,639 (5.9%) occurred in nonmetropolitan counties. Rates of aggravated assault are greatest in the South (44.5%). The Northeast (14.2%), Midwest (18.9%), and Western (22.5%) regions of the United States have lower aggravated assault rates.[84]

Temporal Effects

Of 2007's 775,060 aggravated assaults analyzed in the Crime Victimization in the United States report, 45.6% occurred between 6 a.m. and 6 p.m., 39.8% occurred from 6 p.m. to midnight, 12.6% occurred from midnight to 6 a.m.[85]

Chapter 7::
Risk Factors of (Simple) Assault

By Jill Drucker | Rutgers University

Summary of Key Factors: Restaurants, bars, and nightclubs; School buildings and school property; Entertainment venues; Gender; Age; Marital status; Socioeconomic status.

Operational Definition

Simple assault is defined as an "attack without a weapon resulting either in no injury, minor injury (for example, bruises, black eyes, cuts, scratches or swelling) or in undetermined injury requiring less than two days of hospitalization."[86] Simple assault also includes attempted assault without the use of a weapon.[87]

Aggravating/Mitigating Risk Factors Based on a Review of Empirical Literature

Offense Locations

Restaurants, Bars, and Nightclubs: Restaurants, bars, and nightclubs are conducive to violence, including simple assault. Alcohol consumption causes heightened emotionality, risk taking behavior, limited perception of options during an altercation, a reduced fear of consequences and sanctions, and an impairment of communication which prevents individuals from talking their way out of a potentially violent situation. The environment of these facilities are often characterized by overcrowding, a lack of physical comfort, competitive situations, a low number of staff, tolerance of delinquent behavior, and a low level of police regulation which all contribute to possible violence and assault. Establishments that cater to prostitutes, traffic in stolen goods or drugs, or incorporate aggressive entertainment are at a higher risk for violence. While a higher concentration of restaurants, bars, and nightclubs does not necessarily correlate with higher violence, if establishments have the same closing time, then patrons, possibly from different social groups, may encounter each other on the street leading to violent altercations.[88]

School Buildings and School Property: According to the *Sourcebook of Criminal Justice Statistics*, 19.8% of simple assaults occurred inside of school buildings or on school property in 2007.[89]

Entertainment Venues: Entertainment venues such as stadiums, arenas, sporting grounds, and concert halls are conducive to simple assault as they are characterized by overcrowding, a high level of physical contact between attendees, alcohol availability, high-energy events, and the adversarial nature of athletic competitions.[90]

Victim Characteristics

Gender: Males experience higher rates of simple assault victimization than females.[91]

Age: Individuals aged 12-19 show the highest rate of simple assault victimization followed by individuals aged 20-24. Rates of simple assault victimization rapidly decrease after age 24.[92]

Marital Status: Largely due to their lifestyle or routine activities, individuals who have never married or are divorced or separated have higher rates of simple assault victimization than those individuals who are married or widowed.[93]

Socioeconomic Status: Households with a cumulative income of less than $7,500 have the highest victimization rates of simple assault.[94]

Temporal Differences

Simple assault that is related to alcohol consumption or patronage of a bar or nightclub are more likely to occur during weekend nights.[95]

Setting Effects

Urban environments, classified as metropolitan cities with populations exceeding 50,000, have the highest rates of simple assault as compared to suburban and rural communities.[96] According to the FBI's National Gang Assessment of 2009, gangs commit as much as 80% of the crime in many communities. The FBI notes assault as an example of a typical gang-related crime. Assault is often committed against rival gangs or rival drug distributors in the gang's territory.[97] Communities with high rates of drug use and drug distribution experience higher levels of violence, which includes assault. Assault may occur as a result of disputes between drug dealers over territory, disputes within dealing hierarchies to enforce regulations, disputes over payment, arguments over drug quality or quantity, during attempts to steal drugs or drug paraphernalia, or due to violence associated with drug use.[98]

Chapter 8::
Risk Factors of Auto Theft

By Shuryo Fujita | Rutgers University

Summary of Key Factors: Vehicle Availability, Locations of Older Vehicles Parked, Locations of Most Frequently Stolen, Vehicles Parked, Land-Use Type, Proximity to High Schools and Bars, Parking Lots, Nighttime Entertainment Venues, Property Value, Household Income, Single-family Households.

Operational Definition

Auto theft is defined for the purposes of this brief as the completed theft of passenger vehicles (including sedans, station wagons, coupes, convertibles, sport utility vehicles, minivans, and pickups). Auto theft may be used interchangeably with the following terms: car theft, vehicle theft, and motor vehicle theft.

Aggravating/Mitigating Risk Factors Based on a Review of the Empirical Literature

Vehicle Availability: Rates of auto theft in an area (census tracts/cities) increase as the number of vehicles per square mile in the area increases.[99]

Locations of Older Vehicles Parked: Risks of vehicles being stolen increase as they become older.[100] About two-thirds of stolen vehicles in the U.K. and Australia are more than 10 years old when stolen. These vehicles also dominate as the most stolen vehicles in the U.S.[101] This implies that an area where older cars prevail is likely to be at the most risks of auto theft.

Locations of Most Frequently Stolen Vehicles Parked: Similar to older vehicles, certain model of vehicles are far more likely to be stolen than others,[102] suggesting that identifying an area where such vehicles are parked would lead to an area of higher risk for auto theft.

Land-Use Type: Street blocks with more vacant lots, restaurants/bars, youth hangouts (theaters, arcades, and schools), retail stores, manufacturing/storage facilities, or apartments tend to have higher auto theft rates.[103]

Proximity to High Schools: Areas within one block of high schools tend to have more auto thefts.[104]

Proximity to Bars: Areas within one block of bars tend to have more auto thefts.[105]

***Parking* Lots:** Large parking lots tend to be a hotspot of auto theft. These include (1) parking lots with over 100 stalls,[106] (2) trolley station lots, and (3) the lots of "big box" retail stores and shopping malls.[107] When taking into account the size of lots and the length of time parked, risks of auto theft at trolley lots or long term (commuters/transit) parking lots and lots close to a freeway are especially higher than other parking lots. At the micro level, parking lots with high levels of security (perimeter fencing, exit bars, CCTV, and good lighting) have been found to have fewer auto thefts.[108]

Nighttime Entertainment Venues: An area with such facilities as theaters, restaurants, and bars/night clubs, especially where they are found grouped together in busy night districts, experiences higher rates of auto theft.[109]

Property Value: Areas (census tracts/blocks) with higher median property values tend to have more auto thefts or higher theft rates,[110] perhaps because more attractive vehicles are found in these places. On the other hand, the median owner-occupied property value has been found to act as a mitigating factor of auto theft at the census block group level, meaning that the higher the value in a census block group, the lower the auto theft rate or fewer auto thefts in that area.[111]

Household Income*:* Areas (census tracts/block group) with lower median household income tend to have higher auto theft rates.[112]

Single-family Households: This variable, often used as a proxy measure of family disruption, has been found to act as an aggravating risk factor of auto theft at the census tract, blockgroup, and street block level.[113] Areas with higher percent/number of single-family households tend to have higher auto theft.

Setting Effects
The risk factors of auto theft described above have been tested in different settings (both rural and urban regions) at different units of analysis (i.e. census tract, blockgroup, and street block level). However, it should be recognized that the nature of auto theft can vary by geographic region, state, and city, and that auto theft is not a uniform offense. It includes a number of subtypes (e.g., theft for joyriding, transportation, use in commission of other offenses, stripping for parts, export, etc.), each involving different risk factors. For example, five of the top 10 states with the highest auto theft rates per vehicles registered in 2007 were adjacent to the U.S.-Mexico or U.S.-Canadian borders. In these states, a risk factor such as proximate to U.S. border, which can facilitate the theft for export, might play a bigger role than other factors. Auto theft in a city characterized by homogeneity in low income levels or property value might be less likely to be influenced by socio-economic factors.

Temporal Differences
The majority of auto thefts (61 percent) occur at night between 6:00pm and 6:00am, with more than one-third of thefts occurring between 12:00am and 6:00am (BJS, 2010). Statistics shows that

75 percent of near-home thefts occur between 6:00pm and 6:00am. Auto thefts in public parking and work/office parking lots are 4 times and 8 times more likely to occur during the daytime than nighttime, respectively.[114]

Chapter 9::
Risk Factors of (Residential) Burglary

By William D. Moreto | Rutgers University

Summary of Key Factors: Measures of social disorganization, Proximity to pawn shops, Proximity to public transportation, Land use type (residential), Time of day, Day of week, Proximity to police stations.

Operational Definition

Burglary can be broadly defined as the illegal and unlawful entry into a home or structure to commit a felony or theft[115]. Burglary is manifested in several ways and can occur in several distinct settings and contexts. Both residences and commercial/retail establishments can be burgled. Moreover, the broad categories of residences and commercial/retail establishments can further be disaggregated into discrete sub-categories. For instance, residential burglary can be broken down into occupancy (single-family and multi-family); design (attached, separated or semi-separated residences); and structure (houses, apartments, condominiums and public housing).

Any residence, business or establishment can conceivably fall victim to an act of burglary; however, in reality, there are certain areas and places that are more conducive for offenses to occur[116]. For instance, four distinct factors have been identified that affect the variation in risk of a location being victimized: (i) surrounding area; (ii) household/premise characteristics; (iii) immediate design and planning features and; (iv) other aspects of lifestyle affecting the location[117]. For the purposes of investigating urban residential burglary, the surrounding area should be the main focus since the household/premise characteristics and immediate design and planning features of a location are at a micro-level that only explain one particular location's risk.

Aggravating/Mitigating Risk Factors Based on a Review of the Empirical Literature

By focusing on a city-level unit of spatial analysis, an analyst will be able to explicitly identify contextual factors that contribute to the risk of an area to residential burglary. This forward-looking approach results in the ability to forecast locations of future events based on the characteristics of places and not on prior events like conventional hot-spot mapping. It is important to note that crime correlates can be weighted. However, if such a method is used, it is up to the analyst to determine the level of significance and the subsequent risk value for each correlate in relation to one another in a meaningful and empirical manner.

Based on prior empirical research, five crime risk correlates have been identified to be associated with urban residential burglary:

Measures of Social Disorganization: Research has indicated that residences in socially disadvantaged and disorganized areas have high levels of crime due to low levels of collective efficacy and informal surveillance, low levels of socioeconomic status, high levels of ethnic heterogeneity and high levels of residential mobility[118]. Further, residents in such areas may not have the resources to safeguard their homes with adequate security measures[119]. In addition, socially disadvantaged areas may have more offenders living within or in near proximity of the area; thus, increasing the overall levels of risk of an area[4]. Importantly, research has also found that offenders do not travel far in order to offend and do so based on a crime template derived from their daily routines, traveling paths and overall awareness space[120]. Lastly, the residents of such areas may lack the appropriate security measures needed in order to deter and/or prevent being victimized resulting in multiple victimizations. As described, there are several ways to conceptualize and operationalize social disorganization[121], and it is up to the researcher to identify factors specific to the research setting and its context. However, it is important to remember that if factors of social disorganization are to be incorporated within a risk-terrain model, data must be up-to-date and recent.

Proximity to Pawn Shops: Burglars not only want to burgle a residence in a relatively quick fashion in order to avoid detection, but they also want to discard of any stolen property as quickly as possible. While most burglars may initially seek out cash, since it can be immediately used, they may also find objects that can be easily taken and sold in exchange for money. This may be especially true in impoverished areas, where objects that are of higher value or "hot products" may be at greater risk of being stolen due to their perceived value[122]. Pawn shops, especially ones that have lax policies, are avenues for burglars to dispose of stolen goods in a swift and immediate manner[123]. As such, it is generally understood that proximity to a pawn shop will increase the risk of an area.

Proximity to Public Transportation: Public transit stations may place certain locations at more risk since such connectors provide a way for offenders to access neighborhoods more readily, while also providing a means for exit[124]. Offenders may be able to expand their crime template by using public transportation as a means to move in and out of nearby (or possibly at even greater distances) neighborhoods. Unlike suburban residential burglary, urban burglars may not need to secure and use their own means of transportation to move larger products (i.e. televisions); and hence, are able to use public transportation as a means to move about.

Land Use Type (Residential): Since residential burglary can only occur at residences, land use is vital to include as a risk correlate. Parcel data can be particularly useful.

Time of Day / Day of Week: Burglars are more likely to burgle a home when it is not occupied[125]. While the occupation of a specific household is dependent on the individual lifestyles of the occupants[126], it is argued that specific time-periods can be aggregated to identify risky times due to the general routine activities of most communities[127]. For instance, an average work day could range from 8AM to 6PM (accounting for possible travel-time); therefore, the risk levels of an area as an aggregate would be higher during this time period. Additionally, since the average work week in the U.S. is Monday to Friday, it can be argued that households are more likely to be victimized during these time periods due to lack of guardianship.

Proximity to Police Stations: These have been shown to mitigate risks of urban residential burglary. Findings indicate that burglars take into account the patterns of police activity when offending[128]; thus, it can be argued that the increased presence of authorities, the increased likelihood of authorities being present and the increased ability of authorities to respond quickly can be considered mitigating factors resulting in a decrease of risk in an area.

Temporal Differences

Twelve-month or smaller time periods should be selected carefully to account for seasonal fluctuations (i.e. winter months v. summer months); commercial-retail times of the year (i.e. winter holidays) and work/school-related changes (i.e. summer holidays). Time periods can inherently change the dynamics of an environment. For example, summer months will result in increased guardianship in the form of children (possibly even a parent) staying home. Individuals' also go on vacations at different times of the year, namely during the summer and winter months leaving their homes unattended. Lastly, commercial-retail seasons results in an influx of "hot products" being purchased for gifts (i.e. "Black Friday", "Cyber Monday", and Christmas). As can be seen, the mere concept of season can vary and is dependent on the way it is defined.

Setting Effects

It is vital at the onset of any study to not only identify the specified issue that is being addressed, in this case residential burglary, but also the setting in which the study will occur. Distinguishing between urban and suburban neighborhoods will also affect the eventual framework, both theoretical and practical, during any analysis. Further, an appropriate area of study must be determined. This is especially true in any form of geographic analysis as the different levels of spatial aggregation will require different data and techniques and will provide different outcomes[129]. While a more specific level of analysis could be conducted (i.e. at a neighborhood level), an analysis at the city-level will be sufficient in order to prove the utility of RTM.

At a more specific level, an entire neighborhood could be assessed to determine which individual residences are at more risk based on certain factors; however, such a subjective analysis may be more suited after a general risk terrain is modeled and specific locations can be addressed. For example, a high risk area of a city may be identified based on the amalgamation of crime correlates creating an environmental setting conducive for residential burglary. Based on this information, it may be possible to identify residences within such an area that may be at even more risk solely based on individual characteristics of that home (i.e. security measures, points of entry, proximity to alleyways etc). Furthermore, such neighborhood-level analyses could utilize specific risk terrains based on prior empirical evidence that acknowledges issues related to repeat victimization (including, near-repeats, early repeats, delayed repeats)[130].

Conversely, a broad application of RTM at a state-level could also be conducted, but may not yield any meaningful information due to the fact that the area of study is simply too large. Further, it may be difficult to identify crime correlates at a state level that produce meaningful information regarding a criminogenic environment. Indeed, it can be argued that assessing a local-level problem like residential burglary through a state-level lens potentially results in the neglect of interactions and relationships that may be of importance[131]. Additionally, state-level analysis may not necessarily yield useful intelligence that authorities and policy-strategists can utilize for appropriate responses.

It is recommended that the most efficient and useful way to make use of RTM in investigating the risk of urban residential burglary based on the surrounding environmental context is by conducting an analysis at a city-level. It is believed that at this level of spatial analysis, the identification of crime correlates and temporal features will produce information that is not only insightful but also practical.

Chapter 10::
Risk Factors of Drug Dealing in Open-Air Markets

By Yasemin Gaziarifoglu | Rutgers University

Summary of Key Factors: Camouflage and escape, Gun violence, Owner-Occupied Housing, Proximity to prostitution areas; Street robbery areas, Budget motels, convention centers, hotels, coffee shops and bars, Transportation hubs and arterial routes, schools, recreation areas, shopping malls.

Operational Definition

$\mathcal{D}$rug markets may take different forms (in certain instances more than one form) regarding *the geography of the market* and the *nature of the transaction* between the buyer and the seller[132]:

- *Closed* markets where the buyer and seller know each other through friends and acquaintances,
- *Open markets* where the buyer and seller do not know each other,
- *Mobile markets* where the buyer and seller agree on the details of the transaction - including the location of the transaction- over the phone and,
- *Open-air markets* where the transactions take place in geographically well defined open-air areas.

For the purposes of this chapter, open-air drug dealing covers all types of illegal drug transactions that physically take place in open-air.

Aggravating/Mitigating Risk Factors Based on a Review of Empirical Literature

Proximity to Prostitution Areas: Studies suggest that one of the main reasons for involving in prostitution is financing drug addiction[133]. Accordingly since many prostitutes are addicted to drugs, proximity to prostitution areas may be a strong correlate for drug dealing in open-air markets.

Proximity to Street Robbery Areas: When the motive of robbery is to acquire cash in exchange for drugs, proximity to street robbery areas is a strong correlate of drug-dealing in open-air markets, especially when small scale drug dealers (the possible robbery of both cash and drugs) and customers are targeted as victims.[134]

Proximity to Budget Motels, Convention Centers, Hotels, Coffee Shops and Bars: As indicated earlier prostitutes constitute a high risk group for drug abuse. Accordingly proximity to the hang around locations of prostitutes such as budget motels, convention centers, coffee shops and bars etc. may be a strong correlate for drug dealing in open-air markets.[135]

Proximity to Transportation Hubs, Arterial Routes, Schools, Recreation Areas, and Shopping Malls: The presence of legitimate and daily activities and the easy access to the market area attract buyers to markets around these routes and facilities.[136]

Camouflage and Escape: To avoid the risk of being , most buyers and sellers prefer local environments which facilitate an easy money and drug exchange such as; dim lighting, concealing landscape, and abandoned buildings (for the use of drugs after purchase) .[137] In a similar vein to avoid the risk of apprehension most buyers and sellers prefer streets and roads in which they will be able to watch for the police and complete the transaction quickly.

Gun Violence: Research relates youth gun violence to street drug markets.[138]

Owner-Occupied Housing: Since drug dealers prefer the least supervised environments, in neighborhoods where owner-occupied housing dominates public housing, the probability of the establishment of open-air drug markets is less.[139]

Temporal Effects

As indicated earlier open-air markets gather around transportation hubs and arterial routes, accordingly
illicit drug markets are more likely to be open when "the arterials and nodes have a great deal of licit routine activities, and will be closed when the routine activities of the area are at their lowest and if this is the case, the limits of temporal displacement are set by the legitimate routines of the area in which the marketplaces are found".[140] But in the case where open-air markets supply the needs of drug addicts, the physical dependency of the hard drugs may necessitate the drug markets to be open 24/7. Nevertheless depending on the demanded product, the operation times of the markets may vary.[141]

Setting Effects

Open-air markets are specifically preferred in cases where the buyer is either an addict or wants to get the product quickly. In most cases open air-markets are also open markets accordingly for the buyers to locate the seller, most of the time sellers stick to particular locations and when they have to move they will try to limit the distance they move accordingly displacement will be limited to the high routine activity area.[142]

As indicated earlier since transportation hubs and arterial routes provides easy access to drug markets open-air drug markets are often located in inner city or urban areas. Additionally open air markets are more likely to be located in economically depressed neighborhoods where the presence of vacant buildings and the lack of informal surveillance facilitate the drug market.

Furthermore "markets that have a reputation for selling drugs can grow large in size and the concentration of activity in a small area will be hard to hide". [143]

Chapter 11::
Risk Factors of Larceny-Theft

By Jill Drucker | Rutgers University

Summary of Key Factors: Public transportation and public transportation stations; Areas of tourism; Restaurants, bars, and nightclubs; Shopping centers and malls; Parking lots; Bicycle-parking facilities; Apartment yards, parks, fields, and playgrounds; Schools and school property; Goods sold; Proximity to pawnshops and markets for stolen goods.

Operational Definition

Larceny-theft is defined as "the unlawful taking, carrying, leading, or riding away of property from the possession or constructive possession of another."[144] Larceny-theft includes bicycle theft, theft of motor vehicle parts and accessories, shoplifting, pocket-picking, purse snatching, and the stealing or attempted stealing of any property that is not taken by force, violence, or fraud.[145]

Aggravating/Mitigating Risk Factors Based on a Review of Empirical Literature

Public Transportation and Public Transportation Stations: Modes of public transportation and public transportation stations are conducive to theft because of overcrowding, limited visibility, a general lack of supervision, admissibility to all who pay a small entrance fee, and easily predicted behavior of potential victims for offenders to anticipate.[146]

Areas of Tourism: Tourists are profitable targets because they typically carry large amounts of money and other valuables. As tourists are on vacation they are characteristically more relaxed and off guard making them more vulnerable. Tourists are also less likely to report victimization or testify against perpetrators in order to avoid further problems or a return trip to the area.[147]

Restaurants, Bars, and Nightclubs: Establishments such as restaurants, bars, and nightclubs are considered high-risk facilities for larceny-theft. Restaurants, bars, and nightclubs are at high-risk because of their density for theft opportunities, patron's leaving their personal belongings unattended or at a considerable distance away from their person due to a lack of storage areas, the divided attention of the patrons due to noise, social interaction, dancing, or the consumption of alcohol, and a high population turnover that allows offenders to go unnoticed. Facilities with sufficient storage areas were associated with less theft.[148]

Shopping Centers and Malls: Shopping centers, especially those that are busy with a large number of customers, have higher rates of shoplifting. Shopping centers with their storefronts on the open-street attract more shoplifters than enclosed malls due to the greater opportunity to escape. Specific stores are at greater risk if they have many exists, exits that can be accessed without bypassing checkout, high displays that conceal customers, crowded areas around displays, restrooms or changing rooms, a high volume of items on the floor and near entrances, and blind areas that cannot be surveilled by staff.[149]

Parking Lots: In 2009, 9.0% of larceny-theft involved the stealing of motor vehicle accessories, and 27.3% involved the stealing of property from motor vehicles excluding motor vehicle accessories.[150] Large parking lots experience a considerable number of thefts from vehicles. In addition to the size of the parking lot, lots which contained cars parked for longer periods of time, lots that were open for a higher number of days, lots with unregulated access and limited or no security patrols, lots with multiple exit sites, and proximity to major roadways were increasingly susceptible to theft from autos. Such lots may include those designated for commuters, those located near large retail stores, shopping centers and malls, and those located at schools or universities.[151] Parking lots with attendants, improved lighting, limited access to pedestrians, electronic access systems, perimeter security, CCTV systems, and locations near other commercial building which provide natural surveillance are less likely to experience high rates of theft from vehicles.[152]

Bicycle-Parking Facilities: In 2009, 3.4% of larceny-theft offenses involved the stealing of bicycles. Bicycle-parking facilities at public transportation stations, university campuses, recreational facilities, and shopping areas are may be targeted for theft. The use of locks, proper locking practices, improved parking equipment, and increased guardianship through the use of security guards and surveillance techniques are mitigators of bicycle-theft from parking facilities.[153]

Apartment Yards, Parks, Fields, and Playgrounds: In 2007, 7.8% of pocket picking and purse snatching offenses occurred in apartment yards, parks, fields, or playgrounds.[154]

Schools and School Property: In 2007, 9.0% of pocket picking and purse snatching offenses occurred inside school buildings or on school property.[155]

Goods Sold: The most popular merchandise shoplifted from stores is concealable, removable, available, valuable, enjoyable, and disposable (able to be sold or bartered for money). Such merchandise includes tobacco products, health and beauty products, recorded music and videos, and clothing and apparel, especially those with designer labels.[156]

Proximity to Pawnshops and Markets for Stolen Goods: Stolen goods are typically sold within 30 minutes of their theft in local markets for stolen goods, including pawnshops.[157]

Setting Effects
Areas of high drug use and drug dealing may experience higher levels of larceny-theft as some of the most prolific offenders of larceny-theft are drug users who sell and barter stolen items for

drugs or money to buy drugs.[158] Neighborhoods or communities of low socioeconomic status are more likely to experience property crime. Households whose occupants earn less than $7,500 cumulatively per year are the most likely to experience property crime.[159] Areas with high levels of tourist activity are also more likely to experience larceny-theft as tourists are high-risk victims for their lack of security concern and large amount of valuables carried on their person.[160]

Temporal Differences

Thefts on modes of public transportation and in public transportations occur more frequently during morning and evening rush hours as well as from midnight to 6 am where sleeping or intoxicated passengers are targeted.[161] Bicycle theft typically peaks during the summer months of June, July, and August. The rate of bicycle theft at a particular location can also be impacted by other factors, such as the start of a school semester.[162] Most shoplifting occurs during when stores are at their busiest including times during the latter half of the week (between Wednesday and Saturday), during seasonal shopping rushes (pre-Easter, pre-summer, and pre-Christmas times), and as juveniles commit a considerable amount of shoplifting, during times such as non-school days, late mornings, and afternoons into the evening.[163]

Chapter 12::
Risk Factors of Loitering

By Jill Drucker | Rutgers University

Summary of Key Factors: Shopping centers and malls; Video arcades; Public parks, playgrounds, and amusement parks, School grounds; Apartment complex common areas; Public libraries; Convenience stores and fast food restaurants; Transportation facilities; Open-air drug markets; Gang activity; Prostitution; Homelessness.

Operational Definition

$\mathcal{F}$or the purpose of this research brief, loitering is defined as standing in public with no apparent purpose.[164]

Aggravating/Mitigating Risk Factors Based on a Review of Empirical Literature

Mitigating Factors Associated with Loitering Locations

Locations with poor comfort levels, convenience, and attractiveness are associated with lower levels of loitering behavior. For example, locations with limited places to sit or lean, little or no protection from the weather, intense lighting, unpopular music playing, enforced parking regulations, high levels of visibility, and increased surveillance techniques such as the use of CCTV.[165]

Locations Commonly Associated with Loitering[166]
• Shopping Centers and Malls
• Video Arcades
• Public Parks, Playgrounds, and Amusement Parks
• School Grounds
• Apartment Complex Common Areas
• Public Libraries
• Convenience Stores and Fast Food Restaurants
• Transportation Facilities

Open-Air Drug Markets: Open-air drug markets are characterized by the presence of a seller or sellers in a specific geographic area where potential buyers can easily locate a drug from the seller or sellers. Consequently, drug sellers will loiter in these areas in order to be identified by potential buyers and likewise, potential buyers may loiter in an area looking for an individual who is selling the drug or drugs he or she is seeking to purchase.[167]

Gang Activity: Gang members frequently engage in loitering in order to stake claim to a particular geographic area, to recruit new members, to intimidate other rival gangs, and to strike fear in local residents.[168] Gangs may also engage in loitering when writing graffiti to mark their turf, convey threats, disrespect rival gangs, or show pride for their own gang.[169]

Prostitution: Loitering often occurs when prostitutes remain in a specific geographic area and try to entice and solicit potential clients or when clients remain in a specific geographic area looking for the services of a prostitute. Pimps may also engage in loitering when trying to arrange meetings between a prostitute and a client.[170]

Homelessness: Homeless men and women spend more time on the streets and in public areas as they often have nowhere else to go. Homeless individuals may pass time on the streets and public places or may engage in panhandling behavior to procure money.[171]

Setting Effects

Open-air drug markets are frequently found in inner city or urban environments with poorly maintained, high-density low-income housing.[172] While gang activity is found in suburban and rural communities, gang activity is also a predominant element in inner city or urban environments with the majority of gang members identified as being from the underclass.[173] Loitering behavior may also be more common in these environments because of a lack of entertainment, activities, or facilities for youths and teenagers and a lack of supervision.[174]

Chapter 13::
Risk Factors of Murder and Non-Negligent Manslaughter

By Jill Drucker | Rutgers University

Summary of Key Factors: Gang activity; Gun accessibility; Drug trade; Drug and alcohol use; Unemployment.

Operational Definition

*F*or the purpose of this research brief, murder and non-negligent manslaughter are defined as "the willful killing of one human being by another" excluding deaths caused by negligence, suicide, or accident as well as justifiable homicides.[175]

Aggravating/Mitigating Risk Factors Based on a Review of Empirical Literature

Gang Activity: From 1993 through 2003, gang members perpetrated approximately 373,000 of the 6.6 million violent victimizations that occurred each year.[176] Gangs are often responsible for violent incidents involving the use of firearms, especially those incidents involving youths.[177] From 1994 through 1997, almost two-thirds of youth murders in Minneapolis, Minnesota were gang-related. Gang-related homicides can be traced back to illegal money making ventures or long standing gang rivalries.[178] Deadly drive-by shootings where an individual or individuals fire a gun from a vehicle at another vehicle, person, or structure are commonly committed by gang organizations to strike fear in rival gangs, as a means of appearing fearless, to show gang loyalty, as acts of retaliation, and over territory disputes.[179]

Gun Accessibility: In 2009, firearms were used in 67.1% of the homicides analyzed by the FBI.[180] Research findings indicate firearm availability is positively associated with homicide rates. Locations with higher levels of firearm ownership are plagued with higher homicide rates.[181]

Drug Trade: Drug markets are often associated with violent offenses, particularly homicides. Those involved in the drug trade are more likely to resort to violence due to competition for customers and drug markets and as a way to solve disputes.[182]

Drug and Alcohol Use: Drug use may be related to increased incidences of homicide. In 1997, the percentage of federal prison inmates convicted of murder who reported being under the influence of drugs at the time of their offense was 29.4% while the percentage of state prison inmates convicted of murder who reported being under the influence of drugs at the time of their offense was 26.8%.[183] The most frequently cited circumstance surrounding the commission of a homicide is an argument. Arguments include brawls caused by the influence of alcohol or narcotics.[184]

Unemployment: In a study of homicide in eight major cities in the United States, researchers found that as employment declined homicide rates increased and as employment increased homicide rates dropped.[185]

Demographic Factors

Of the 13,636 total homicide victims analyzed by the FBI in 2009, 6,556 (48.1%) victims were Black, 6,568 (48.2%) were White, and 360 (2.6%) were classified as Other. In regards to gender, 10,496 (77.0%) of victims were male and 3,122 (22.9%) were female. The highest percentage of homicide victims were in the age range from 20-24 with 2,426 homicide victims in 2009.[186] Of the 15,760 total homicide offenders analyzed by the FBI in 2009, 5,890 (37.4%) were Black, 5,286 (33.5%) were White, and 245 (1.6%). Males comprised 10,391 (65.9%) of the total offenders while females comprised 1,197 (7.6%). In regards to age, the highest percentage of homicide offenders were in the age range from 20-24 with 2,682 homicide offenders in 2009.[187]

Setting Effects

In 2009 an estimated 13,408 murders and acts of non-negligent manslaughter occurred in metropolitan areas while only 1,035 occurred in nonmetropolitan counties and 798 occurred in cities outside metropolitan areas.[188] Murder rates, particularly those involving firearms, were higher in the southern United States and on the west coast. New England, the Mountain region, and the East North Central regions of the United States saw lower murder rates.[189]

Temporal Differences

The majority of gun violence occurs between 7 p.m. and 1 a.m., according to the Kansas City Gun Experiment.[190] Drive-by shootings also frequently occur at night as the darkness can prevent the offenders from being detected or identified.[191] Homicides are more likely to occur on national holidays and weekends as there are more personal interactions. In addition, the spring and summer months, excluding June, were found to have the highest homicide rates.[192]

Chapter 14::
Risk Factors of (Street) Prostitution

By Yasemin Gaziarifoglu | Rutgers University

Summary of Key Factors: Road design, Camouflage areas, Proximity to drug dealing areas; Transportation hubs; Budget motels, convention centers and hotels; Coffee shops and bars.

Operational Definition

Sex markets may take three forms regarding the geography of the market:

- *Street trade* where the client locates the prostitute initially on the street,
- *Off-street trade* where the client locates the prostitute initially at specific facilities such as brothels, massage parlors, saunas, hostess clubs etc. and,
- *Mobile trade* where the client locates the prostitute initially by responding to an ad on an online website, local paper or a card left at a public location such as phone booths.

For the purposes of this chapter, street prostitution is defined as the illicit sexual transactions in which the client locates the prostitute initially on the street; either face to face or by curb crawling.

Aggravating/Mitigating Risk Factors Based on a Review of Empirical Literature

Proximity to Drug Dealing Areas: Although many different factors are identified as the pressures to enter prostitution, studies suggest that one of the main reasons for involving in prostitution is financing drug addiction[193]. Accordingly since many prostitutes are addicted to drugs, proximity to drug dealing areas may be a strong correlate for street prostitution.

Proximity to Transportation Hubs: Street prostitution areas are more common around train and bus stops.[194]

Proximity to Budget Motels, Convention Centers and Hotels: Since budget motels offer relatively lower rates, accept cash and have a much more unrestricted environment due to layout and management features, budget motels attract prostitution activities.[195] Additionally prostitution activities are also common around convention centers and hotels "especially when mostly male conventions are held".[196]

Proximity to Coffee Shops and Bars: Prostitutes take breaks in these facilities.[197]

Camouflage Areas: Sexual transactions take place in dark, dimly lit or abandoned areas such as parking lots, alleys[198] and abandoned buildings[199].

Road Design: More sexual transactions take place on roads "that allow drivers to slow down or stop, ideally where the driver's side of the vehicle is closest to the curb"[200].

Temporal Effects

Street prostitutes generally work six to eight hours a day, five to six days a week.[201] The peak hours change from place to place.

Setting Effects

Street prostitution is more common in socially disorganized neighborhoods such as areas with weak communal ties, industrial areas or declining residential areas. Still these neighborhoods are not highly crime-ridden areas as clients will be afraid to seek transactions in such settings. Accordingly street prostitution takes place in areas of transition rather than areas with high crime rates. Street prostitution areas mostly have a radius less than a mile, and it's possible to observe more than one prostitution area in large cities[202].

Chapter 15::
Risk Factors of (Forcible) Rape

By Liza Chowdhury | Rutgers University

Summary of Key Factors: Alcohol consumption, prior victimization, presence of male organized peer groups such as fraternities and sports teams, availability of private rooms such as dorm rooms, knowing the motivated offender, being alone with offender after 6p.m., living in an urban area, being a female between the age of (16-24), first few weeks of college semester (months of late August and early September).

Operational Definition

*F*orcible rape is defined as unwanted intercourse that occurs as a result of (1) force or threat of force, (2) the victim being physically unable to indicate lack of consent (e.g., due to intoxication), or (3) the victim being made incapable of consent because she/he was forcibly administered alcohol or drugs.[203]

Subcategories of forcible rape are:

- *Acquaintance rape*: Usually involves an attacker who is a classmate, friend, boyfriend, ex-boyfriend or other person known to the victim. Incidents usually occur when two people are in the same place such as a party or a dorm room.
- *Date rape*: Rape that occurs at the end of a (friendly/romantic) date.
- *Gang rape*: Multiple men taking turns to forcibly rape a woman.
- *Stranger rape*: The attacker is not an acquaintance of the victim.[204]

For the purpose of this brief, correlates of forcible rape will be divided based on data provided by college campuses and national samples because of the unique dynamics of forcible rape incidents that occur on college campuses compared to elsewhere.

Aggravating/Mitigating Risk Factors of Forcible Rape on College Campuses Based on a Review of the Empirical Literature

Alcohol: In more than three-quarters of forcible rapes at colleges, the offender, the victim or both had been drinking. Alcohol-related rape cases on campuses involved victims who were frequently drinking enough to get drunk, drinking to the point of being unable to resist forceful sexual advances, using drugs and/or drinking (both the victim and the assailant).[205] Reasons why alcohol is present in so many college rape cases includes: men become more sexualized when drinking, alcohol increases misperceptions, some men believe in stereotypes about women that drink, alcohol is used as a justification or an excuse, alcohol causes poor sending and receiving of friendly and sexual cues, alcohol decreases women's ability to resist rape.[206] Alcohol is usually involved in acquaintance rapes on campus because the victim feels some sort of comfort level in drinking with the acquaintance. In stranger rape cases, the victim usually has not had any alcohol to drink.

Repeat Victimization: College women most at risk of rape are those who were previously victims of childhood or teen sexual assault. Prior victims are nearly twice as likely to be raped in college than those with no previous history of sexual assault.[207]

Presence of Athletic Teams, Fraternities: Sexually abusive men often are friends with and loyal to other sexually abusive men and get peer support for their behavior, fostering and legitimizing it.[208] Researchers suggest that certain all-male living arrangements foster unhealthy environments conducive to rape. College athletes are disproportionately reported to campus judicial officers for acquaintance rape. As for fraternities, a disproportionate number of documented gang rapes involve fraternity members.[209] Fraternities are usually known for having private settings near the campus and holding unsupervised parties with abundant amounts of alcohol.

Setting Effects

Environmental factors that can facilitate rape on college campuses include parties at an off-campus house, on or off-campus fraternity, availability of alcohol at parties, availability of a private room, loud music that drowns out the woman's calls, and, potentially, a cover-up by the house's residents, who may choose to maintain group secrecy over reporting the rape.[210] By contrast, a date rape typically involves two people who are just becoming acquainted, and the offender rapes the victim in a car or residence after the date. Stranger rapes tend to occur in isolated areas of campus such as: parking lots, campus garages or in the woman's dorm room. Thirty-four percent of completed rapes and 45 percent of attempted rapes take place on campus. Almost 60 percent of the completed campus rapes that take place on campus occur in the victim's residence, 31 percent occur in another residence, and 10 percent occur in a fraternity.[211]

Temporal Differences

College students are the most vulnerable to being victims of rape during the first few weeks of the freshman and sophomore years. In fact, the first few days of the freshman year are the riskiest. Research has shown that rapes of college women tend to occur after 6 p.m., and the majority occur after midnight.[212]

Aggravating/Mitigating Risk Factors of Forcible Rape Based on a Review of the Empirical Literature Regarding National Samples of the General Population

Urban/Rural: As with other types of violent crime, the size and type of jurisdiction are related to the rates of arrest for forcible rape and other sex offenses. Larger cities with the largest populations have the highest rates of forcible rape in the United States.[213]

Victim/Offender Relationship: Most rape incidents involve offenders that the victim already knows. In cases with children under 12 years of age, law enforcement agencies reported that family members victimized most of these young victims. Victims age 16-24 (i.e., the largest age group of rape victims) had a prior relationship with the rapist, but they were more likely to have been acquaintances than family members. [214]

Victim's Residence/Setting Effects: More than half of rape/sexual assault incidents were reported by victims to have occurred at their own home or within one mile of their home.

Temporal Differences

Based on 1995 NIBRS data, two-thirds of rapes/sexual assaults were found to occur between 6 p.m. and 6 a.m. Nearly a third of the rapes took place between midnight and 4 a.m., with little variation in time of day by victim-offender relationship or by location of occurrence. The period from 8 p.m. Friday to 8 a.m. Saturday had the largest number of rapes in a 12-hour block. Law enforcement data indicate that the highest volume of rape reports in 1995 (9.9% of the annual total) were recorded in August and the fewest (6.8%) were recorded in December.

Chapter 16::
Risk Factors of (Street) Robbery

By Yasemin Gaziarifoglu | Rutgers University

Summary of Key Factors: Proximity to drug dealing areas; Prostitution areas; Public transport; Bars, pubs and exotic clubs; Schools, banks and cash points; Post-offices, Leisure and fast-food outlets.

Operational Definition

Street robbery is defined as occurring in a public or quasi-public place (e.g., on the street or in a vehicle) and requires the convergence of the following four conditions:

- The goods stolen should belong to an individual or group of individuals rather than a corporate body;
- The actual or implied use of force should be directed against the victim or to the property, but not the victim;
- The robbery should take place in public space excluding the interior of vehicles;
- The offender and victim might be strangers or might know each other.

Aggravating/Mitigating Risk Factors Based on a Review of Empirical Literature

Risks in Relation to Criminal Victim Selection

Individuals involved in risky lifestyles might be involved in activities that are likely to be linked to disorderly/criminal behavior.[215] According to criminals, people already involved (or getting ready to be involve) in illegal activities are seen as perfect robbery targets since they are believed to be less likely to report crimes.[216] Additionally robbers perceive police officers as less likely to intervene in robberies involving drug transactions.[217]

Proximity to Drug Dealing Areas: When the motive of robbery is to acquire cash in exchange for drugs, proximity to drug dealing areas is a strong correlate of street robberies, especially when small scale drug dealers (the possible robbery of both cash and drugs) and customers are targeted as victims.[218]

Proximity to Prostitution Areas: According to criminals, people seeking illegal sexual activities are ideal robbery targets since they will be carrying cash for the transactions and they are believed to be more reluctant in reporting the crime incident.[219] Additionally since many prostitutes are addicted to drugs[220], high-prostitution areas may be a strong correlate for street robbery.

Risks in Relation to Non-Criminal Victim Selection

According to criminals, when they are in need of fast money, law-abiding citizens might be the most suitable victims as they will be less dangerous (less likely to respond) when compared to people involved in criminal activities.[221]

Proximity to Public Transport: Proximity to public transportation has been cited as a major contributing factor for street robberies for a variety of reasons. Criminals specifically travel to public transport stations to commit crime. Offenders target victims waiting around isolated bus stops and train stations. Additionally, the vicinity of public transport areas turn into crime attractors and crime generators with the constant flux of people and the presence of other illegal activities such as illicit drug markets and ticket touts.[222]

Proximity to Bars, Pubs and Exotic Clubs: Offenders prefer to target their victims when they are drunk and pay less attention to their personal safety. [223]

Proximity to Schools: Offenders prey on students along the routes and short-cuts between main university teaching sites and residence halls.[224]

Proximity to Banks and Cash Points: Proximity to cash points increases the likelihood of street robberies as the suitable targets will be cash-rich when leaving these sites.[225] A majority of offenders are most interested in locating targets carrying a substantial amount of money to acquire the dollar sum they need in just one offense.[226]

Proximity to Post Offices: Bag snatches from elderly people most often happen around post offices.[227]

Proximity to Leisure and Fast-Food Outlets: Young, school-aged, people and young adults are often targeted around leisure and fast-food outlets.[228]

Setting Effects

According to UN reports, crime levels are generally higher in urban environments than rural ones in all countries, with the highest levels of crimes occurring in cities experiencing rapid growth. Additionally, victims of crimes in cities have a higher probability of being victimized in public space, according to international victimization surveys.[229] Most of the street robberies occur in urban areas in the US, Wales, and England.[230]

Movement is primarily shaped by street grids in cities, and integrated streets attract more movement because of their ease of accessibility. Internationally, integrated streets tend to be the safest places with regard to violent crime, but are preferred by petty criminals and thieves. In American cities there is a significantly higher correlation between integrated streets and robberies because of the strong automobile dependent culture--where walking is not the preferred way of transportation.[231] Furthermore, robbers feel more comfortable (and ambiguous) in metropolitan areas--with the camouflage of buildings and skyscrapers.[232]

Temporal Differences

Most robberies generally occur at night and on the weekends. However, in line with routine activities theory and crime pattern theory, which emphasize the space and time convergence of a likely offender and suitable target for the occurrence of a criminal event, it is possible to identify the clustering of street robberies at specific times and days. With regard to street robberies, a specific location considered as a hot spot for street robberies at night may become a low-crime area during the day.

Times & Routines: [233]: In cases where older people (65+) are targeted, robberies mostly take place in the morning and early afternoons; in cases where young people (<18) are targeted, robberies mostly take place between 3 p.m. and 6 p.m. (i.e., with school dismissal); in cases where adults are generally targeted, robberies mostly occur in the evening. Drunken people and migrant workers returning home after payday are mostly targeted at night. Morning and evening rush hours can increase/decrease the likelihood of victimization depending on the level of natural guardianship in the specific city/neighborhood. Regarding land use, the absence of business activities at night in commercial areas with limited residential use might increase the odds of street robberies. [234]

Days & Routines: [235]: Certain holidays (i.e. New Year's Eve, Saint Patrick's Day, Fourth of July, Memorial Day) may increase the odds of victimization because more suitable victims will be available with valuables items to take. Additionally, the likely consumption of alcohol by suitable targets on these holidays increases the vulnerability to victimization. Days with sporting or other special events might have increased odds of robberies due to the availability of targets in public and the likely consumption of alcohol during the events. The beginning and ending days of a school year and the holiday breaks can affect the likelihood of victimization depending on the availability of suitable and vulnerable targets in certain places.

Risk Terrain Modeling Compendium | 2011 | Caplan and Kennedy

Chapter 17::
Risk Factors of Shootings

By Jill Drucker | Rutgers University

Summary of Key Factors: Drug trade; At-risk housing developments; Gang activity; Gun availability; Criminal history.

Operational Definition

$\mathcal{F}$or the purpose of this research brief, a shooting is defined as "when bullets are shot from guns or other weapons."[236]

Aggravating/Mitigating Risk Factors Based on a Review of Empirical Literature

Drug Trade: Violent disputes are often linked with drug dealing and drug trafficking due to enforcement of drug debts, arguments with competitors, and establishing control over territory. Much of the violence associated with gang activity is due to their engagement in drug trafficking and drug sales.[237]

At-Risk Housing Developments: Violent crime in public housing dramatically exceeds levels of violence in other disadvantaged nonpublic housing neighborhoods. Residents of public housing are twice as likely to be victims of gun violence than individuals who do not reside in public housing facilities. The design hypothesis theorizes that the environment and structure of housing projects increases opportunities to offend and thus increases the offending rates of public housing residents as compared to nonpublic housing residents.[238]

Gang Activity: Gangs are responsible for a large percentage of the crime in many urban and some suburban communities in the United States.[239] Gangs often engage in drive-by shootings, when an individual or group of individual fires a weapon from a vehicle at another vehicle, person, or structure, to intimidate or threaten rivals or to establish their gang's turf. Research shows that at-risk youth who are not involved in gang activity are less likely to engage in drive-by shootings than involved gang members. Gang involvement may encourage drive-by shootings due to gun accessibility and condoning of violent behavior.[240]

Gun Availability: Greater firearm availability not only increases the rates of homicide, but also increases the rates of other types of felony gun use.[241]

Criminal History: Perpetrators of weapon-related offenses are more likely to have extensive criminal histories.[242] In addition, youth gun violence is disproportionately present in youths with criminal backgrounds including violent offenses, disorder offenses, and drug offenses.[243]

Demographic Factors: Gun violence is concentrated among young minority males who live in socially and economically disadvantaged communities.[244]

Setting Effects

Urban locations see higher levels of gun violence, both fatal and non-fatal. This increase may be due to the urban area's higher levels of gang conflicts, drug markets, and gun availability.[245]

Temporal Effects

The Kansas City Gun Experiment found that the majority of gun violence occurred between 7 p.m. and 1 a.m.[246] Drive-by shootings frequently occur at night because darkness serves to conceal offenders.[247]

Demonstrates how RTM can be applied to different crime types and settings, and how it can be used for a variety of practical research and analysis purposes.

Part 3

Case Studies and Applications of RTM

Contributing Authors:
Baughman, J.
Caplan, J. M.
Gaziarifoglu, Y.
Kennedy, L. W.
Moreto, W. D.
Piza, E. L.
Sytsma, V.

Chapter 18::
Applying RTM to Street Robberies

By Leslie W. Kennedy and Yasemin Gaziarifoglu | *Rutgers University*

Concerns about armed robbery have permeated the criminological literature over the years, partly as this behavior is so closely tied to the ebbs and flows of the drug trade and is a crime that most urban dwellers fear, threatening their property and their person and leaving traumatic impacts. As its connection to drugs attests, robbery is a crime that accompanies other crimes and permeates all parts of the urban landscape. There have been, over the years, excellent studies examining the factors effecting offenders' motivation and victims' vulnerability in robbery incidents. Where one line of studies examines the robbery risk in relation to the crime attracting nature of some locales such as drug dealing or prostitution areas[248], speculation has also been directed at the crime generating nature of urban features including schools, bars, fast food outlets, and cash points[249]. These studies have all provided important insights into the correlates of this crime but what we propose in this study is to look at robbery in the context of a combination of these factors, examining their relative risk in enhancing the probability that robbery will take place. This analysis will be done using a technique that calculates a risk terrain, combining the important layers of correlates across a continuous map surface, to produce a forecast of the likely areas that robbery will take place. So, this moves beyond simply saying that robbery will occur as a correlation of certain factors to identifying the context in which this crime is most likely to occur. We will examine the contexts of robbery using data from Newark, NJ, a city where robberies have shown the highest increase in the past year with a 12% boost from years 2009 to 2010. Given that a clear distinction between offense subtypes is imperative since every crime is built on different situational factors, this case study selectively focuses on robberies that took place in public space (e.g. streets, sidewalks, parking lots, lots/yards, in front of commercial dwellings). We will consider the importance of different risk layers in forecasting robbery. We will combine these layers into a risk terrain model to which we will add robbery outcomes. We will then examine the predictive validity of our model and compare the increased accuracy of our approach over simple retrospective analysis of past robbery incidents.

Operationalization of the Dependent Variable
Risk terrain modeling is dependent upon the availability of valid data from reliable sources. In this case study the data on 2009 street robberies were available for the months January-August[250].

Operationalization of the Independent Variables
To begin forecasting future risk of street robberies, it was necessary to consider existing theory and literature that would help to understand this form of crime. According to the review of the empirical literature discussed above there are 7 factors that research has shown correlate with

street robberies: *proximity to/high density of drug dealing areas; prostitution areas; bus stops; rail stations; bars, pubs and exotic clubs, leisure and fast-food outlets; universities; banks*. In risk terrain modeling, including all risk factors does not always produce better models. The model may still be meaningful and could serve operational needs, but the effectiveness of the model comes from including only the "most correlated" factors and excluding all others. This phenomenon of "less-can-be-more" in RTM has been proved empirically by Kennedy, Caplan and Piza[251]. Accordingly, at the beginning of this case study a series of Chi-squared tests were conducted to identify the variables most significantly correlated with the outcome event.

For chi-squared tests, a blank vector grid of cells that covered the entire study area was created using the "Create Vector Grid Tool" in Hawth's Analysis Tools for ArcGIS. This assigns attributes to the vector grid cells that note whether a cell intersects with any of the features on the "risk map layers", accomplished by "selecting all cells of the vector grid that 'intersect' with point features on the street robberies map". After running 7 chi-square analyses, only 5 of the 7 proved to be significantly correlated with street robberies ($p \leq .05$). Accordingly, in this case study, these five key factors are used: locations of retail business venues (bars, liquor stores, markets, and restaurants), locations of bus stops, locations of banks, locations of drug arrests, and location of prostitution arrests. The "drug arrest" and "prostitution arrest" independent variables include the arrests that took place in the first eight months of 2008 to predict the street robbery incidents in 2009. The locations of the other 3 independent variables were also available in address-level datasets for the year of 2008.

Operationalizing these datasets to raster map layers was done using standard tools available in ArcView's Spatial Analyst Extension. Data were first geocoded to street centerlines of Newark, NJ (obtained from Census 2000 TIGER/Line Shapefiles) to create point features representing the locations of retail business venues, bus stops, banks, drug arrests and prostitution arrests on five separate maps. The Density Tool in ArcView's Spatial Analyst Extension was then used to create a raster grid for each map and assign values to identically-sized raster cells based on the intensity, or local concentration, of points near each cell's location. This density scheme for operationalizing geocoded tabular data into raster map layers was repeated for each variable, producing

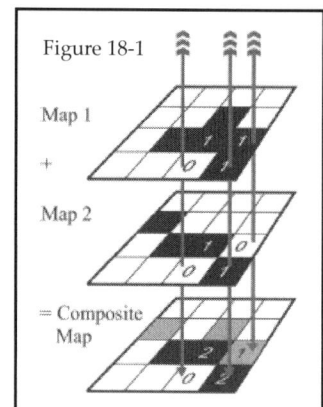

Figure 18-1

maps with cell values assigned according to the immediate or nearby concentration of key variables in each respective cell. Cells within each raster map layer were then classified into four groups according to standard deviational breaks. This process was repeated for all five density map layers to produce five new raster maps of Newark with all locations designated as low to high risk for street robberies. Since the cells of different raster map layers were the same size and were classified in a consistent way, they could be summed to form a composite risk terrain, as exemplified in Figure 18-1.

The areas including Newark Liberty International Airport and Port Authority were excluded from the study extent as these areas do not fall within Newark Police Department jurisdiction. A risk terrain map was created using data from 2008. The predictive validity of this risk terrain was tested using counts of street robbery incidents during 2009 that were appended to the cells of the 2008 risk terrain using the Spatial Join function in ArcView. Cells of the final risk terrain map, then, had two values attributed to it: 1) risk value and 2) number of street robbery incidents during the consecutive time period. Figure 18-2 illustrates the risk terrain produced from the RTM approach using 2008 data, together with the street robberies in the first eight months of 2009. As shown in Figure 18-2, future street robbery incidents appear to be located in areas that the risk terrain map forecasted to be higher risk.

Figure 18-2

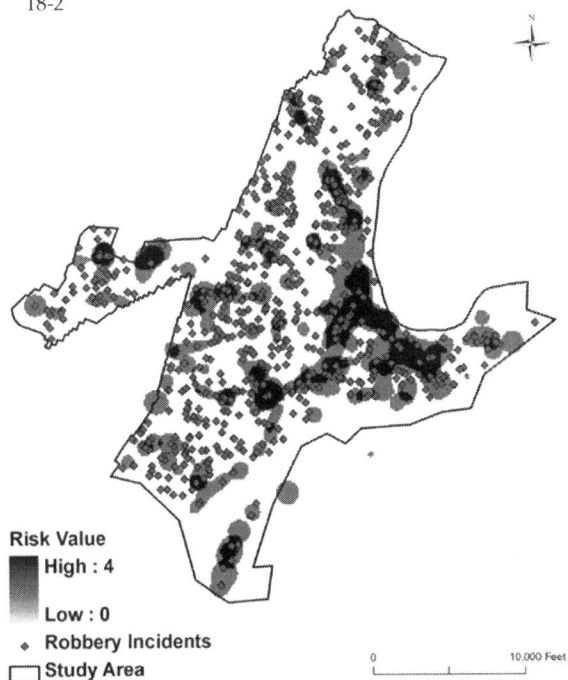

2008 Risk Terrain and 2009 Street Robbery Overlay

Risk Value
High : 4
Low : 0
◆ Robbery Incidents
☐ Study Area

0 — 10,000 Feet

Before testing the statistical validity of our model with these two attributes; a Global Moran's I test was conducted using ArcMap's Moran's I tool to control for "spatial autocorrelation". Simply put distributions among geographical units, such as grid cells, are usually not independent, meaning that values found in a particular cell are likely to be influenced by corresponding values in nearby cells and Moran's I measures this autocorrelation[252]. Since the Z score indicated a statistical significance (p<.05) and the Moran's I index was more than "0", it was concluded that there was a significant tendency towards clustering of street robbery incidents in the city of Newark. Accordingly, a spatial lag variable for each cell was created via the "Generate Spatial Weights Matrix" tool in ArcMap. This variable was added as the third attribute to the cells of our final risk terrain map to include it in our regression model as a control. Logistic regression analysis allowed us to measure the extent to which the Period I risk terrain model explained the patterns of street robbery incidents during Period II (Ind. Var. = "Risk Value" [0-4]; Spatial Lag Variable = [.25-.5]; Dep. Var. = "Presence of Any Street Robbery" [Yes or No]). As shown in Table 18-1, the odds ratio suggests that for every increased unit of risk at a 100ftx100ft place, a future street robbery is almost 2.3 times more likely to occur (p<0.001). The spatial lag control variable was not found significant.

Table 18-1: Logistic Regression for Risk Value on Street Robberies				
Period I Risk Terrain				
	B	S.E.	Sig.	Exp(B)
Risk Value	0.82	0.036	0.000	2.272
Spatial Lag	-187.323	12631.65	0.988	0.000
Constant	41.25	3157.912	0.990	8.22E+17
-2LL: 7853.965; Nagelkerke R square: .045				

$\mathcal{A}$lthough crime incidents occur at specific geographic points, most of them are recorded in reference to the addresses of certain facilities and dwellings, and in most cases we do not have the data on exact locations. So, to realistically test the efficiency of the risk terrain model with further statistical analysis, the limitations of administrative data should be taken into account.

Accordingly the predictive validity analysis was conducted using *street segments* as units of analysis. The average street segment length in Newark (when we exclude Newark airport and Port Authority) was 422 feet.

Before testing the statistical validity of our model; first the cells that intersect with a street segment were selected and then for each street segment the average risk value was calculated using the spatial join function in ArcMap. Figure 18-3 shows the average risk values of street segments.

Before conducting the logistic regression analysis for street segments, a Global Moran's I test was conducted using ArcMap's Moran's I tool to control for "spatial autocorrelation". Since the Z score did not indicate a statistical significance (p>.05) and the Moran's I index was more than "0", it was concluded that there was not a significant tendency towards spatial autocorrelation. Accordingly this time it was not seen necessary to add a spatial lag variable to the regression model as a control.

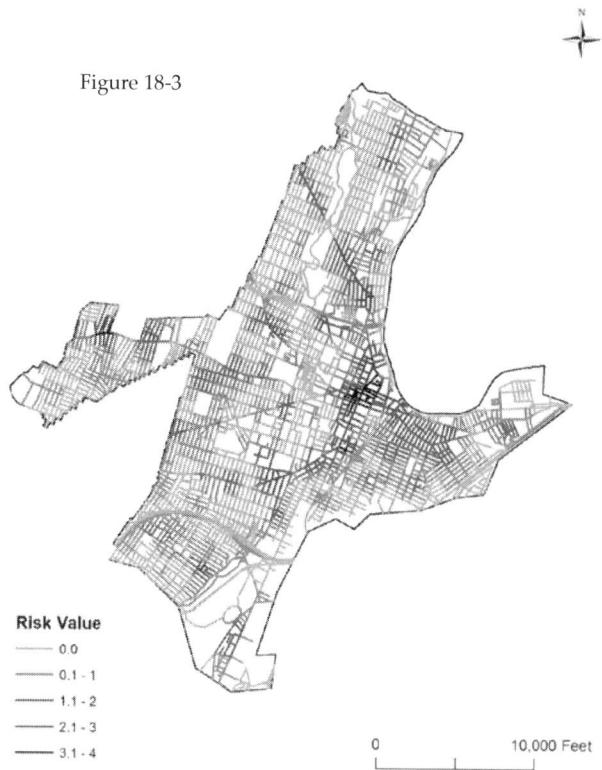

Figure 18-3

Risk Value
— 0.0
— 0.1 - 1
— 1.1 - 2
— 2.1 - 3
— 3.1 - 4

0   10,000 Feet

A logistic regression analysis was conducted using street segments as the unit of analysis to measure the extent to which the Period I risk terrain model explained the patterns of street robbery incidents in Period II (Ind. Var. = "Average Risk Value" [0-4]; Dep. Var. = "Presence of Any Street Robbery" [Yes or No]). As shown in Table 18-2, the odds ratio suggested that for every increased unit of average risk at a street segment, the likelihood of a future street robbery increased by 16% (p<0.01).

Table 18-2: Logistic Regression for Risk Value on Street Robberies					
Period I Risk Terrain					
		B	S.E.	Sig.	Exp(B)
	Average Risk Value	.153	.049	0.002	1.166
	Constant	-2.044	.055	0.000	.129
-2LL: 3580.227; Nagelkerke R square: .004					

*O*ur results indicate that robberies are tied to locations, and certain features in the environment combine to increase risk of this crime that can be used to forecast future occurrence of these events. Our findings support the importance of place-based approaches to combating violent crime, and our approach to converting risk values to administrative units increases the efficacy of this approach for law enforcement. In the past decades, studies involving crime analysis have been almost uniformly dedicated to the identification and analysis of spatial crime concentrations. Studies in general define "place" either zero-dimensionally as a "point in space" such as a commercial building or a residential dwelling, or uni- or bi-dimensionally as "an area" such as a census block, police district, or sometimes even a city. The latter component of that definition might be also differentiated as "space"[253]. With the increased interest in place-based policing, place has also been defined in micro-level-units of addresses or clusters of addresses such as buildings or addresses; block faces, or street segments; or clusters of addresses, block faces, or street segments[254]. Using the techniques described here, it is possible to aggregate up to meaningful places to improve the accuracy of targeting areas of concern and responding accordingly.

Regarding the backcloth of the crime incident, the specific situation—originally referred to as behavior setting—has been generally seen in a hierarchical relationship with places and space. Accordingly, the behavior setting which provides the background of an incident is rooted in place and each place is rooted in space "a larger area governing long-run routine activity patterns of potential participants in conflict situations"[255]. As Bernasco and Block (2010)[256] state, in geographic criminology "the spatial unit of analysis should match the theoretical perspectives that guide the analysis." Accordingly, rather than designing a study around "what's available" or "what is easier," researchers should aim for models which are grounded in theory and which are flexible enough to move between different levels of analysis when the analysis and needed information products require it.

Doing a risk terrain model first identifies the pool of risk factors that are related to a specific crime incident at the micro-level rather than being constrained by predefined geographic boundaries set by street segments or neighborhoods. This gives researchers the tools to identify the significant risk correlates within different spatial and temporal extents. The simultaneous analysis of statistically significant risk factors enables the researcher to evaluate the compounded criminogenic qualities of places irrespective of all other places within a terrain[257]. With its flexibility, the RTM approach enables the practitioners and researcher to adjust to the limitations of data and to respond to the needs of the law enforcement system, in particular. So, as demonstrated, if patrols are easier to define by street segments, RTM easily identifies where the highest risk street segments for robbery are. Going beyond describing risk events or combining possible risk correlates, RTM turns into a spatial intelligence tool by equipping the researchers with skills to statistically test the significance of their models and law enforcement with skills to allocate their resources proactively with emancipation from spatial and temporal research constraints.

Such an approach to crime analysis has specific implications for cities like Newark that have long been plagued by high levels of violent crime. Since 2006, the Newark Police Department has incorporated a large number of place-based interventions in their efforts against violence. These approaches range from increased officer presence, high levels of foot patrols, situational-crime prevention techniques (such as street closures and surveillance activities), and proactive narcotics enforcement. But, these approaches are difficult to sustain in times of manpower reductions. Identification of risk clusters that would encourage street robberies can aid police leaders in their resource allocation by identifying high-priority areas both currently receiving and in-need of additional coverage. In the case of Newark, a number of risk clusters fall within existing target areas of the Police Department's various place-based interventions. However, other high-risk places currently receive no more than basic police attention in the form of patrol, retroactive investigations, and ad hoc suppression efforts. With the approach offered in this paper, the crime analysts can provide targeted maps that direct attention to specific street segments for added attention. With such data in hand, police mangers in Newark and elsewhere can more-precisely deploy proactive, place-based interventions. There is the additional benefit of this approach in that RTM allows for a continuous evaluation of the success of these interventions through a continuous temporal cycle of analysis that can be performed using data from affected areas. Analysts can also add other factors to the analysis that are dynamic and not fixed, as are the features that we used in this analysis. For example, they could include measures of arrests for related crimes, such as drugs, and could include information about such things as the activity of street gangs. This framework provides a more flexible way to assess and forecast robbery locations using techniques that are uncomplicated and theoretically informed.

Chapter 19::
Applying RTM to Residential Burglary

By William D. Moreto | Rutgers University

$\mathcal{R}$esidential burglary is arguably one of the most popular index crimes that crime analysts and criminologists have attempted to *predict.* However, with the exception of some scholars[258] the majority of prior research has focused on 'hot spots' or incident-based maps and has neglected to *operationalize* the environmental backcloth[259] in which burglaries actually occur. The current pilot study contributes to the literature by addressing the facilitating context of residential burglary and illuminates environmental factors that contribute to and/or mitigate against burglary events from occurring. The study uses the Risk Terrain Modeling (RTM) approach to forecast urban residential burglary (herein known solely as burglary) in the city of Newark, New Jersey. By

using this method, the current study moves beyond the reliance on past or instigator events by generating a greater understanding and appreciation for the underlying contextual environment in which particular crimes are more likely to occur.

The City of Newark was chosen as the setting of the current study since it is the largest city in New Jersey. Considered to be one of the most culturally diverse cities in the United States, the city has made substantial improvements in recent years in several areas, including the economic and industrial sectors. However, Newark continues to struggle with

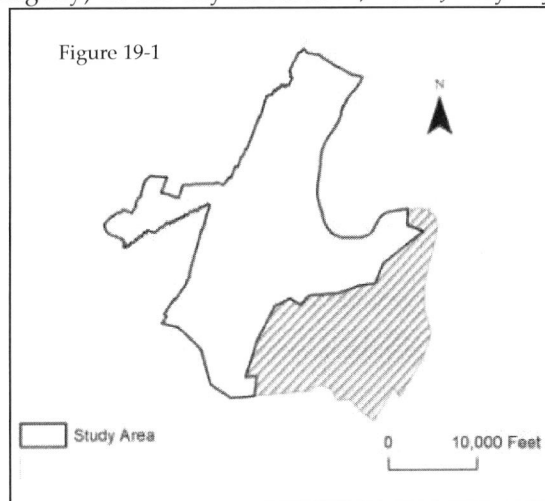

Figure 19-1

poverty and crime. For example, burglary rates for 2009 were 1,947 per 100,000, compared to national average for similar size cities in the United States of 727.3 per 100,000 (UCR 2009). Recently, the city has laid off 167 police officers as a result of budget cuts resulting in the further limitation of resources available to the Newark Police Department. Thus, cost-effective analytical techniques that can increase the capacity of the practitioners by providing meaningful and useful information that can be used for appropriate and efficient responses are desired. As shown in Figure 19-1, the actual study area included only those locations that are within the jurisdiction of the Newark Police Department, so areas including the Newark airport and Port Newark were excluded.

Prior to any application of RTM, a thorough review of the existing literature should be conducted in order to elucidate potential variables, both aggravating and mitigating, that could be included in a subsequent spatial analysis. The experience of the analyst and of practitioners should also be considered in order to consider other potentially relevant factors[260]. Importantly, the inclusion of variables should be grounded in theory to help clarify the possible mechanisms and relationships to the outcome of interest, in this case, burglary. For the current case study, there were four key factors that were operationalized to identify an environment conducive for urban residential burglary. Three as aggravating factors (at-risk housing complexes, bus stops, and pawn shops) and one as a mitigating factor (guardian infrastructures). It must be noted that the aforementioned variables are not an exhaustive list of all key variables associated with burglary based on the literature review conducted; however, these were sufficient for the current pilot study.

The most up-to-date data of burglaries from the Newark Police Department was up to August, 2010; however, for the current study, the data was limited to a six-month time period (January 1, 2010 through June 30, 2010). Location data was used to create the risk terrain map for Period 1 (January 1, 2009 to June 30, 2009), which would be used to forecast residential burglary for Period 2 (January 1, 2010 to June 30, 2009), as shown in Figure 19-2. Similar time periods were used in order to control for any seasonal variations and related

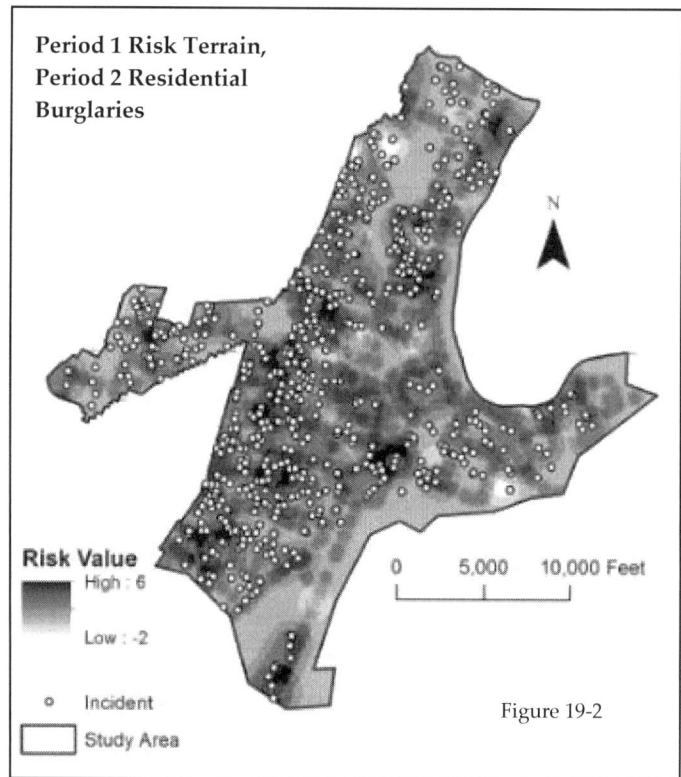

Period 1 Risk Terrain, Period 2 Residential Burglaries

Risk Value
High : 6
Low : -2

o Incident

☐ Study Area

Figure 19-2

events (i.e. spring break, beginning of summer holidays, etc). ESRI's ArcGIS 9.3 was used to create the map layers and subsequent RTM map. ArcMap's Spatial Analyst Extension was utilized to convert the datasets into raster map layers. Data were first geocoded to street centerlines of Newark, NJ (obtained from Census 2000 TIGER/Line Shapefiles) to create point features representing the locations of bus stops, pawn shops and guardian infrastructures (police department precincts, fire department fire halls and hospitals) on three separate maps. The fourth risk layer, at-risk housing complexes, was based on data provided by the Newark Police Department and the Newark Housing Authority[261]. Privately owned crime-prone complexes were also included due to knowledge of them being associated with illegal drug markets in Newark[262], which may also be linked with residential burglary as offenders may burgle a home in order to sustain their drug-use[263]. Buffers were created around the point and polygon features described and were based on proximity distances that are believed to be at high (HH), high-low (HL), low-high (LH) and low risk (LL) based on the literature and theory.

ArcMap's Density Tool was used to create a raster grid for each map and assign values to identically-sized raster cells (145 feet x 145 feet). The average length of Newark streets was not used due to highway street segments acting as outliers and skewing street measurements; therefore, half the approximate *median* length of a Newark city block (290 feet) was used for the current study. The raster cells were created based on the local concentration of points near each individual raster cell's location. Each risky and mitigating variable was geocoded similarly. Maps were created with raster cell values based on the immediate or nearby accumulation of risk and mitigating variables in each individual cell. Each map layer was then reclassified into two groups with cells given a value (2, 1, -1, -2 or 0) based on their respective risky or mitigating values[264]. This process was done for all four variables resulting in eight new raster map layers. Importantly, since the cells for all raster map layers were equal in size and were classified in a similar fashion, they could be added together using the Raster Calculator tool to form the subsequent risk terrain map needed to conduct the evaluation on the validity of the RTM.

A binary logistic regression analysis was conducted to assess the predictive validity of the risk terrain map produced from 2009 data on residential burglary incidents that occurred within the first half of 2010 in Newark, NJ. As shown in the Table 19-1, the odds ratio suggested that for every one unit increase in risk, the likelihood of a burglary incident occurring increased by 15% (p <.001). It should be noted that a Moran's I test was conducted and no spatial autocorrelation was found, therefore no spatial lag was incorporated in the current analysis[265].

Table 19-1: Period 1 Risk Terrain for Period 2 Incidents								
2-Log Likelihood = 5187.80 Nagelkerke R Square = .006; n = 13948	B	SE	Wald	df	Sig	Exp(B)	95% C.I. for Exp(B)	
							Lower	Upper
Risk Value	0.14	.03	25.20	1	<.001	1.15	1.09	1.2

The current study shows the utility of RTM in its ability to identify areas where residential burglaries are more likely to occur in the city of Newark, NJ. The use of RTM methods implicitly results in crime analysts and ground-level practitioners to separate themselves from relying on instigator events to occur *before* they can respond. Essentially, RTM enables the potential for proactive, intelligence-led forms of policing to occur as opposed to traditional reactive-based approaches which rely on crimes to occur. Additionally, the identification of risky areas may also identify vital locations with important stakeholders that otherwise may not be recognized (i.e. place managers). Importantly, the current study also accounted for mitigating factors. Arguably, criminology as a discipline has traditionally been focused on factors that increase the risk at a particular area, while neglecting the influence of mitigating factors, especially during the *same* analysis. RTM allows the ability for crime analysts to include both risk-related and mitigating factors in a single analysis thereby being sensitive to the dynamic and inter-dependent relationship of contextual factors. In other words, RTM recognizes that a *criminogenic context* may encompass both forms of risk and security.

It is important to note that the concepts of repeat victimization and the near repeat phenomenon still need to be accounted for. Up to this point, RTM has yet to deal with this issue. Any assessment of residential burglary must take the aforementioned concepts into consideration and they will be addressed in future research. Indeed, it may be found that RTM may complement the current literature on both prospective mapping and residential burglary by establishing the much-needed baseline risk levels that may result in even more meaningful analysis and interpretation of the so-called 'communicability of risk' (Bowers et al. 2004).

As has been shown, RTM is much more than merely making a map. Theoretically grounded and premised on empirical literature, RTM presents a potentially more efficient and effective alternative to conventional retrospective mapping techniques. By identifying areas that are more susceptible to particular crimes, appropriate responses by both formal (i.e. police) and informal (i.e. place managers) stakeholders can be initiated *before* an incident occurs. In effect, RTM moves crime mapping away from its reliance on past crimes and presents the opportunity to utilize theory, technique and technology in a concerted and proactive way.

Chapter 20::
Applying RTM to Aggravated Assault

By Victoria Sytsma | *Rutgers University*

*T*his research brief presents a pilot study employing the technique of Risk Terrain Modeling[266] (RTM) to the offence of aggravated assault within the city of Newark, NJ. This pilot contributes to the existing literature by producing greater insight into the spatial intersection of a variety of environmental facets conducive to the outcome of aggravated assault. Further, by spatially engaging potential risk factors favorable to the occurrence of a criminal event, one can provide strong explanatory conjecture without having to rely upon past criminal incidents.

The combination of lower inhibitions due to alcohol, over-crowding, poor communication, and the possibility for the presence of other crimes such as prostitution and drug dealing makes bars and social clubs an environment ripe for aggravated assaults to occur.[267] In addition, drug markets contribute to aggravated assaults through drug deal disputes and turf wars turning violent.[268] For this pilot study, three risk factors for the spatial occurrence of aggravated assault are operationalized here; the locations of drug arrests, narcotic hotspots, and the locations of bars and social clubs. It must be noted that this is not an exhaustive list of the risk factors linked to aggravated assault by any means. This is a pilot study and accordingly these findings may be built upon in future research.

The area under study here is the city of Newark, NJ. Despite recent reductions in violent crime, at 413 aggravated assaults per 100,000 in Newark in 2008 versus the national average of 275, Newark continues to face challenges with violent crime (UCR, 2008). It must be noted that the Newark Liberty

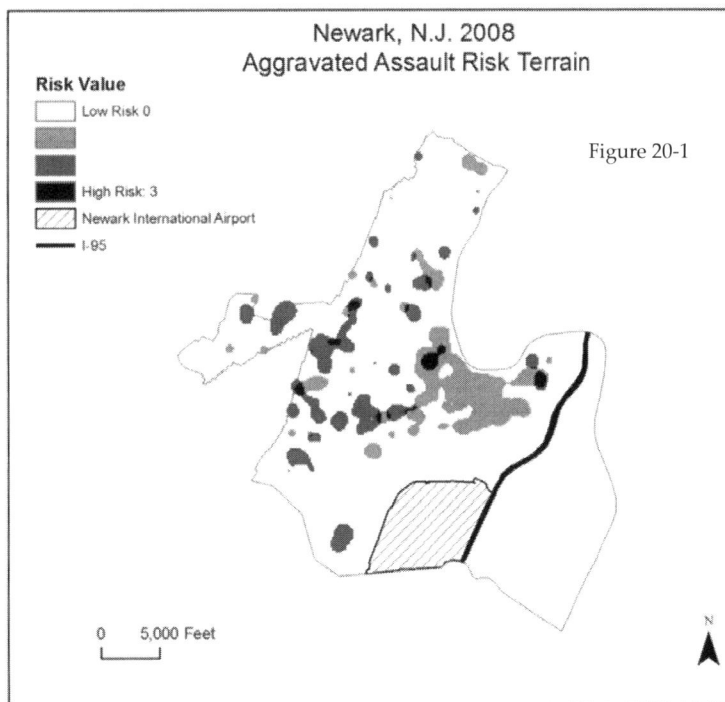

Newark, N.J. 2008
Aggravated Assault Risk Terrain

Risk Value

Low Risk 0

High Risk: 3

Newark International Airport

I-95

Figure 20-1

0   5,000 Feet

N

International Airport is not patrolled by the Newark Police Department and these findings cannot be generalized to that area of Newark. Further, the area of Newark south of highway I-95 is home to Port Authority; an area also not patrolled by the Newark Police and thus the results do not apply to this location as well.

The period under study here for the location data is 2008 and the risk calculation produced for this period was tested for predictive validity against 2008 aggravated assault point data to see if the risk calculation indeed significantly predicted aggravated assault to occur within the 2008 landscape. The ArcView Spatial Analyst Extension was used to convert data to raster and it was geocoded to street centerlines of Newark, NJ (obtained from Census 2000 TIGER/Line Shapefiles). Each of the three risk factor layers were then reclassified into a dichotomous variable, operationalized as 0=not highest risk, 1=highest risk; with '1' referring to all values greater than 2 standard deviations from the mean. In the case of the *narcotic hotspot* risk layer, because it was a polygon shapefile as opposed to point data, no standard deviations were used –a location was either a hotspot or it was not. The Raster Calculator function in ArcMap was used to combine each risk factor into a Risk Value layer which can be seen in Figure 20-1.

The predictive validity of this RTM was tested by converting the Risk Value layer into a vector polygon grid with each cell representing 140 square feet –approximately half a Newark city block. The 2008 aggravated assault point data was joined with this polygon grid of 38,047 cells to determine if criminal events spatially intersect with risk. As seen in Table 20-1, a logistic regression was run and it was found that for every one unit increase in risk value, the odds of an aggravated assault occurring increases by 116%; these results were statistically significant.

Table 20-1: Logistic Regression for Risk Value on Aggravated Assault

	B	S.E.	Wald	df	Sig.	Exp(B)	95% C. I. for EXP(B) Lower	Upper
Step 1[a] RiskValue	.773	.035	485.531	1	.000	2.165	2.021	2.319
Constant	-4.051	.041	9600.986	1	.000	.017		
-2 Log likelihood= 8064.931; Nagelkerke R^2 = .050								

This pilot study gives credence to the use of RTM, particularly in police agencies such as Newark where budgets require efficient methods to determine where patrols are needed. However, because this is merely a pilot study, other risk factors surrounding aggravated assault may be investigated in the future. The adaptive nature of RTM makes this method amenable to investigating risk factors grounded in theory and literature, but also risk factors which arise out of police and crime analysts' experiences with a criminal event or location. Finally, based on the forecasting nature of this method, RTM might be used for crime *prevention* based on the environmental contexts of a given area, as opposed to merely relying on past crime events to prevent where future crime will occur.

Chapter 21::
Police Resource Allocation

By Eric L. Piza, Leslie W. Kennedy, and Joel M. Caplan | *Rutgers University*

*T*here has been an increased interest in developing techniques using spatial analysis programs to identify and target areas where crime concentrates. The most popular approach has been hotspot mapping based on high spatial crime density to direct police attention to certain locations to suppress crime and deter offenders[269]. Sherman[270] examined the ways in which different types of crime concentrate in hotspots and concluded that what is important in understanding crime outcomes are onset, recurrence, frequency, desistence, and intermittency, in the context of how these processes influence the concentration of crime. This perspective, drawing together routine activities, rational choice, and crime careers approaches has been the gold standard of crime analysis for years. However, while hotspot mapping has allowed police to address the concentration of crime, it has generally turned attention away from the social and structural contexts in which crime occurs. Predictions about crime occurrence are then based on what happened before in locations rather than on the behavioral or physical characteristics of places within communities.

As better data and more sophisticated mapping techniques have come available, opportunities have emerged to move beyond approaches that rely on mapping past incidents to empirical and evidence-based strategies that forecast where crime will emerge in the future. Caplan, Kennedy and Miller[271] have proposed that risk terrain modeling (RTM) offers a way of looking at criminality as less determined by previous events and more a function of a dynamic interaction between social, physical and behavioral factors that occurs at places. They suggest that the ways in which these variables combine can be studied to reveal consistent patterns of interaction that can facilitate and lead to crime. This analytical strategy more directly addresses the role of place-based context in crime forecasting, tying back to the basic premises in environmental criminology that social and physical characteristics of communities influence how crime emerges, concentrates and evolves[272].

The study briefed here examined how the RTM approach to spatial risk assessment can be implemented into police operations by addressing three important issues that address the validity of RTM that sets it apart from current approaches to spatial crime analysis. First, it addressed the selection criteria used in determining which risk layers to include in risk terrain models. Second, it compared the "best model" risk terrain derived from the analysis to the traditional hotspot density mapping technique by considering both the statistical power and overall usefulness of each approach. Third, it tested for "risk clusters" in risk terrain maps to determine how they can be used to target police resources in a way that improves upon the current practice of using density maps of past crime.

$\mathcal{N}$ewark is the largest city in the State of New Jersey, covering 26 square miles, with an estimated 2009 population of over 280,000 persons[273] and the largest municipal police force in the state, with more than 1,300 sworn officers as of 2009. The City has a long standing reputation as a tumultuous urban environment. The new millennium saw both murders and non-fatal shootings increasing every year from 2000 to 2006, according to police department figures. But under the direction of newly appointed Police Director Garry F. McCarthy, formerly the lead crime strategist at the NYPD, the mission and structure of the department changed and an intelligence-led policing mantra was adopted.

Since these initiatives went into effect, Newark experienced a significant reduction in violent crime. According to department figures, overall crime decreased 19% from 2006 through 2009, with murders and shootings decreasing 28% and 40% respectively. While some may instinctively think otherwise, cities experiencing reductions in violence such as Newark can benefit from analytical methods like risk terrain modeling as much as jurisdictions facing crime increases or stagnation. As violent crime trends downward, so does the margin of error for police (especially police with limited resources). Public desire for crime reduction is ever-present, as is the political motivation for maximizing public safety. For these reasons, a technique that accurately forecasts the locations of future incidents (not just future totals) can be a valuable tool for agencies looking to build upon their recent successes.

Here, we focused our attention on gun violence due to the obvious seriousness of the offense and its (still) high level of occurrence in Newark. Despite ending 2008 with its second lowest murder total since 1965 (67), Newark's murder rate of 23.9 (per 100,000 residents) more than doubled the national average (11.5) for cities with populations greater than 250,000[274]. Firearm usage directly dictates the murder rate in Newark, with police data showing 84% of the city's murders resulting from gunshot wounds from 2007 through May 2010. While recognizing recent successes in violent crime reduction, city officials and residents consider current levels of gun violence to be unacceptable and rank violent crime along with the related issues of gangs and drugs as the most serious issues facing the city.

The Newark Police Department maintains an extensive Geographic Information System (GIS) which contains numerous data layers. Such a system presents a unique situation: The abundance of data allows one to configure numerous risk models, each utilizing a different combination of data layers. At the same time, the analyst faces the daunting task of identifying the "best" combination that produces the model with the strongest predictive capabilities. The more layers accessible within a GIS, the more frustrating this situation can be.

Given the size of Newark PD's GIS (as of the date of this study 50 separate layers appeared in the system) we first attempted to get a general sense of the place-based factors related to shootings in the city. The professional insight of experienced police officers in conjunction with a review of relevant empirical research led us to identify seven risk factors that we believed would accurately forecast the locations of shooting incidents in Newark: (1) locations of drug arrests, (2) proximity to "at-risk" housing developments, (3) "risky facilities," (4) locations of gang activity, (5) known home addresses of parolees previously incarcerated for violent crimes and/or violations of drug distribution laws, (6) location of past shooting incidents, and (7) locations of past gun robberies. These risk factors were operationalized into separate risk map layers in a manner consistent with the steps detailed in the *Risk Terrain Modeling Manual* (www.riskterrainmodeling.com).

Research Objective 1: Select the Best Risk Terrain Model

Although seven risk factors were initially identified to be correlated with shootings, we sought to select only those that were most significant and influential. Chi-Squared tests were conducted to identify the place-based risk factors most significantly associated with shooting locations and to develop four models: Model 1 included all of the seven risk factors; Model 2 included risk factors that were significant at $p<0.05$ (Drug Arrests, Gang Territory, At-Risk Housing, Risky Facilities, Shootings, and Gun Robberies); Model 3 included risk factors that were significant at $p<0.01$ (Drug Arrests, Gang Territory, At-Risk Housing, and Risky Facilities); Model 4 included risk factors that were significant at $p<0.01$ and whose proportions of cells experienced 20% or more shootings at places with each risk factor, respectively (Drug Arrests, Gang Territory, and At-Risk Housing).

Model 4 proved to be the best model, as results of binary logistic regression showed consistently higher odds ratios compared to the three other models and across four consecutive three-month time periods. For every increased unit of risk in a 140'x140' cell (i.e. place) in Newark, the likelihood of a shooting occurring there within the next three months increased by more than 48%, with a 95% confidence interval of 38%-60% (N=17,524; $p<0.001$). As hypothesized, including only the risk factors with relatively high and significant correlations to the outcome event produces the best place-based risk assessment of future events.

Research Objective 2: Compare Risk Terrain Maps to Retrospective Hotspot Maps

The Model 4 risk terrain was compared to retrospective density maps of past shooting incidents because if RTM does not outperform retrospective hotspot maps then its operational value to police is negligible and, thus, not worth the effort that the production of "best model" risk terrains mandates. Retrospective mapping was defined by using the locations of past events to predict locations of future similar events. To make this comparison, separate retrospective maps were created for Periods 1 through 4 (three months each from July 1, 2008 through June 30, 2009) in the same manner that the Model 4 risk terrain maps were produced. Then, consistent with the approach used by Caplan, Kennedy & Miller[275], four categories of "high risk" cells were designated for each map and tested: The top 10 percent (n=1,752), top 20 percent (n=3,504), top 30 percent (n=5,262) and top 40 percent (n=7,009). This allowed for a numerically equal comparison of

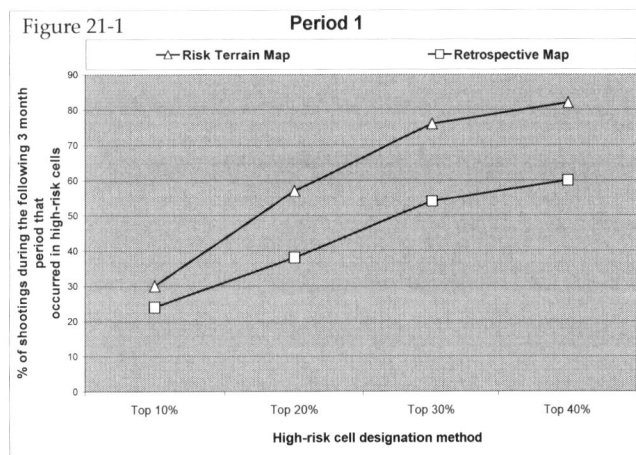

Figure 21-1

cells designated as "high risk" between the two methods—retrospective density maps and risk terrain maps. It also added pragmatic operational value to the results by identifying the coverage area (10 percent through 40 percent of the city) needed to maximize any observed benefits so that finite police resources can be allocated most efficiently.

As exemplified in Figure 21-1, the risk terrain maps outperformed retrospective maps across each high risk cell designation method and across all time periods. As much as 36 percent more shootings occurred in high-risk cells identified by the risk terrain model compared to the retrospective map.

Research Objective 3: Use Risk Terrain Maps for Spatial Intelligence

With nearly 300 shootings annually in Newark, even a small five percent improvement over existing analytical practices equates to 15 shootings that will probably occur within known 140'x140' places. In the context of shootings, which run a high risk of fatality, there could be a significant dividend if police take adequate preemptive measures to mitigate one or more risk factors in these places. Herein lies the leading question for Objective 3: How can the intelligence produced by RTM be communicated in a meaningful way to police and used for strategic decision-making and tactical operations?

If police want to target areas with existing high crime, then using simple retrospective density maps of these events will show the general areas where crime is most concentrated and suitable for common suppression methods (e.g. increase police patrols, ordinance enforcement, curfews, zero-tolerance enforcement of ordinances and misdemeanors, knock & talks). The challenge that police agencies have is to allocate resources to areas with high crimes in order to suppress them, and also to areas that pose the highest risk for crimes to occur in the future[276]. Risk terrain modeling especially permits the latter. This encouraged us to think more about using "risk clusters" instead of crime hotspots to allocate police resources, and we used Local Indicators of Spatial Autocorrelation (LISA), or Local Moran's I, to test whether RTM could generate this type of information. LISA can distinguish between statistically significant clusters of high values surrounded by high values (HH), low values surrounded by low values (LL), high values surrounded by low values (HL), and low values surrounded by high values (HL). This kind of information can be especially useful to police strategists within the context of risk terrain modeling because it allows for categorizing (and ultimately

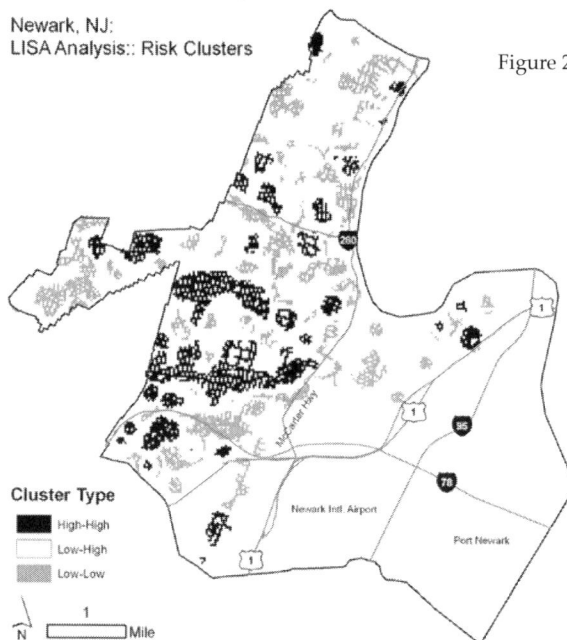

Newark, NJ:
LISA Analysis:: Risk Clusters

Figure 21-2

Cluster Type
- High-High
- Low-High
- Low-Low

prioritizing) the most risky, most vulnerable, or least risky places.

Figure 21-2 shows results of a Local Moran's I test performed on the period 1 Model 4 risk terrain map with all zero-valued cells excluded. It is apparent from this map that risk can, in fact, cluster and that the nature of these clusters can better inform plans for police response. For example, officers might seek to leverage the social and human capital and other strengths of low-risk places that are nearby high-risk places in their efforts to mitigate one or more of the risk factors in both "risk cluster" spots. Or, because lower-risk clusters still have some criminogenic risk factors in them, police can monitor these places as they target nearby high-risk clusters to preempt any displacement or dispersion of risk factors (or new crime incidents) that could occur.

Conclusion

*T*he computation of the conditions that underlie crime patterns is a key component of risk terrain modeling (RTM), with the ability to weigh the importance of different factors at different geographic points in enabling crime events to occur. These attributes themselves do not create the crime. They simply point to locations where, if the conditions are right, the risk of crime or victimization will go up. Risk terrain modeling offers an approach that provides a means of testing for the most appropriate qualities of space (i.e. risk factors) that contribute to these outcomes through a statistically valid selection process. It also promotes the idea of the concentration of risk leading to these problems, in a way that these "risk clusters" can be used to help forecast future crime and direct interventions, such as police patrols, to these high risk locations.

Information from risk terrain maps can also be used to support the resiliency and expansion of the mitigating attributes that are in the low risk areas. The risk clustering approach can direct police to anticipate crime problems early and address the correlates of crime outcomes (note that these can vary by the type of crime being studied). Since risk can cluster in meaningful ways, RTM can ground risk-based policing much more into the contexts in which police operate rather than concentrating police on behavior that they are trying to control.

This study offers a number of advances to thinking about spatial analysis of crime. It serves as replication of risk terrain modeling from what was offered by Caplan, Kennedy, and Miller[277], but improves on it by addressing both the analytical and practical aspects of this approach. This study identified a procedure for selecting some variables out of many to include in the risk terrain model; it compared RTM to hotspot mapping and suggested a way to utilize both in concert—rather than the need to have RTM replace density mapping; and it considered how risk clusters can be used in strategic decision-making in police organizations. See the full manuscript for a more detailed presentation and discussion of the results in which we concluded with an in-depth exploration of how one might develop strategies for incorporating risk terrains into operational policing.

Chapter 22::
Violent Crimes Initiative

By Jonas Baughman | *Kansas City, Missouri Police Department*
and Joel M. Caplan | *Rutgers University*

Each year the Kansas City, Missouri Police Department (KCPD) conducts what has informally been named a Violent Crimes Initiative (VCI). The KCPD Violent Crimes Division and Narcotics & Vice Division spearhead the VCI in collaboration with other agencies including the ATF, FBI, and ICE. The VCI is deployed in designated ("target") areas of the city to curtail and prevent violent and narcotics-related crimes such as homicides, aggravated assaults, shootings, armed robberies, and narcotics sales or possession that were known to have occurred frequently in the recent past. Activities conducted during the three-day operation include execution of search warrants, buy busts, and intelligence-gathering activities.

In previous years, the methodology used to determine the VCI's target areas was to produce basic kernel density maps of all violent crime across the entire city. Command staff would then visually scan these maps for the "hottest" hotspots and select those areas as the VCI's target areas. While certainly telling of Kansas City's past violent crime locations, density mapping failed to address one key goal of the VCI: to identify emergent crime locations and to <u>prevent</u> violent crimes from becoming endemic. To achieve this goal, an approach to spatial analysis other than conventional density maps of past crimes was needed. It was this void in KCPD's analytical toolkit that risk terrain modeling (RTM) filled with ease.

The 2010 VCI was only recently implemented, so data are still being collected and analyzed to determine its effectiveness at suppressing and preventing crimes (this is the topic of a forthcoming research paper, currently in progress). Here, we present a demonstration of how RTM was applied to the KCPD's 2010 VCI using the ACTION[278] risk analysis model.

Assessing Vulnerabilities, Exposures, and Threats

In the past, planning the VCI's activities and target areas relied solely on violent crimes known to the police that already happened. However, the 2010 VCI incorporated these and other data sets including DRAGNET reports[279], intelligence/activity from the KCPD's Narcotics & Vice Division, and vacant house lists from City Hall to assess the city's vulnerabilities and threats to public safety. This more comprehensive analysis and understanding of past events and their contexts were incorporated into risk terrain models and maps that informed decisions about where to target the VCI. Figure 22-1 shows the highest-risk clusters within a VCI target area.

In recognition of RTM's value for strategic decision-making and operational planning, new data sets are already being compiled or identified for inclusion in subsequent risk terrain models to inform future VCIs. For example, it is anticipated that much of the information in the citizen calls for service to the Kansas City 3-1-1 Action Center—a popular service used for quality of life issues such as vacant houses, uncollected trash, abandoned property, broken street lights, or public disorder –can be used as risk factors in a RTM.

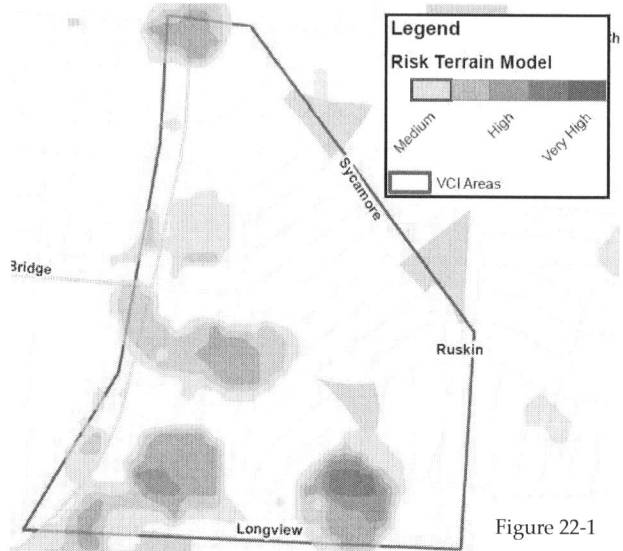

Figure 22-1

Making Connections

*A*fter assessing the city's vulnerabilities and public safety threats, including known crime hotspots, VCI planners looked for connections among human (i.e. wanted subjects) and place-based targets of the VCI. Data was explored in a GIS to note any criminal behaviors and/or categories of calls for service that appeared spatially related to violent crime incidents (e.g., Disturbances with a Weapon, Suspicious Person with a Weapon, or Sounds of Shots). Gang turfs and residences of known violent offenders were also mapped in a GIS and explored for spatial relationships to violent crime incident locations.

The VCI planning meetings were effective outlets for accomplishing this step of the ACTION model due to the variety of stakeholders present, including KCPD command staff and other community partners.

Setting Tasks to Respond and Prevent

*I*n retrospect, setting tasks to prevent crime at high-risk places deserved more attention than it received at the early stages of the VCI, especially compared to efforts to respond to crime at known hotspots. Although many tasks addressed offenders' behaviors at hotspot places, too few tasks sought to mitigate one or more risk factors at these and other high-risk places that helped to attract and enable criminal activity (e.g., many vacant houses or poor street lighting). Instead, the 2010 VCI activities mirrored those of previous years, which were limited to the expertise and capacities of law enforcement, rather than a more multidisciplinary approach: 1) Execution of search warrants; 2) Knock & Talks[280]; 3) Buy Busts or other sting operations; 4) general intelligence gathering regarding violent or narcotics-related crime; and 5) Neighborhood canvassing by KCPD Homicide Unit squads for information regarding current or Cold Case Homicides. Patrol Divisions have, however, maintained police presence and continued certain VCI activities for preventative purposes in target areas and high-risk clusters, even after the VCI officially ended. These patrols are guided by new risk terrain maps of regularly updated data sets.

Measures of VCI activities were collected and are currently being analyzed as layers in new risk terrain models to evaluate their spatial and temporal impacts on locations of future crimes. Preliminary results suggest that VCI activities were most effective at suppressing crime and preventing the emergence of new crimes when they simultaneously targeted crime (density) hotspots and the highest-risk places identified by the RTM (even if crimes were not reported there)--thereby limiting opportunities for dispersion or displacement to other likely crime-prone places.

Collecting Information about the Event

*D*iscussions have already begun about how to refine risk terrain models and incorporate risk terrain maps into planning, implementation, and evaluation activities for the 2011 VCI. For now, KCPD is waiting for enough time to pass before it declares the 2010 VCI a success or failure. Long-term effects are as important to KCPD as short-term outcomes, and the RTM approach will permit empirical assessments of changes to high- and low-risk places over time. In addition to police statistics that traditionally measured VCI activities, such as number of arrests or pieces of intelligence collected, RTM offers new evaluation methods that more closely match the department's ideal definition of success—to suppress existing crime and prevent its reemergence in the same places or elsewhere in the city. For now, the following can be said of the VCI: 74 people were arrested; 145 warrants were cleared; more than $48,000 and thousands of grams of narcotics were seized; and new information was obtained about 5 unsolved homicides.

Refining the Organization and Notifying Others

*A*s a result of its successful application to all stages of the VCI, RTM has quickly become a valuable and favored tool used by KCPD officers and crime analysts. In particular, two Patrol Divisions are now working with the CSTAR Unit[281] and using RTM to strategically and tactically deploy patrol officers to high-risk places. In the past, officers frequently patrolled their Divisions essentially at random between 911 calls for service. Now, risk terrain maps inform officers of the places that are most conducive to crime—regardless of the history of past crimes or the types of people who frequent these areas. Officers simultaneously maintain a visible presence in high-crime places as well as places that are most at risk for new crimes to emerge (that is, until steps are taken to preemptively mitigate risks). The Violent Crimes Division also expressed a desire to use the RTM approach to spatial risk assessment for studying the place-based contexts of new robbery and assault patterns so they can take immediate steps to prevent repeats.

KCPD's use of RTM has also been shared with the greater Kansas City community through the internet and local media outlets. For more information, see the "RTM in Action" section of the riskterrainmodeling.com website for links to news stories and blog posts.

Conclusion

$\mathcal{K}$CPD's first attempt to incorporate RTM into policing operations was very positive, and it is with great enthusiasm that KCPD adds RTM to its analytical toolkit. All of those involved were impressed with the practical theoretical framework, meaningful and actionable products, and ease of use. KCPD has already made progress with integrating RTM into strategic planning, risk reduction, and evaluation activities. Patrol divisions are now iteratively using risk terrain maps to address crime by (preemptively) focusing on known risk factors of crime at high-risk places; partnerships with outside agencies (e.g., Codes Enforcement, Public Works) address factors of risk outside the police department's purview. The long term goal is to use RTM to continually assess place-based risks and mitigate them with multi-faceted and interdisciplinary approaches. KCPD is convinced that strategically allocating existing resources to areas where crime problems are likely to emerge will result in fewer problems, period.

Chapter 23::
Evaluating Place-Based Interventions by Controlling for Environmental Context

By Joel M. Caplan | Rutgers University

*H*indsight is 20/20, as the saying goes. So, in reference to the risk terrain model presented in Chapter 1, to say that interventions to suppress and prevent shootings could have been strategically targeted in Irvington to maximize benefits seems a bit unfair. However, police agencies operating in Irvington did in fact have a targeted strategy to suppress and deter shootings. Now with risk terrain modeling (RTM) and a detailed understanding of the spatial influence of criminogenic features (i.e., see Chapter 3), there is a spatial analytic method for evaluating it. The Township of Irvington is relatively small (about 2.9 square miles), sandwiched between a slightly bigger suburban township and the larger city of Newark. But its murder rates for 2007 were 38.7 per 100,000 persons compared to the national average for similar sized cities across the country of 4.9 (UCR, 2008). Primarily for this reason, Irvington drew a considerable amount of attention from political leaders and law enforcement officials who set up a special task force to police this jurisdiction in addition to the smaller municipal police force. During 2007 the task force consisted of uniformed state troopers who patrolled targeted areas in both a highly visible saturation capacity and in aggressive undercover operations. Drug arrests at these targeted areas were the task force's principal method of intervention; The purpose was to incapacitate likely shooters and likely victims (since shootings were mostly gang- and drug-related) by means of arrest, conviction, and incarceration. While this strategy yielded an overall reduction of violence[282] in the Township since prior to the task forces' inception and the number of shootings has remained fairly constant since (about 25 bi-annually), its effect on the spatial distribution of new shootings remained unknown.

Knowing that certain criminogenic features attract and enable shootings above-and-beyond the routine activities of offenders, victims or police, Irvington's environmental context must be controlled for when evaluating geographically targeted interventions such as the task force's aforementioned drug arrests. A validated risk terrain model of Irvington's fixed criminogenic contexts is especially useful for such an evaluation. The risk terrain map in Chapter 1 was "fixed" because it was produced from criminogenic features that did not change during the year. For example, the count and locations of school buildings did not change during 2007. In Irvington, (probably like many other jurisdictions), schools, bus stops, bars, etc. are not demolished or erected on a regular basis. Therefore, the aforementioned risk terrain model with predictive validity articulated the fixed criminogenic contexts for shootings at micro-level places throughout Irvington. RTM can be used to create a contextual control measure of environmental risks of crime for the purpose of evaluating police interventions at places. The fixed context risk terrain map can be used as a base map—a backcloth, if you will (Brantingham & Brantingham, 1981)—to evaluate the spatial impact of the task force's targeted drug arrests during the first half of 2007 on subsequent shooting locations during the second half of 2007. Six months is a reasonable time frame to measure this effect because the NJ State Police routinely report 6-month crime trends to the public (e.g., www.njsp.org/info/stats.html#cit) and revise policing operations and tactics accordingly.

$\mathcal{T}$he first step to evaluate the spatial effect of targeted drug arrests on shooting incident locations is to operationalize the intended spatial influence of drug arrests and produce a respective map layer to be added to the fixed context risk terrain model. The basic information sought from evaluating this intervention is whether it was a success, defined by an overall reduction of shooting incidents without displacement or reemergence. This spatial evaluation seeks to answer: What effect did targeted drug arrests during January through June 2007 (Period 1) have on the locations of shooting incidents during July through December 2007 (Period 2)?

There were 32 known locations of shootings during Period 1 and 26 during Period 2; a slight reduction bi-annually. As shown in Figure 23-1, the spatial distribution of shootings during the two time periods changed, with more incidents clustered in the Northeastern part of the township during Period 2 than had occurred there during Period 1. It is hypothesized that places with higher concentrations of targeted drug arrests had a mitigating (i.e. deterrent) effect on the criminogenic contexts at these places and, therefore, shootings would have been less likely to occur. Drug arrest locations were geocoded to street centerline shapefiles and then used to produce the density map in Figure 23-2 showing the places with density values greater than +2 standard deviations from the mean drug arrest density value throughout the township. These "highest density" places were reclassified with a value of "1" and all other places were assigned a value of "0". Parameters for this map were similar to map layers already included in the fixed context risk terrain map, described previously in Chapter 1: "places" were defined by a cell size of 100 feet and density was calculated with a search radius of 1110 feet, about three blocks.

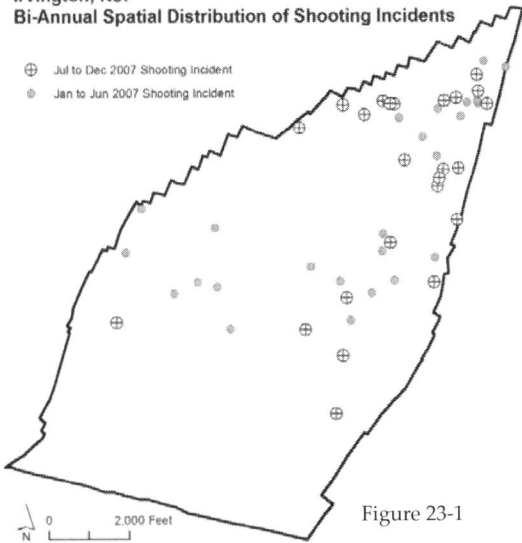

Irvington, NJ:
Bi-Annual Spatial Distribution of Shooting Incidents

⊕ Jul to Dec 2007 Shooting Incident
⊛ Jan to Jun 2007 Shooting Incident

N   0   2,000 Feet

Figure 23-1

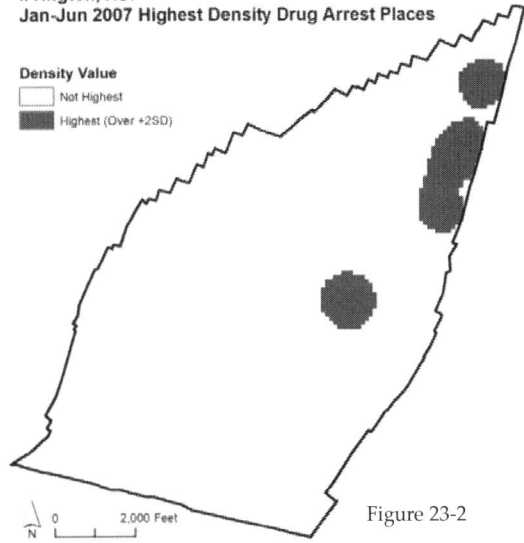

Irvington, NJ:
Jan-Jun 2007 Highest Density Drug Arrest Places

Density Value
☐ Not Highest
■ Highest (Over +2SD)

N   0   2,000 Feet

Figure 23-2

To test the hypothesis that places with higher concentrations of drug arrests deterred future shootings, the drug density map was subtracted from the fixed context risk terrain map to produce a new risk terrain map with values ranging from -1 to +4. As shown in Table 23-1, this new risk terrain model (let us call it the "Hypothesis RTM") is statistically significant, though not as much as the original fixed context risk terrain model produced in Chapter 1. The Nagelkerke R Square of the "Hypothesis RTM" was 0.032; the fixed context RTM was 0.081. The Nagelkerke R Square provides a measure of how well future outcomes are likely to be predicted by the model. This means that the "Hypothesis RTM" only explains about three percent of the variance in future shooting locations compared to more than eight percent explained by the fixed context RTM.

On reflection, it is apparent that comparing the Hypothesis RTM to the fixed context RTM is like comparing apples to oranges. As with any other statistical tests, we should only consider the results of the hypothesized model against the alternative, or null, hypothesis. The null hypothesis for the task force's intervention is that places with higher concentrations of drug arrests attract future shootings. To adjust to this null hypothesis, the drug density map was added to the original fixed context risk terrain map to create a "Null Hypothesis RTM" with values ranging from 0 to 5. As shown in Table 23-1, the "Null Hypothesis RTM" has statistically significant predictive validity, with a Nagelkerke R Square value of 0.073.

Table 23-1: Logistic Regressions for Period 1 Hypothesis RTM on Period 2 Shootings

		B	S.E.	Wald	Sig.	Exp(B)	95% C.I. for Exp(B)	
							Lower	Upper
Hypothesis RTM: Drug Arrests as Mitigating Factor (Nagelkerke R Square = .032; df=1)	Risk Value	.645	.222	8.465	.004	1.906	1.234	2.942
Null Hypothesis RTM: Drug Arrests as Aggravating Factor (Nagelkerke R Square = .073; df=1)	Risk Value	.715	.154	21.608	<.001	2.045	1.512	2.764

Compared to the Hypothesis RTM, the Null Hypothesis RTM explains the variance in shooting locations much better. Targeted drug arrests at certain areas appears to have actually attracted new shooting incidents to these same places. This seems counterintuitive and there are likely many explanations for this happenstance. Methodologically, a limitation of the risk terrain model is that it did not account for very small increments of time, so it is possible that shootings were deterred while police were in an area, but then ensued shortly after they left. Or perhaps many targeted drug arrests created new "open turf" that other drug dealers fought over to control. Targeted drug arrests may simply not be an appropriate response to gun shooting crimes. Recall that the fixed context risk terrain model (i.e., in Chapter 1) did not include any risk factors directly related to drug crimes. Yet police sought to suppress and deter shootings with targeted drug arrests. A more effective intervention might have been to utilize evidence-based practices to mitigate one or more of the criminogenic risk factors that were included in the fixed context RTM; thereby reducing the availability of places that are conducive to shootings. This might include increasing shooters' risks of apprehension through strategic interventions at places within one block from bus stops, bars, clubs, fast food restaurants, and liquor stores; increasing police patrols along travel routes to and from schools—especially within the immediate three-block areas; or taking civil actions to shut down the most historically problematic bars—giving priority to establishments within places having risk values of 4.

𝒫hysical structure, as well as public activities, will have an effect on the ways in which crime occurs[283]. While this seems to be fairly obvious, it has been difficult to show empirically how this connection works because of data problems and the complexity of the issue. Measuring and modeling criminogenic features according to their spatial influences, as discussed in Chapter 3, addresses this difficulty. It also lends itself to multi-level modeling in GIS with techniques such as RTM which models the combined influences of criminogenic features and activities at places. When RTM is performed with fixed criminogenic features, it can serve as an environmental control measure for evaluating spatial impacts from place-based interventions. This approach can be used to determine the effectiveness of programs and the efficacy (or waste) of certain types of resources used.

Chapter 24::
Joint Utility of Hotspot, Near Repeat, and Risk Terrain Modeling Techniques for Crime Analysis

By Joel M. Caplan, Leslie W. Kennedy, and Eric L. Piza | *Rutgers University*

Work on crime hotspots has generated a great deal of interest in the spatial analysis of crime, leading to a revolution in the ways in which scholars and practitioners consider the origins and dispersion of crime. This work has been driven by sophisticated geographic information systems (GIS) software and advanced statistical techniques. The extension of the hotspot analysis approach has been the examination of "near repeats"[284] or contagion effects which explain how past crime incidents can serve as predictors of new crime incidence. Near repeat models assume that if a crime occurs in a location, the chances of a new future crime occurring nearby increases; many near repeat incidents over time could result in crime hotspots. In the studies completed to-date, researchers have found evidence to support the near repeat phenomenon in crimes such as burglary and shootings[285]. While hotspot mapping and near repeat analysis have allowed police to more efficiently target criminogenic places, often the main consideration in responding to crime at these places focuses on controlling the offender or hardening the targets[286]. Attention to known offenders and likely victims is vital in controlling future crime problems, but this cannot succeed outside of an understanding of the combined effects of the social and physical environments in which the offender operates; the pressures that come to bear on the offender from his or her social network; and the influence of community and police actions to control his or her behavior. Extending the researcher beyond events, criminologists have more recently begun to address the importance of concentration effects of crime patterns based on underlying social context[287]. This type of research is based on a form of analysis pioneered by Brantingham and Brantingham[288] that considers the underlying social and physical "fabric" as a framework for action.

In these aforementioned approaches to crime analysis, there is a dichotomy in the way crime analysts attempt to forecast crime locations that is relevant to the emerging discussions concerning predictive policing[289] and risk terrain modeling. One approach suggests that the best way to predict future crime occurrence is to use past behavior, either in terms of actual incidents or collections of incidents (i.e., hotspots) as indicators of future behavior. An alternative approach is to consider the contextual landscape in which crimes are occurring and identify factors that would be conducive to crime. Conventionally, this contextual approach has identified environmental factors (beyond past crime incidents) that might increase the place-based opportunities for new crimes or support new offending.

Two elements need to be clarified to move forward. The first relates to the idea that event dependence is not a linear process but rather, in the interaction that takes place between crime incidents and context, a constantly changing risk dependence that emerges from the actions of all parties and criminogenic features about a location. The second relates to the role that crime incidence has on supporting future crime occurrence. With a better understanding of these elements and how they fit into the broader evolution (and often separate event-dependent or contextual approaches to crime analysis and forecasting), it becomes clear that each method has unique operational utility for policing, even if the end analytical goals are the same. In this chapter, we address these issues through an exploration of the strengths and weaknesses of each approach in terms of the short- and long-term predictive validity and practical utility of point pattern analysis, hotspot mapping, near repeat analysis, and risk terrain modeling. Further, we address the information products that each method offers with a demonstration of place-based violent crime forecasting. There is no room in the crime analyst's toolkit for competing tools; rather, there is a growing need for skilled practitioners to apply each tool to the most appropriate task in the stepwise endeavor of crime analysis. Findings from the demonstration presented here provide related guidance for answering questions about where, when, and why violent crimes occur in a jurisdiction.

Crime Concentration, Event Dependence, and Contextual Risk Dependence

$\mathcal{A}$ common thread among ecologists, opportunity theorists, and related scholarly thinkers argues that the unit of analysis for a crime event is a place—not the event itself, and that the dynamic nature of that place constitutes opportunities for crime[290]. Also common to many studies[291] is the view that opportunities for crime are not equally distributed across locations[292]. Drug markets provide an example of how crime both concentrates at certain places but also evolves in a way that sustains risky places and promotes violent behavior, acting as both attractors and generators of illegal activity[293]. The clustering of such activity in particular areas is supported by the unique combination of certain factors that make these places opportune locations for crime occurrence[294]. That is, the potential for, or risk of, crime comes as a result of all the characteristics found at these places. Hotspots of crime, then, serve more as a proxy measure of places where the dynamic interactions of underlying criminogenic factors exist, or persist over time. In this way, groups of past crimes serve as predictors of new crimes because their common denominator is a geography that is conducive for criminogenesis. A sole analytical focus on crime hotspots, in contrast, is like observing that children frequently play at the same place every day and then calling that place a hotspot for children playing, but without acknowledging the presence of swings, slides and open fields—features of the place (i.e. suggestive of a playground) that attract children there instead of other locations absent such entertaining features.

Farrell, Phillips and Pease[295] offer two suggestions as to why it is that particular targets are more likely to be repeatedly involved in crime. The first explanation for repeat victimization is what they refer to as 'risk heterogeneity'. Victims (or targets) may have certain characteristics that increase the possibility that they will be victimized and victimized repeatedly. These characteristics are thought to exist prior to the initial victimization and are enduring—lasting both before and after initial and later victimizations, regardless of steps that might be taken to reduce a risk profile. A second explanation focuses less on individual characteristics and more on the context in which the victimization takes place. They refer to this as "state dependence" and note that, "...in the context of re-victimization presumed to be state-dependent, the basic question concerns reasons for the choice of the same [or different] perpetrators offending more than once against the same target[s] in preference to other targets (386)". Rather than enduring traits characterizing victims as in the first explanation, state dependence implies that victimization changes victims to make them increasingly attractive. This can be viewed in terms as simple as suggesting that individuals with certain risky experiences find that there is not much they can do to adjust their environment to reduce their vulnerability. The "state dependent" situation may apply to locations as well as to individuals. Locations may contain characteristics that make them more likely to attract crime than other, less suitable, areas.

If we consider the past experience with crime as an isolated indicator of future victimization, this would parallel crime analysis approaches based on event dependence, such as hotspots. As an extension of, or companion to, hotspot analysis, the phenomenon of contagion effects has been labeled "near repeats"[296] and explains how past crime incidents can serve as predictors of new crime incidence[297]. As Johnson[298] points out, the two theories of repeat victimization offer two views of near repeats. The first argues that repeat victimization results from a contagion-like process. For example, after the first burglary, the risk of another crime is boosted. This occurs as offenders will return to take advantage of the good opportunities in this target. In contrast, a second explanation suggests that victimization will recur based on a time-stable variation in risk. In a sense, target attractive locations are flagged. Near repeat models assume that if a crime occurs in a location, the chances of a future crime occurring nearby increases. Many near repeat incidents over time could result in crime hotspots.

Investigations of near repeats provide an important extension of hotspot analysis as it allows for a more dynamic approach that takes into account the temporal link between crime events and does not just assume that behavior that takes place in close proximity (i.e., hotspots) at whatever time in a set frame (e.g., a month, a year) has anything to do with other behavior located nearby. But, near repeats also is restricted to the view that re-offending or re-victimization is event dependent. As a forecasting tool, it provides evidence for future behavior but it relies on the occurrence of crime as a foundation for predicting future behavior.

Crime explanations can also be accounted for by different factors that tie different components of environmental risk together to explain individual, group, and institutional influences and impacts on crime events[299]. Risk suggests the likelihood of an event occurring given what is known about the correlates of that event. Risk terrain modeling builds upon ideas that are central to hotspot mapping and near repeat analysis in that space and time matters, but it assumes a divergence in the extent to which locations contain attributes that are likely to contribute to criminogenesis by looking beyond the clustering or proximity of past events themselves. Theoretically- and empirically-grounded risk terrain maps show places where conditions are conducive for crime events to occur in the future, and offer a statistically valid way to articulate and communicate criminogenic and vulnerable areas at the micro-level.

Albeit, there is a long-standing debate in criminology concerning what promotes certain crime outcomes. But it is not enough to say that risk of crime increases when the number of criminals increase (i.e. routine activities); that future crimes will always remain where past crimes happened (i.e. hotspot mapping); or that crime incidents are always catalysts for near repeats. What is more likely to occur is that the odds of crime occurring in areas that share criminogenic attributes is higher. This is different from saying that crime concentrates in highly dense hotspots. Rather, it suggests that individuals at greater risk to committing crime will congregate in riskier locations.; that is, locations whose conditions for criminal behavior (lower risk of apprehension or retaliation) are better than at other places. Obviously, offenders occupy space and bring to certain locations characteristics that might threaten others and disrupt social interaction in these locations. They may also engage in illegal activities (such as gang or drug activity) that change the risk character of these locations (and also attract attention). But these, too, are qualities of space that are present regardless of whether or when a crime incident actually occurs or is detected by police at these places.

While forecasting methods based on hotspot or near repeat analyses focus on the presence or absence of past events, risk terrain modeling (RTM) focuses on the dynamic conditions (or attributes) of the environment where a crime event could occur. The unit of analysis is the geography, not the event. This removes "event dependence" from the analytical equation and permits other indicators of criminogenesis to be studied as clues for future crimes to occur at specific locations. Commonsense suggests that hotspot mapping, near repeat analysis, and risk terrain modeling are reasonable methods and research confirms their predictive power[300]. With the proliferation of all three of these methods in law enforcement agencies around the world, it is high-time for criminologists to better understand (and capitalize on) their unique and joint capacities. It is our intention here to begin this venture. In the remainder of this chapter, we present the operational utility of each of these three approaches to crime analysis and forecasting. We analyze the same data sets using each approach in isolation to explore the information products that each method yields. Through careful consideration of results from empirical measurement, we determine the validity and applicability of each approach for crime analysis and forecasting.

$\mathcal{T}$his demonstration emerged out of collaboration with the New Jersey State Police in 2007. The focus of this collaboration, and the analyses presented henceforth, is Irvington, New Jersey, an urban community of 2.9 square miles with a population of 65,000 that became a particular concern of local and state law enforcement. Murder rates for 2007 were 38.7 per 100,000 persons, compared to a national average for similar size cities across the country of 4.9 (UCR, 2008). The community is adjacent to a slightly larger suburban township and the larger city of Newark. The town has a large number of shootings and other violent crimes and it contains a vibrant drug market. In addition, it is also the hometown of a large number of known gang members. The combination of these factors and the growth of violence within Irvington—without noticeable or alarming dispersion or displacement to other nearby towns, led the New Jersey State Police to set up a special task force to police this area as a supplement to the smaller and overtaxed municipal police.

The task force consisted of uniformed troopers who patrolled targeted areas based on prior acts of violence and a shooting response team that investigated all shootings where a victim was injured by gunfire. The task force is unique for a state police agency in that these troopers worked out of a station house in the center of the township and were assigned fulltime to this detail, often for a period of several years. As a result of this task force operation, there was an increase in drug arrests and a reduction of shootings in Irvington. This reduction in violence[301] was dramatic at the onset of the operation; however, it leveled off and remained fairly constant since. State Police executives looked for more robust analyses of their data, specifically the ability to use forecasting to direct police operations. It is in this context that we have empirically tested the predictive validity and operational utility of hotspot mapping, near repeat analysis, and risk terrain modeling.

Violent crime data includes aggravated assaults, homicides, robbery, shootings, and weapon possession, and was provided by the NJ State Police through the Regional Operations Intelligence Center and the datasets they maintain, validate and update regularly to support internal crime analysis and police investigations. There were 52 violent crime incidents from April to August 2007 and 57 violent crime incidents from April to August 2008. These address-level data were geocoded to a street-centerline shapefile of Irvington, NJ, obtained from the Census 2000 TIGER/Line shapefiles that were created from the Topologically Integrated Geographic Encoding and Referencing (TIGER; http://arcdata.esri.com/data/tiger2000/tiger_download.cfm) database of the United States Census Bureau. The Irvington Outline shapefile was obtained from this same source.

Point Pattern Analysis (Event-Dependent)

Figure 24-1 is a pin map showing violent crime incident locations during April to August 2007. Visual inspection of the map suggests that violent crimes are not uniformly distributed throughout Irvington and may be clustered in certain areas. One way of empirically measuring the global distribution of violent crime incident locations is to conduct a Nearest Neighbor (NN) analysis. Results of a NN analysis presented in Table 24-1 suggest that the distribution of violent crimes in Irvington is significantly clustered.

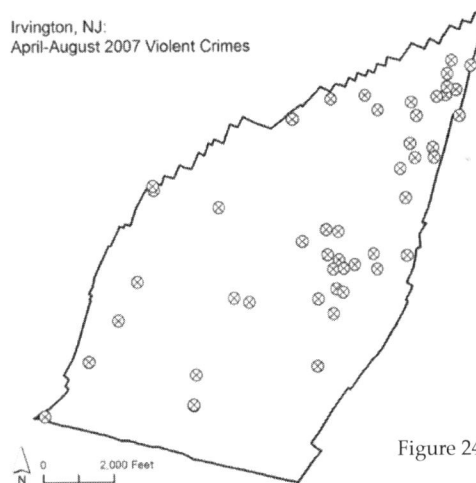

Irvington, NJ:
April-August 2007 Violent Crimes

Figure 24-1

Table 24-1: Nearest Neighbor Results Summary (Euclidean Distance)	
Observed Mean Distance:	492.27
Expected Mean Distance:	601.95
Nearest Neighbor Ratio:	0.82
Z Score:	-2.51
p-value:	0.01

Conventional Hotspot Mapping (Event-Dependent)

*H*otspots are areas with high concentrations of crime. Hotspot mapping is the use of cartographic techniques to create and visualize crime clusters. Conventional hotspot mapping uses the locations of past events to predict locations of future similar events and is usually operationalized as the production of density maps. Density mapping serves as a useful follow-up to visual reviews of pin maps and NN analysis because it identifies where the highest concentrations of crime incidents are occurring at more localized places within the study area. Density maps are based on the distribution of individual incidents and are, therefore, able to show with greater detail than a pin map how crimes are spatially clustered across a landscape.

Figure 24-2 presents a density map of violent crimes (N=52) in Irvington, NJ from April through August 2007. The density map is symbolized according to standard deviational breaks, with all places colored in black having density values greater than +2 standard deviations from the mean density value—which statistically puts these places (i.e., raster cells of 100ft x 100ft) in the top 5% of the most densely populated with violent crimes. The gray color represents places with density values between +1 and +2 standard deviations; white places have density values below +1 standard deviation.

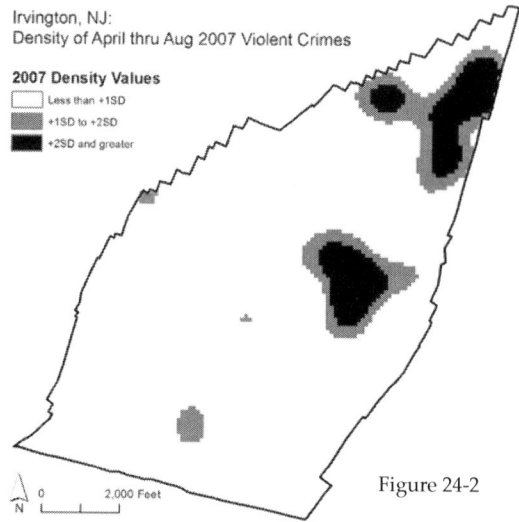

Irvington, NJ:
Density of April thru Aug 2007 Violent Crimes

2007 Density Values
Less than +1SD
+1SD to +2SD
+2SD and greater

0   2,000 Feet

Figure 24-2

As Table 24-2 shows, density hotspot mapping yields respectable place-based forecasts of 2008 violent crimes. In the 100ftx100ft places on the map in Figure 24-2 that had a density value above +2 standard deviations (i.e., the top 5% of density values), 23% of violent crime incidents between April through August 2008 occurred within these same places (Pearson Chi-Squared value=13.50; df=1; p<0.01). Supported by existing literature and routinely practiced by police departments, density and hotspot mapping has particular value in identifying the places where police resources should be targeted to immediately in order to suppress crime at regularly problematic places. But conventional hotspot mapping is a-temporal. Brantingham and Brantingham[302] referred to this as the "stationarity fallacy" that emphasizes the fact that hotspots are combinations of unrelated incidents that occurred over time and are plotted in hotspots as though they are somehow connected beyond sharing a common geography. In overcoming this fallacy, the identification of criminogenic places should incorporate time.

Table 24-2: Chi-Squared results

Place Type (N=4035)	P-value	Any Violent Crime in 2008?	
		No	Yes
Density > +2SD	Fisher's=0.001; Pearson-.000	335 (8.4%)	12 (22.6%)
At least one cell has expected counts less than 5.; Place=100ftx100ft cell			

Near-Repeat Analysis (Event-Dependent)

$\mathcal{N}$ear repeat refers to when a crime incident occurs nearby a precursory crime location within a specific period of time. Near repeat analysis adds a temporal aspect to point pattern and hotspot analysis by suggesting--with a certain level of statistical confidence, that new crimes happen within a certain distance of past crimes and within a certain period of time from the prior incident. Although near repeat analysis relies on instigator events to happen first before any analysis can take place, this retrospective event-dependent test can be especially useful for informing future police activities under the assumption that the general nature of crime patterns in a jurisdiction will remain the same.

According to results of a near repeat analysis of Irvington violent crime incidents during April through August 2007 using the Near Repeat Calculator, Version 1.3 (http://www.temple.edu/cj/misc/nr), there is evidence of an over-representation of violent crimes at the same place up to 7 days after an initial incident ($p<0.05$); the chance of another violent crime incident was about 500 percent greater than if there were no repeat victimization pattern. Near repeat violent crimes were also overrepresented between 8-14 days and within 801 to 900 feet of the initial incident ($p<0.01$), and there was a 153 percent greater chance of a new violent crime incident occurring within 0-14 days at 801 to 900 feet away from the initial incident ($p<0.05$).

If this near repeat pattern of violent crimes persists beyond the time period from which the crime incident data was obtained and used to ascertain the existence of the near repeat phenomenon, this information can be useful for operational policing in the immediate aftermath of a new violent crime event. Furthermore, if April through August 2008 violent crimes were assumed to occur with the same near-repeat pattern as April through August 2007 violent crimes, then near-repeat analysis could inform the allocation of police resources to prevent near repeat crimes during 2008. Though, there was not, in fact, a near repeat pattern of violent crimes from this five-month period in 2008, according to results from the Near Repeat Calculator. A limitation of near repeat analysis for reliable crime forecasting is the notion of the time-window effect, which refers to the idea that relationships of incidents will vary based on the specific time frame in which they are observed. Near repeat analysis can, however, validate conclusions informed by nearest neighbor analysis and hotspot maps that violent crime incidents cluster spatially <u>and</u> temporally, thereby ruling out concern about a "stationarity fallacy"[303] and strengthening the construct validity.

Risk Terrain Modeling (Contextual Analysis)

$\mathcal{A}$ny location in Irvington could conceivably be host to an act of violence; however, there are certain places that are more conducive for violent crimes to occur than others. Place-based characteristics of the environment will affect individual-level decisions and criminal behaviors (and vice versa), and ultimately the locations of instigator events. For comprehensive crime analysis, event-dependent methods such as point-pattern analysis, hotspot mapping, and near repeat analysis, should be combined with contextual methods.

Risk terrain modeling (RTM) considers attributes of the environment as they relate to creating context for crime. RTM builds upon underlying principles of hotspot mapping, environmental criminology, and problem-oriented policing, but offers an alternative statistically valid way to articulate and communicate criminogenic and vulnerable areas at the micro-level. Risk terrain maps can be used to forecast areas with the greatest potential for violent crimes to occur in the future, not just because police statistics show that similar crimes occurred there in the past, but because the environmental conditions are ripe (if they remain unchanged) for violent crimes to occur there tomorrow.

Figure 24-3 is a risk terrain map for violent crimes that was produced in accordance with the steps described by Caplan and Kennedy's Risk Terrain Modeling Manual (www.riskterrainmodeling.com). The risk terrain map was produced from a binary-valued unweighted risk terrain model, using the ad hoc method and five risk factors that previous empirical research found to be correlated with violent crimes. These risk factors are: Gang members; bus stops; schools; public housing; and facilities of bars, clubs, fast food restaurants, and liquor stores. The risk terrain map is symbolized according to unique risk values, which range from 0 (lowest; white) to 5 (highest; black). Clusters of places with similar values might be considered high-risk clusters, or hotspots of high risk, as depicted in Figure 24-4.

As shown in Table 24-3, logistic regression results suggest that for every unit increase of a place's (i.e., 100ft x 100ft cell's) risk value, the likelihood of a violent crime occurring there in April through August 2008 increased by more than 99 percent. According to results of a Chi-Squared test, 12 percent of the highest-risk

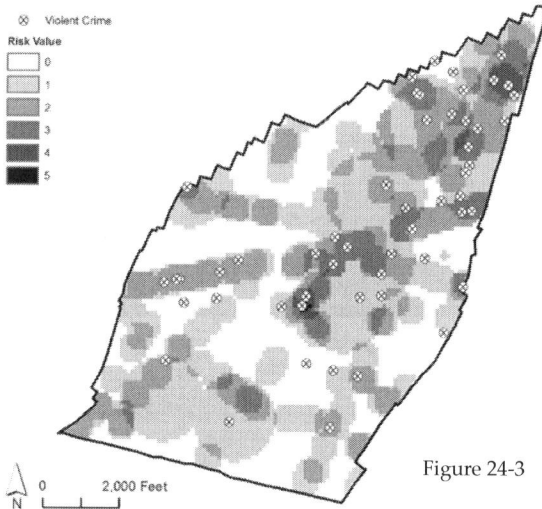

Irvington, NJ:
April-August 2007 Risk Terrain, April-August 2008 Violent Crimes

Figure 24-3

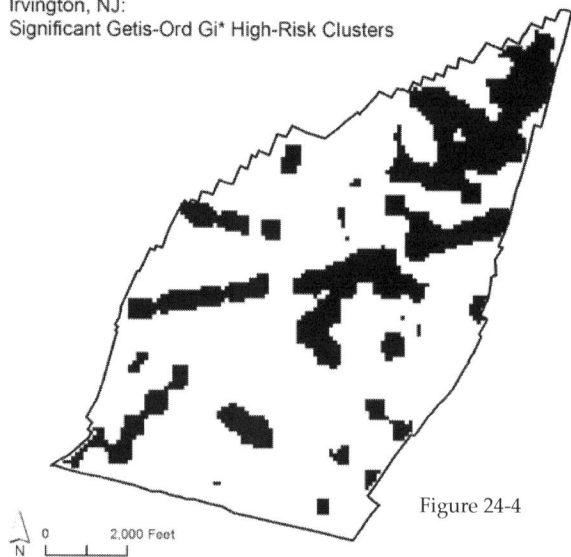

Irvington, NJ:
Significant Getis-Ord Gi* High-Risk Clusters

Figure 24-4

places in Irvington accounted for more than 40 percent of future violent crimes. Given the results of risk terrain modeling, police could give priority to places with higher risk values to mitigate risks there and deter crime with evidence-based intervention practices. Such information can help police commanders stay ahead of crime problems by identifying problematic areas before serious violence emerges. Given that persistent public concerns about safety need to be addressed with limited (and sometimes dwindling) resources, the ability to identify risky areas before they generate significant levels of violence can be invaluable to police. Given the results of risk terrain modeling, police could give priority to places with higher risk values to mitigate risks there and deter crime with evidence-based intervention practices.

Table 24-3: Logistic regression results for 2007 RTM on 2008 Violent Crimes

Variable	B	S.E.	Wald	df	Sig.	Exp(B)	95% C.I. for Exp(B)	
							Lower	Upper
Risk Value	.689	.129	28.721	1	<0.001	1.992	1.548	2.562
-2 Log Likelihood = 536.203; Nagelkerke R Square = 0.054; n = 4039								

Joint Utility of Event-Dependent and Contextual Crime Analysis

*R*esults from the previous event-dependent and contextual analyses suggest that police in Irvington could have strategically allocated resources to key crime-infested places in the short term—given their knowledge of where violent crimes were concentrating at hotspots and the time frame and general area within which near repeat crimes were likely to occur. Then, they could have used risk terrain modeling to target longer-term interventions at high risk places to mitigate one or more risk factors that helped to create criminogenic contexts. However, hindsight is always 20/20 (as the saying goes). The most informative and comprehensive approach to real-time crime analysis for operational policing is not to conduct each analytical technique in isolation. But rather, for police to capitalize on the unique strengths of each so that their information products can inform the procedures and methods of subsequent analyses and a variety of simultaneous policing activities.

For example, hotspots or coldspots of violent crime incidents could direct analysts to places where physical audits of these environments would reveal underlying aggravating or mitigating risk factors. Comparing point patterns of violent crimes to the distributions of other features of the landscape can also reveal environmental vulnerabilities that would permit an analyst to

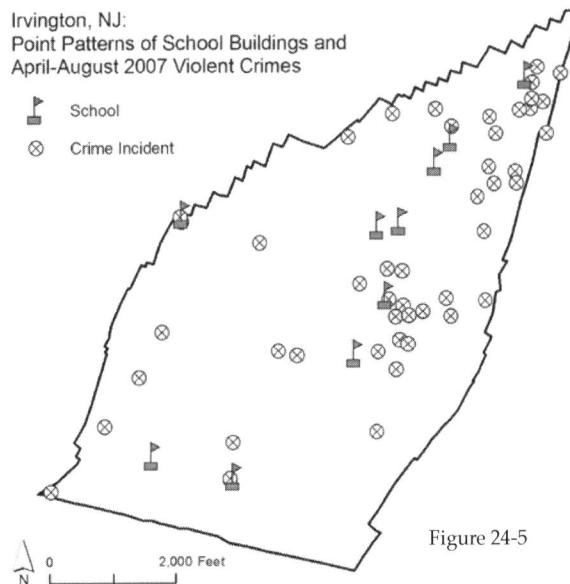

Irvington, NJ:
Point Patterns of School Buildings and
April-August 2007 Violent Crimes

School

Crime Incident

0   2,000 Feet
N

Figure 24-5

hypothesize one or more contextual correlates of the existing violent crime problem. Figure 24-5 demonstrates how visual analysis of school building points layered over a violent crime pin map can be used to derive hypotheses about the attractors and generators of violent crime in the jurisdiction. Other environmental features of Irvington, such as gang members' residences, bus stops, public housing, bars, clubs, fast food restaurants, and liquor stores, reveal similar correlational patterns. Once multiple suspected correlates of violent crime are identified, assumptions about their combined place-based effects on crime occurrence can be tested for statistical significance with risk terrain modeling.

The risk terrain model presented above is a valid predictor of future (April-August 2008) violent crime locations at the micro level, but it is also has predictive validity for April through August 2007 violent crimes (p<0.001; Exp(B)=2.272; Nagelkerke R Square=0.07; n=4039). This is because the criminogenic context for crime as articulated by the risk terrain model does not change drastically over time. Such is the case for Irvington because the five risk factors included in the RTM are not very dynamic; locations of school, bars, restaurants, bus stops, and so on, do not change much from year to year. So, with a fixed context risk terrain model, police commanders can allocate resources with some level of statistical certainty that if new crimes emerge in the very near-term, they are likely to occur in the higher-risk places. In this way, a risk terrain map produces information that can be used for both tactical and strategic decision-making and policing operations.

Baughman and Caplan[304] realized that if risk terrain modeling is used to allocate police resources to high-risk places, it should be done in concert with activities to suppress high crime counts by targeting existing hotspot places. RTM offers police a unique opportunity to prevent violent crimes by allocating resources to places that are most attractive to motivated offenders given certain characteristics of the environment, even if violent crimes are not yet clustering there. At the same time, further insights gleaned from near repeat analysis can be used to anticipate the distal and temporal limits of repeat victimization and near repeat events at certain high-risk places following unpreventable violent crime incidents.

As shown in Table 24-4 and Figure 24-6, near repeat incidents[305] during April through August 2007 were most likely to happen at places with higher risk values according to the risk terrain model (the same model as above). For every increased unit of risk at a micro-level (100ft x 100ft) place throughout Irvington, the likelihood of a near repeat incident occurring there increased by more than 141 percent (p<0.001). So, according to results of the near repeat analysis, near repeat violent crimes were most likely to occur between 801-900 feet and within 14 days of an

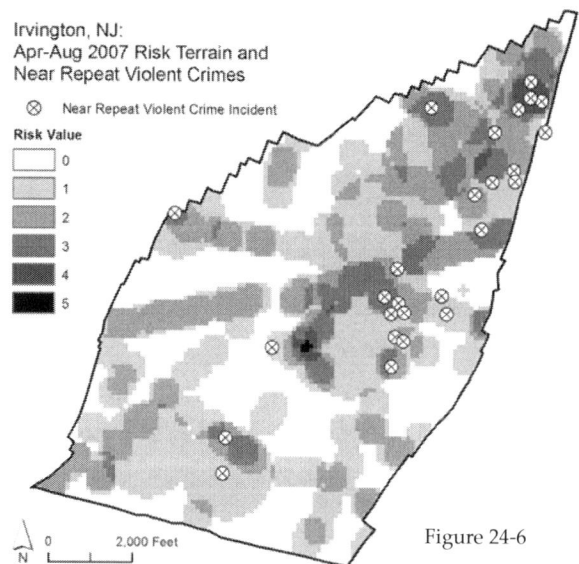

Irvington, NJ:
Apr-Aug 2007 Risk Terrain and
Near Repeat Violent Crimes

⊗   Near Repeat Violent Crime Incident

Risk Value
☐ 0
☐ 1
☐ 2
☐ 3
☐ 4
■ 5

Figure 24-6

instigator event. Risk terrain modeling suggests that near repeat incidents were also likely to occur at the highest-risk places within these bounds.

Table 24-4: Logistic regression results for 2007 RTM on 2007 Near Repeat Violent Crime Incidents

Variable	B	S.E.	Wald	df	Sig.	Exp(B)	95% C.I. for Exp(B)	
							Lower	Upper
Risk Value	.881	.184	23.016	1	<0.001	2.413	1.684	3.459
-2 Log Likelihood = 291.008; Nagelkerke R Square = 0.077; n = 4039; 26 NR incidents								

$\mathcal{T}$he development of new analytical techniques tends to imply that older methods are outdated and, therefore, no longer useful. Sometimes this initiates and encourages the adoption of (much needed) new methods for crime analysis. Other times, it discourages innovative approaches to crime analysis because of the uncertainty among practitioners as to what is actually the "best" and, then, which old approach to doing things the new approach should replace. In contrast to a competitive view over which analytical technique or technology outperforms the other, we conclude that the combined utility of event-dependent approaches to crime analysis, such as point pattern analysis, hotspot mapping, and near repeat analysis, and contextual approaches, such as risk terrain modeling, offer an advanced toolbox for law enforcement information production if the appropriate use of each technique is guided by the specific situation at hand. The best analytical tool is a skilled (human) operator who knows how and when to apply event-dependent and contextual analysis methods, and then what to do with the resultant information product. Point pattern analyses such as pin maps and nearest neighbor analysis help to identify and validate existing crime problems. Density and hotspot mapping show where these problems tend to frequent and cluster. Near repeat analysis adds a forecasting perspective to hotspot mapping by identifying (albeit, in hindsight) a phenomenon whereby certain areas were likely to experience residual crime incidents within a specified period of time. If this phenomenon persists, police commanders can temporarily deploy resources to address these areas, and then allocate resources elsewhere when the high-risk period subsides. Risk terrain modeling articulates the environmental backcloth for criminogenesis and provides a place-based forecasting mechanism. Through the identification of certain features of a landscape that are significantly correlated with crime incidents, police leaders can design policies and allocate resources specifically for the purpose of mitigating risk factors at particular places.

Near repeat and hotspot techniques can play an important role in fostering strategy influenced by RTM. While certain types of past crime events might be one of the many appropriate risk factors in a risk terrain model (e.g., knowledge of past armed robberies might be used to anticipate locations of future shootings), hotspots and coldspots of these events could direct analysts to places where physical audits of these environments would reveal other (underlying) aggravating or mitigating risk factors. Or, in an attempt to most accurately forecast future crime locations, a near repeat analysis of past events could reveal the best time period to model risk for in a RTM. Frequently updated hotspot maps can measure the extent to which precinct commanders are addressing the crime problem, thus ensuring that the suppression strategy is properly implemented. Hotspot maps of crime and officer activity (e.g. arrests) can effectively measure the extent to which officer deployment and enforcement activity is tailored towards observed "risk clusters." Commanders can be held accountable for adequately addressing place-based risk factors as well as existing crime patterns. Such an approach fits nicely into contemporary police functions, such as Compstat meetings and the "S.A.R.A." model of Problem-Oriented Policing[306].

Most often a criminologist's measure of the presence of offenders is designated as the number of crime incidents reported or arrests that are made and tabulated by police in crime reports. But, there are other types of measures to use that are more enduring than the crime incident. Tying predictions of crime to geographic locations provides the basis for connecting attributes of space to actual behavior that occurs at these places, such as high frequencies of crimes (i.e., hotspots) or near repeat victimizations. It also takes the police beyond a tactical response to crime occurrence to one that is more strategic, anticipating where resources will be needed to respond to and prevent newly emerging crime problems.

It has been the case that efforts to understand and control crime (reducing its occurrence) have been most often directed at the crime itself and rarely at the underlying factors that create conditions that are conducive to it. This is not to say that researchers and analysts have been uninterested in these underlying factors or that interventions that have addressed these links are always unsuccessful. However, the focus on crime incidents and their concentration has led to an approach to studying crime that is event-centric. While useful, this approach suffers from the problem that when crime is suppressed, there is no data upon which to forecast future crime using common event-dependent analysis methods. While point pattern, hotspot and near repeat analyses are important for tactical purposes, the effectiveness of the steps taken to control and reduce crime through predictions based on past crime is limited and can be enhanced through the insights provided by contextual crime analysis methods, such as risk terrain modeling.

Part 4

Thinking Ahead

Thought pieces about applications of RTM to research, technology, and practices related to public safety and security.

Contributing Authors:
Heffner, J.
Kennedy, L. W.
Manik-Perlman, T.
Toomey, M.

Chapter 25::
Detecting, Reducing and Preventing Crime

By Leslie W. Kennedy | *Rutgers University*

*I*n looking at the social context of crime, we need to consider the relationships between the correlates that help explain its appearance. Criminal behavior is best understood as a social product that occurs in a patterned fashion, rarely fluctuating wildly from time to time or place to place, an observation that was made 150 years ago by Quetelet[307]. We speculate that this enduring pattern of crime occurs because the underlying factors that increase or decrease the risk of crime are not quick to change and they exert fairly consistent effects on the appearance, spread and persistence of crime. However, although this pattern appears fairly regular over time at the aggregate, there are many factors that contribute on the micro level to the ever-changing landscape of crime. Of interest to us here are how these factors may combine to encourage crime to start; how they provide a backdrop for the ongoing momentum of crime activities over time; and how they can be manipulated to make crime stop. The complexity of the crime emergence problem can be reduced by thinking about crime occurring in context, where an "environmental backcloth"[308] provides the meaningful milieu in which these behaviors occur. In interacting with this backcloth and, through influences that come from the ebb and flow of criminal activity, the features of crime patterns emerge.

It has been the case that efforts to understand and control crime (reducing occurrences) has been most often directed at the crime itself and rarely at the underlying factors that create conditions that are conducive to it. This is not to say that criminologists have been uninterested in these underlying factors or that interventions that have addressed these links are always unsuccessful, as we have seen in recent years with the incremental year over year drop in crime rates in American cities. However, the focus on crime incidents and their concentration, ("hot spots"), has led to an approach to crime that is event centric. While useful, this approach suffers from the problem that there has been a lack of attention paid to why crime occurs in the first place and, when crime is suppressed, there are no data upon which to forecast future crime. While hot spot analysis is important for tactical purposes, as I will address later in this chapter in the assessment of crime control strategies, the effectiveness of the steps that have been taken to control and reduce crime through predictions based on past crime is limited. I will argue here that it can be enhanced through the insights provided by the use of spatial intelligence techniques that identify high-risk areas that are conducive to crime emergence and monitor the success of intervention.

I will divide the review of the efficacy of steps taken to identify and curtail crime emergence by looking at two major issues: 1. A) Why crime starts in certain areas in the first place (emergence) and B) Why crime endures ; and 2. Why crime stops (prevention and deterrence). I will look at these issues in the context of risk terrain modeling that considers the use of risk layers as indicators in identifying areas that may be highly criminogenic (that is, the factors that encourage crime are present and present a high risk), as well as, directing attention to areas in which crime risk is low.

Risk terrains identify locations in which risks that are conducive to crime cluster, raising the possibility that this behavior will appear. But, for a variety of reasons, this is not always the case. The risk clusters may generate crime behavior in certain circumstances but they may also attract law enforcement intervention that precludes crime opportunities or they may signal to potential offenders to be wary of these locations and so they stay away. A systematic review of these risk clusters is possible using a systematic review of the key factors that exist in a location and, assuming that proximity to these factors raises spatial influence, we can measure the extent to which crime is likely to occur.

When we consider crime in terms of context, this influence may not change dramatically over time (unless there are serious attempts made to address the factors contained in these risky locations that are conducive to offending, a point addressed later in this paper) and, therefore, provides a more stable basis upon which to make predictions. But, the combined effects of the ongoing negotiation over risk create a push and pull in locations that influences the appearance, desistance and persistence of crime. Let us start with appearance, or emergence of crime.

Emergence: When Crime starts
The Risk of crime

*I*f we consider that crime is more likely to occur in areas that have high risk, it is evident that for crime to start in an area, something about this location creates the conditions that are ripe for this to happen. It is not a surprise to anyone who understands cities, that they are dynamic and ever changing. Efforts made to improve areas have had the effect of reducing crime. But, equally, when areas have been left to decline, it is evident that crime accompanies this disorder. This outcome underscores the view expressed above concerning the importance of the environmental context in creating conditions for crime to occur. But, risk is not an absolute. Rather, it must be considered in terms of exposure and vulnerability, both of which can influence the consequence (e.g. crime) of its effects. So, our analysis of risk must consider not only the conventional aspects of environmental risk, determined by such things as presence of facilities (such as, bars) that might attract crime. But, we need to consider, as well, that these bars are frequented by people who provide good targets for crime and their presence attracts offenders to these locations.

This metric is not terribly hard to grasp intuitively but it has been hard to conceptualize and operationalize in criminological research. Part of the reason for this has been the difficulties researchers have had in considering the risk factors and vulnerability simultaneously. In addition, the coincident effects of the occurrence of large amounts of crime has provided a distraction for analysts and law enforcement in their attempts to indentify and target criminal locations. As crime data point to where the problems concentrate, it appears logical that police would go there to solve the crime problem. But, their presence is a likely factor in increasing or reducing the risk of crime. Also, their success in dealing with crime may have the effect of making high risk locations of less interest to them but the underlying problems do not go away. So, three things can happen. The crime disappears, it moves, or it subsides to reappear at a later date.

Risk terrain modeling (RTM) considers the factors that are conducive to crime, including an acknowledgement that different crime types may have different correlates that increase the risk of their occurrence. In creating risk maps, RTM can be developed to examine the levels of criminogenesis in an area. It provides a way in which the combined factors that contribute to disorder can be targeted, its connections to crime can be monitored, vulnerabilities can be assessed, and steps can be taken to reduce its worst effects.

Emergence of crime evokes spatial influence, where the context of the environment is likely to increase potential for incidents. In the risk terrain approach, we take the step that is basic to the development of geographic information systems in assuming that certain spatial locations can acquire attributes that, when combined in prescribed ways, define contexts in which certain outcomes are made more probable. So, as an example, the attributes of locations that have many people moving through them in the evening and late night and the presence of many liquor dispensing establishments may denote an area that is seen as an entertainment district that is fun for people to go to for social events.

These attributes combined can be used to predict the types of behavior that we would expect in this location, reducing the likelihood that our predictions about what would transpire there are wrong. In this way, then, we use attributes to assign risk (or likelihood) that certain things will happen in a particular geography. Now, these outcomes may be benign (e.g. people meeting up with friends and enjoying a night out) or they may take on a more sinister character where a combination of certain types of factors creates a context in which the risk of negative outcomes (including crime) can occur.

Attributes themselves do not create crime, they simply point to locations where, if the conditions are right, the risk of crime will go up. Often, this is influenced by factors outside of the context that we are studying, such as the general level of social control that is in place. But, this, too, can be added as an attribute to be considered within the RTM. There is a long-standing debate in criminology concerning what promotes crime outcomes and it is not really enough to say that vulnerability increases when the number of criminals increase. What is more likely to occur is that the risk of crime in areas that share attributes that could be criminogenic is higher as these locations attract offenders (or more likely concentrate them in close locations). This is different from saying that because crime concentrates in highly dense hotspots, crime always attracts crime. It is not necessarily that opportunities for crime are higher here (as there may be fewer victims) but rather that the conditions for criminal behavior (lower risk of apprehension or retaliation) are better in these places than in others where risk factors are the same but the chance of detection are higher.

As we have stated, offenders occupy space and bring to certain locations characteristics that might threaten others and disrupt social interaction in these locations. They may also engage in illegal activities (such as, gangs or drugs) that themselves change the risk character of these locations (and also attract attention from law enforcement). Most often criminologists' measure of the presence of offenders is designated as the number of arrests that are made and tabulated by police in crime reports. But, there are other types of measures that we can use (and that are provided by police). These can include analyzing home addresses of known gang members, locations of drug markets, and locations where known offenders congregate.

As discussed extensively in previous chapters, RTM maps have been used to detect risk clusters of factors related to different types of crimes, such as, robberies or shootings, concentrating on physical infrastructure or the presence of offenders (e.g. gang residences). These studies demonstrate that there is a strong predictive link between these contextual factors and crime, where the risk factors forecast crime outcomes to a much greater degree than what we can expect by looking at retrospective maps. This leads us to conclude that the emergence of crime is linked to these factors. Further we expect that these predictions will be further enhanced if we were to add to RTM maps the components that go beyond infrastructure and include factors, such as, community efficacy and fear in identifying how these types of changes manifest themselves.

These variables that assess the experiences of individuals living in these areas and their ability to respond to threats to their security address a different component of vulnerability from what we discussed above. So, in addition to the presence of potential victims, we can calculate as part of our model, the extent to which people frequenting locations can manage these environments, i.e. the investment that they can and will make in insuring that they are safer. This can range from something as simple as appearing in a location in large numbers (the "safe in a crowd" phenomenon); to being eyes on the street calling in police; or to being active participants in community policing operations that demand more involvement of community agencies in addressing social disorder. Community efficacy becomes a factor in reducing vulnerability through heightening awareness of problems and identifying things that the public can do, with the assistance of authorities, about them. It also has an impact on the extent to which fear can influence the ways in which people use communities and, in countering this, reduce their overall vulnerability to the direct and indirect effects of crime.

Momentum, natural areas, and crime patterns

The advantage of RTM is that it provides us with a view of the landscape that can be considered in terms of factors that contribute to crime that are more enduring than just the characteristics of the people who frequent these locations. When we consider this outcome, we are reminded that it is exactly this same approach that the human ecologists suggested when they talked about "natural areas", a term that appeared in their studies of delinquency in Chicago in the early twentieth century. Natural areas, according to the human ecologists, were settings that had certain characteristics that led to predictable behavioral outcomes, regardless of the character of the people living in or passing through these areas[309]. Risk terrain modeling describes the formation of locations that are more malleable than what the ecologists saw in natural areas but that share the characteristic that they are not pre-defined by the specific characteristics of the people who live there. Rather, they are the product of the social, economic, and physical characteristics of the areas themselves.

This approach suggests a way of looking at behavioral outcomes as less deterministic and more a function of a dynamic interaction that occurs at places. The attributes that we seek to identify are not constant nor necessarily are their interactions set in place over time. However, the ways in which these factors combine can be studied to reveal consistent patterns of interaction, consistent with the view expressed by Brantingham and Brantingham in their development of crime pattern theory[310]. When we consider how risk terrains influence crime emergence, we should consider that risk can vary by the perspective of the individuals involved in interaction. So, we need to consider the ways that offenders, victims, and agents of control approach their environments. Risk assessments are based on routines that set groups of actors learn and enact in managing their daily lives[311]. These can be defined in risk terrains and considered together in the overall model.

Temporal variations in crime

While it may be true that risk clusters vary across geography, it is also true that the same locations can have varying risk levels depending on the time of day or day of week. This may occur because of different activities taking place in varying locations but it is also a function of the large-scale movement of people into and out of these locations when commuting for work, shopping, and entertainment. Andresen and Malleson[312] looked at this issue recently and have developed means by which we can create more accurate assessments of crime exposure, taking into account these population movements. These temporal variations are important for the calculation that we make in our evaluation of risk terrains and can be accommodated for through the use of measures of such things as varying effects of urban infrastructure (bars and liquor stores, for example) that have patterns of use that change considerably from hour to hour and day to day.

Temporal factors can also be considered in our assessment of the effectiveness of our interventions on reducing crime. As we discussed at the beginning of this chapter, the overall levels of crime change slowly over time, on average. Part of this is due to the organizational efficiency of policing that manages urban environments with fairly constant resources, responding in a systematic way. Also, interventions that have the most impact rarely see these effects system wide. Although such things as changes in patrol strategies or the implementation of programs like CCTV extend across the whole jurisdiction, their effects will vary by location. The effectiveness of these changes can only be judged through a careful analysis between sub-areas and over time. The larger changes in effects will be masked by an averaging effect. RTM allows us to dissect this into parts and compare how crime patterns evolve over time.

Displacement or diffusion

Important considerations of temporal effects relate to the issues of displacement and diffusion. We believe that the literature on crime displacement is correct in assuming that it is unlikely to move when successful prevention programs are put in place[313]. However, there is new evidence to question the fact that crime displacement never occurs, based on simulations performed on crime data in Los Angeles[314]. This displacement may not be a modeling aberration but rather a function of selective effects of social context in promoting crime. In our studies of crime in Irvington, NJ and Kansas City, MO we find that within the areas that we define as high risk through our RTM approach, while there is a general reduction of violence in areas that receive police attention in a localized sense, there is a reappearance of crime incidents in subsequent time frame (albeit on a lowered scale) in other areas nearby.

This appearance takes place in high risk areas defined by RTM, removed from the earlier incidents but still in a co-located fashion. The incidents do not appear to jump into cold spots surrounding these high-risk areas, supporting the idea that displacement is not a likely outcome of prevention when the opportunity for this movement is not there.

Criminogenesis

So, emergence can be influenced by vulnerability created by criminogenic, or high risk, conditions. But, as outlined above, vulnerability must be combined with exposure to increase the likelihood of crime. Exposure turns attention from the conditions that promote crime to the targets of crime. This can be considered in terms of risk, as well. Risk is often considered in terms of harm done to victims. The question arises, relative to victims, how do they judge their risk in certain places and what steps do they take to reduce this risk? Is it the case that crime victims simply miscalculate the chances that they are taking, resigned to the dangers that lurk in the areas that they frequent? Or, more likely, do they take steps that allow them to be crime free most of the time, understanding that the environments that they inhabit combine with their risk profile to increase the likelihood of victimization?

If victims misjudge or are unable to control their exposure, the risk of crime in certain vulnerable conditions goes up. The exposure may lead to serial victimization, as well, which suggests that individuals are unable to control either their vulnerability or exposure and are re-victimized, as a consequence. Farrell, Phillips and Pease[315] offer two suggestions as to why it is that particular targets are more likely to be repeatedly involved in crime. The first explanation for repeat victimization is what they refer to as 'risk heterogeneity'. Victims (or targets) may have certain characteristics that increase the possibility that they will be victimized once and then victimized repeatedly thereafter. These characteristics are thought to exist prior to the initial victimization and are enduring, lasting both before and after initial and later victimizations, regardless of steps that they might take to try to reduce their risk profile.

A second explanation focuses less on the individual characteristics and more on the context in which the victimization takes place. Farrell et al refer to this as "state dependence"[316]. Farrell and his colleagues note, "…in the context of re-victimization presumed to be state-dependent, the basic question concerns reasons for the choice of the same [or different] perpetrators offending more than once against the same target[s] in preference to other targets"[317]. Rather than enduring traits characterizing victims as in the previous explanation, state dependence implies that victimization changes victims to make them increasingly attractive to offenders. In this way, we can see this as increased vulnerability as the risk context increases the potential for crime. This can be viewed in terms as simple as suggesting that individuals with certain risky experiences find that there is not much they can do to adjust their environment to reduce their risk of victimization.

Vulnerability, then, may come more from frequenting areas where offenders mix, preying on one another. But, this is obviously not the complete answer. Importantly, the locations in which crime concentrate are areas that are less desirable to inhabit in the first place. That means that individuals who cannot afford to vacate these locations assume a risk in living there, increasing their chance of victimization and likelihood of revictimization. So, it is in locations such as drug markets that are known as locations not only of high offender activity but also high victimization. The violence that emerges in these areas is part of the drug market conditions but it is also the case that the very presence in these locations increases vulnerability to related crimes, such as robbery and burglary. This intermixing of crime types on these areas supports the continued appearance of crime.

Low Risk Cold Spots

When we consider crime emergence, we need to think about not just those locations that promote crime, or act as crime generators, but also those that do not. It is not always the case that risk levels will stay constantly high, as some of the factors that we would consider (such as, location of offenders or police activity) might move around a fair amount. But, as we discussed above, it is reasonable to expect that most high risk areas stay that way for some period of time. It is also evident from previous research that these areas are often surrounded by cold spots, locations in which crime occurrence (and risk) is low. There is plenty of literature to suggest that crime does not displace from high risk to low risk areas[318], a point that we will explore below.

The reasons for the existence of cold spots are probably a result of the absence of factors that promote the crime in the first place. As Weisburd[319] points out, it is unrealistic to assume that if we tackle crime problems in a super-market through effective police intervention that this crime will appear on the next street if there is no supermarket there. A distant supermarket might suffer the consequence of this intervention but it seems unlikely. But, cold spots appear for reasons more than the lack of targets. The persistence of cold spots would appear to relate to the low levels of risk of key characteristics that promote crime. Or, they may be locations in which there are key factors that mitigate crime occurrence, such as high levels of community involvement in prevention or proactive policing. If these factors are present, the fact that they are not conducive to crime over time further supports the idea that geography matters.

Interestingly, there appears to be a boundary formation process that creates and maintains cold spots around areas in which crime concentrates. The cold spots that form these boundaries can be defined by the "absence" of crime hot spots but this is not a very stable measure. Instead, we should look for risk levels that define areas as unlikely to be locations where crime emerges. If we look for examples of cold spots we can point to such things as business districts that have private security or areas around schools or universities. The formal surveillance that these institutions provide is combined with the informal network of people using these areas who are aware of their security and expect protection.

The sustained levels of low risk in these areas support the notion that, even in high crime areas, locations can be made safe. An interesting example of this is found in the newly located sports and entertainment facilities that have been placed in inner city areas. While the areas around these complexes remain high risk, the corridors into and out of these locations, as well as the venues themselves, appear to have maintained good records of safety for staff and customers alike (examples of these include inner city facilities in Newark, Los Angeles, Detroit, and so on).

Cold spots can be maintained by police activity but they are also a product of activities that break up criminal risk.

Risk Reduction: When Crime Stops
Prevention

When we have looked at the interventions that have made use of RTM as a means of identifying key locations of high risk, we have uncovered some interesting outcomes (one of which was unanticipated) in the ways in which the police have used this information to respond to these crime forecasts. After calculating risk terrains and identifying areas that the police can target for special patrols and other interventions (e.g., Kansas City, MO and Arlington, TX), it turns out that the RTM is effective in reducing the crime under consideration. The Kansas City violent crime reduction initiative (VCLI) that used RTM to define the areas for intervention found a drop in crime in these areas. This finding compared favorably to previous attempts at implementing this initiative but on the basis of less structured assessment of risk. In Arlington, a similar positive outcome appeared in their shopping mall crime prevention initiative that demonstrated a drop in crime from previous years.

High risk areas are targeted and, therefore, receive more attention from the police, including more patrols, higher public contact, and overall greater visibility through discussions in the media. But, what we did not anticipate in our original assessment of this approach was that even though fixed factors in the environment that raised the risk levels are not changed through these interventions, the crime rates drop. What happens is that the police go into these areas and make arrests, focusing on offenders who might be driving up the crime rate. Now, what this means is that they are really not doing anything about changing the character of the target area in the short run other than removing offenders. Still, their overall crime control effectiveness increases as their efforts are more targeted and they are able to sustain their programs for longer in smaller areas.

So in these applications of RTM, the risk maps were used by police to tell them where to go to find the offenders. But, risk reduction should involve more than mobilizing police as other agencies (for example, parole, social support agencies, child welfare, and so on) can monitor programs in areas over time to reduce the risks that such things as poverty, recidivism and so on might have on crime, an important but still limited response to the problem. So, to date, RTM has proved useful for finding where crime is likely to occur but has not been extended to dealing with the conditions themselves. This seems to be an important next step for RTM, using it for prevention with a longer time frame for assessing its overall effects on crime outcomes.

To extend RTM to prevention beyond arrest, it is important that we start to include data about communities that extend beyond crime and into social conditions that are formed by important factors in the community. One example that has come to our attention is the extent to which the new 311 numbers, that are used to identify community problems, can be mined for complaints that point to locations of disorder, areas in which the conditions that support crime may locate. If we are able to more clearly understand how disorder forms, this may give us a greater understanding of where crime is likely to locate. It has been said about the revival of New York, after the difficult times in the 1970s and 1980s, that the problems with crime were not only a function of poor policing but also a product of the failure of other civic agencies to do their jobs. Allowing communities to suffer from a decaying infrastructure, poor code enforcement, inadequate sanitary support, and illegal street commerce can promote the types of problems that intensify the risk clusters that support crime.

Proactive Approaches to Risk Reduction

As we have seen from the intervention programs discussed above, the actions of police have an important role to play in affecting the risk terrain. They can deter offenders, embolden victims, and assist in the hardening of targets. These tactics can have the overall impact of reducing crime occurrence, but we need to separate what we would see as risk reduction strategies from prevention and response. The risk reduction approach that follows from an RTM approach suggests that we identify the contexts in which crime is likely to appear, based on forecasts from risk terrain modeling. We then propose strategies to address these conditions and interrupt the interactions that lead to crime outcomes. In contrast, the currently popular prevention strategies operate on the basis of responding to crime occurrence, targeting areas based on what has happened previously as a way of suggesting that if it happened in this location once, it will happen there again.

An important aspect of this risk reduction approach is that while it can accommodate the ideas of situational crime prevention in targeting certain locations for intervention, the program extends beyond a focus on opportunities for crime and targets all aspects of the context that raises the risk that crime might occur. So RTM provides a multi-layered approach that identifies the relative contribution of any risk factor to crime occurrence and helps suggest ways in which locations can be targeted to reduce these risks. The resulting Risk Reduction Strategy (RRS) considers the effects of guardianship, victim characteristics, locations, and proximity of offenders in a way that is dynamic and the ability to monitor changes in these effects through reiterations of the risk maps makes the risk reduction steps transparent and assess their effectiveness.

In our tests of risk terrain methodologies that predict on the basis of predictive factors we have replicated the results of Johnson et al[320] suggesting that contextual predictive models are more accurate in predicting future crime than are models based on previous crime occurrences. This would argue, then, for a need to consider how we would incorporate this form of predictive modeling into a policing strategy that allocates resources (and deploys devices such as surveillance) in a proactive rather than reactive manner. This might involve techniques that incorporate risk terrains into a Compstat approach that considers what the high risk areas are based on reasoned analysis of key elements that interact to form certain types of crime locations.

This can also consider ongoing changes in a location that might be a function of salient events, such as, a major disaster, a weather event, or seasonal changes. It can also happen when larger macro changes occur, such as, what has happened with the mortgage crisis that has impacted housing in inner city areas, in particular. Tying predictions to geographic locations provides the basis for connecting attributes of space to actual behavior that occurs at these places. It also takes the police beyond a tactical response to crime occurrence to one that is more strategic, anticipating where resources will be needed to respond to and prevent newly emerging crime problems.

We can monitor some of these changes through the use of real time data sources. As suggested above, we can begin with the information that comes from 311 call centers. Unlike the 911 system, 311 provides an opportunity for people to report on issues that range from lack of garbage pick-up to potholes in the street. This information on disorder would provide an important source of data on the physical and social context of locations. Added to this information, data that are compiled through social media sources, including cell phone surveys or twitter feeds, also offer a real time source for compiling risk layers.

A final resource would be information gleaned from CCTV feeds. Currently CCTV data are used almost exclusively to monitor ongoing activity and provide an historical record of single incidents. This information could be analyzed for patterns about areas that would be useful in creating risk indices. Obviously, all of these approaches run the risk of breaching privacy concerns and imposing too much control in neighborhoods but handled in a controlled way, the data produced by these approaches can provide important insights into locations that are not available through other data sources.

Conclusion

Examining crime from a risk perspective provides us with a way of understanding the ways in which risk factors combine in context to encourage, prevent, or simply maintain crime outcomes over time. Risk terrain modeling provides a mechanism for studying the interaction among these factors, tying them all to a common geography. It also allows us to develop systematic risk reduction strategies to cope with crime in ways that alter the influence that different risks have on crime.

Chapter 26::
Transforming RTM with Server-Based Geoprocessing

By Tamara Manik-Perlman and Jeremy Heffner | Azavea

Risk Terrain Modeling (RTM) can be an important part of efforts to transform a law enforcement organization into a knowledge-based enterprise that more efficiently allocates resources by relying on "information about its current functioning and its environment to set goals, to evaluate actions and to plan its resources"[321]. Caplan and Kennedy have emphasized that "intelligence is a constant process of data collection, analysis, distribution, and assessment"[322], and that implementing intelligence-led policing enables law enforcement organizations to make their efforts proactive rather than reactive[323].

The publication of theoretical and technical guidelines for RTM represents a major step toward better equipping any crime analyst with access to a geographic information system (GIS) to conduct meaningful forecasting. Nevertheless, running such a model on the desktop presents a number of challenges to a systematic, organization-wide intelligence-led policing effort. From a software perspective, RTM currently exists only as a toolbox for a single desktop GIS application, Esri's ArcGIS platform, and requires specialized GIS and crime analysis experience in order to generate models. Operationally, RTM is thus limited to a single officer or crime analyst on a dedicated workstation. In this environment, the results of RTM can be exported only as a static map to be shared throughout an organization in digital or printed form.

The goal of most police organizations is to operationalize the findings produced by RTM in order to effect on-the-ground change. Caplan and Kennedy cite "the ACTION model as offering a framework by which police organizations can embed evidence-based analysis of risk into their organizations"[324]. The ACTION model emphasizes an iterative process of data collection, analysis and notification—this means not only transmitting RTM findings to patrol officers and the community at large, but also gathering information from those on the ground in order to refine the model. These communication flows could be made more efficient if the collection and dissemination of key RTM data and outputs were moved from the workstation to web and mobile applications.

Recent advances in computing and spatial analysis technology—namely distributed processing and mobile technology—make it possible to implement an intelligence-led policing model, such as ACTION, more comprehensively. Azavea's ongoing research to optimize GIS data processing performance by distributing computation across multiple threads, processors and servers demonstrates the potential to make RTM available as a scalable, web-based application. This would provide a number of advantages to law enforcement agencies. First, it would make the automated application of RTM simultaneously available to multiple users across a network. Second, it would provide faster processing and response times even with large datasets or greater geographic extents, enabling crime analysts to more easily experiment with and fine-tune models. Third, and perhaps most importantly, it would enable the display of interactive risk terrain maps on mobile devices and make them available to officers in the field, where they could be updated on-the-fly based on current conditions. This chapter will outline several potential approaches to enabling processing to occur with sufficient speed that an RTM application could be deployed to a much broader audience within a police department.

From Desktop to Server

Caplan and Kennedy offer a good primer on raster-based geoprocessing and, in particular, on the map algebra functions that enable individual risk factors to be assigned weights and combined into a composite risk terrain layer. The tools that they have created leverage the Toolbox, ModelBuilder and other features integrated into the ArcGIS Desktop for adding new functionality. However, desktop implementations of RTM are substantially limited by the processing power and hardware of the machine on which they are being run. These hardware limitations can circumscribe the ability of crime analysts to select analytical parameters that are most appropriate to their model. For instance, in their demonstration example, Caplan and Kennedy state that "100x100 foot cells were the smallest area that our computers could process reasonably fast"[325]. While this level of granularity was appropriate for their purposes in modeling crime in Newark, New Jersey, the same level of granularity could pose significant processing challenges when applied to a city with a larger geographical extent—for instance, Los Angeles, at approximately 500 square miles, is nearly 20 times the size of Newark.

Moving RTM from a desktop to a server is not an inherently challenging task—the basic map algebra functions that allow a crime analyst to combine a variety of weighted factors into a single, composite risk terrain layer are available within commonly-used server environments such as Esri's ArcGIS Server. Such tools for running GIS models in a server environment do allow analysts within an organization to publish tasks and to share models. Nevertheless, it is still essentially an environment aimed at trained GIS analysts. While processing times can be accelerated, at a minute plus, they remain unsuitable for deployment to large numbers of users through a web browser. For an analyst using ArcMap on a workstation one minute is a tolerable response time; these same processing times would be frustrating to and inappropriate for use by officers running models in the field (a scenario we will discuss in more detail below). Providing an experience that can meet the expectations of everyday users requires advances in the approach to computing models.

In addition to implementing the basic RTM process described in the *Risk Terrain Modeling Manual*, an ideal methodology would also facilitate experimentation with the data—enabling users to explore and improve models iteratively by running, assessing, tweaking and rerunning them. Such an approach exemplifies the model of intelligence refinement described previously. Azavea has conducted substantial research into how to implement user interfaces that make this approach possible by optimizing geoprocessing tasks through the use of both distributed processing of models and emerging techniques such as employing graphics processing units (GPUs) to conduct geoprocessing.

Distributed Computing

*I*n a traditional desktop software application, completing multi-step calculations like those used in RTM requires several steps to be completed one-by-one, in a serial manner. Further, each step is performed by a single processor. For the RTM process in a medium-sized city, this can typically take one minute or more. This execution time is especially influenced by the number of risk factors, the geographic extent of the model, and the cell size of calculation. For example, in generating a raster surface to cover the city of Philadelphia with 100-foot raster cells, we create nearly one million cells. When we consider that evaluating the model for each of these cells incurs multiple computations, the execution time is not surprising. However, it is possible to improve on this. Contemporary CPUs include multiple "cores" on each CPU chip and each core is capable of handling many simultaneous activities. Distributed computing, also known as "concurrent" and "parallel" computing, can accelerate processing tasks, such as RTM, by splitting the data into many smaller chunks and simultaneously processing all of the smaller pieces across multiple CPU threads, cores, and servers and then reassembling the results for display to the end user. When successfully applied, this approach can significantly reduce the time required to return a result to the user, as well as enable an application to support many more users simultaneously. By splitting the raster calculations into multiple chunks of work that can be farmed out to many processing "worker agents," we can dramatically improve the user experience. In 2006, Azavea received funding from the US Department of Agriculture[326] to develop a methodology for optimizing the execution of one type of raster calculation—the weighted overlay operation—through several tactics, including the development of a faster raster file format, a simpler way to pass messages between different modules in a system, and the use of distributed processing. These research efforts resulted in the development of DecisionTree, a calculation engine that produced impressive speed gains, reducing the calculation time on several raster data layers with 25–50 foot cell sizes for a city the size of Philadelphia from 10 to 60 seconds down to 500 milliseconds—20 to 120 times faster.

DecisionTree works by receiving requests through a REST application programming interface (API), then dividing the calculation tasks up among distributed worker agents. As a worker agent completes its assigned processing task it returns the result and, potentially, is given a new task. Once all of the tasks are completed, the results are reassembled into a single raster and returned to the user. These results can be returned in a variety of formats, and can be visualized in a web browser along with a base map layer accessed through a map server. However, it is a basic engineering principle that the optimization of one aspect of a problem frequently sub-optimizes other ones. This effort was not an exception to this principle. The initial version of DecisionTree achieved these speed optimizations by sacrificing the ability to support a broad range of data types, on-the-fly reprojection, mixed cell sizes and many of the other features that define a generalized GIS solution. Further, it was able to perform only a single type of operation, weighted overlay.

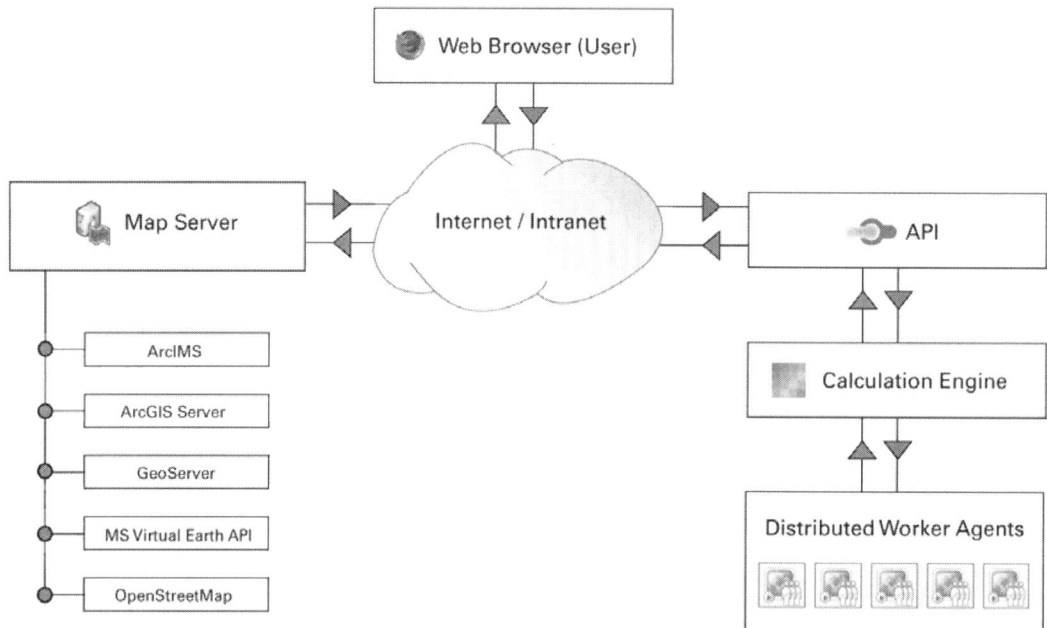

Figure 26-1: The DecisionTree distributed processing architecture

In the past year, Azavea has invested additional research and development in rebuilding DecisionTree from the ground up, and has overcome a number of these limitations. Rebuilt using Scala, an emerging language that integrates features of object-oriented programming and functional programming, the calculation engine continues to leverage the power of distributed processing to optimize raster calculations. The engine is now able to accept rasters in a variety of formats, including widely used standards like GeoTIFF, and can process a range of types and values. DecisionTree also now supports an array of map algebra operations as well as some vector processing operations, making it more suitable for use in RTM. Most importantly, calculation times improved by another order of magnitude, with what was a 400-500 millisecond calculation dropping to about 40-50 milliseconds. The levels of performance realized in systems like DecisionTree enable RTM to potentially be extended from the desktop to the web and mobile devices, and to be embedded within applications that offer an entirely different user experience.

General Purpose Computing on Graphics Processing Units

Graphics Processing Units (GPUs) represent a second high performance computing technique that could potentially be applied to accelerating the RTM processing tasks. GPUs are typically only leveraged to power computer displays or to render scenes within computer games. However, it is now possible to use these GPUs for certain kinds of processing, apart from games. The strength of GPUs arises from the fact that they have not just two or four cores, but as many as 500 or 1,000 cores on a single chip. These are more specialized chips than a CPU, but they are well suited to certain kinds of calculations. Geographic rasters are not unlike the images rendered for games or movies, being composed of values assigned to each cell (pixel) within a rectangular matrix. By not only splitting RTM processing into multiple chunks but also optimizing calculation steps through the use of GPUs, the response time can be further reduced. The approach of utilizing GPUs for non-graphical computation is called "general-purpose computation on graphics processing units" or GPGPU.

In 2010, Azavea researched the feasibility of leveraging GPUs to increase the performance of raster operations through a National Science Foundation grant[327]. The initial findings were quite promising. While the feasibility study did not implement all operations required to execute a full risk terrain model, component operations of the RTM process were implemented and benchmarked against the equivalent ArcObjects components, the basic building blocks of the ArcGIS platform. For rasters similar in size to our 100-foot Philadelphia raster example, execution time was sped up on the order of 20 times for both local sum operations and local weighted overlay operations and up to 70 times faster for neighborhood operations. Such a speed-up in combination with distributed computing opens the door for dramatically different interactions with the RTM model.

Evolving the Model
Speed Is Transformative

*T*he RTM methodology relies on the ability of crime analysts to identify appropriate risk factors, operationalize them into risk map layers, weight them appropriately, and assemble them into a complete risk terrain model. While it is possible to conduct this process in an ad hoc manner, the "empirical" method of selecting factors based on the results of statistical tests is generally superior. Similarly, many crime analysts would welcome help indexing and standardizing variables, and calculating appropriate weights. Additionally, risk terrains could be improved by testing and adjusting for the effects of seasonality. Each step in the process of optimizing a model is time consuming, and many crime analysts may have only enough time and resources to develop a model that is "good enough." The improvements in processing speed discussed above offer the possibility of improving the model optimization process by at least partially automating the process of selecting and operationalizing variables and testing various model scenarios.

A core step in the risk terrain modeling process is identifying risk factors that correlate with historic incidents. These risk factors then become layers in the risk terrain model. The team at Rutgers has done much to publish key risk factors for major crime classifications (including in Part 2 of this compendium) and certainly factors with a strong backing of criminology research warrant consideration. A particular jurisdiction, though, may experience incidents that differ from established patterns due to the unique qualities of their geography. Sifting through numerous potential risk factors manually would be tedious and a poor use of limited time resources. For example, the Census Bureau's American Community Survey now publishes Census block group level tabulations for tens of thousands of demographic variables. Enabling a computer system to iterate through such a library of available datasets to score their usefulness would do much to focus an analyst's attention on highly correlated yet novel risk factors for their jurisdiction to potentially include in a model.

Further, in a manual risk modeling process, incorporating a particular data set requires a user to decide upon the best raster representation for the factor. For example, bar locations may be integrated by using a circular 400-foot buffer around each point. Locations of known gang members may be operationalized by applying a kernel density calculation with a particular search radius. Just as in risk factor selection, manually exploring the space of possible ways to operationalize a particular risk factor would be prohibitively time consuming (though it should also be focused by theory and prior empirical research, and not simply a data-mining endeavor).

When we then consider that a risk terrain model is made up several weighted risk factors drawn from a large data catalog, each with a particular operationalization approach, we quickly realize that optimizing such a model is not trivial. The predictive power of a model is certainly a good measure of success, but if the best predictive model is too complex to be understood operationally, its usefulness is greatly diminished[328]. Thankfully, computer science provides an approach to balancing multiple desired qualities in a model while searching through the space of possible model configurations in a systematic way.

Genetic Algorithms

$\mathcal{A}$ genetic algorithm is a method for searching a solution space that mimics the process of natural evolution. In nature, for example, if you captured a group of foxes from the wild, selected the tamest half of the group, bred them, and repeated the process through many generations you would end up with a group of tame foxes – foxes that are friendly enough to be pets, according to the research project started in Novosibirsk, Russia in 1959 that conducted such an experiment[329]. The concepts of genetic inheritance, mutation, and biased selection are core to the process of natural selection and are imitated within a genetic algorithm.

In a similar way, we can conceptualize a risk terrain model as a set of genes: the risk factors selected, the data processing methods applied to each factor, and the layer weightings used to combine them. With natural selection the genes passed on to each successive generation are determined by "fitness" for adapting and surviving within a particular ecosystem niche. A genetic algorithm mimics this effect by assigning a fitness score to each generation of models. Different models exhibit different strengths. One model might be highly predictive. Another model might be very simple to understand. We can balance these criteria to form a composite score for each model and then select the models that best meet our diverse criteria. The most "fit" versions of the model are combined to develop the next generation of models. Just as we could select tame foxes to breed with one another, we can select high scoring models and combine their qualities to form new models, which, hopefully, will be better than their parents. This process can be continued over many generations, testing thousands of combinations and allowing the best models to bubble to the top of the heap.

We previously applied such a genetic algorithm approach to the early warning system within HunchLab[330]—a web-based crime analysis, early warning and risk forecasting platform. In HunchLab, we allow an analyst to cover an entire jurisdiction with a series of circular catchments, called Hunches, which form a lattice across the geography. As new incidents are recorded in the database, we detect particular areas that are experiencing statistically elevated levels of activity and send alerts to the appropriate staff members[331]. The exact placement of this lattice is somewhat arbitrary and a particular circular Hunch catchment might have been better placed 100 feet to the left or expanded to include a larger geographic area. Through funding from the National Science Foundation (award number IIP-0750507), we explored the application of genetic algorithms to "mutate" the area of interest and other parameters such that we can focus the user's attention on the area that is experiencing the most unusual activity. By testing thousands of possible Hunch variations this approach enables us to provide additional insight to a user by showing how variations in the original Hunch change the statistical validity of the tests, focusing attention on the most important locations and events.

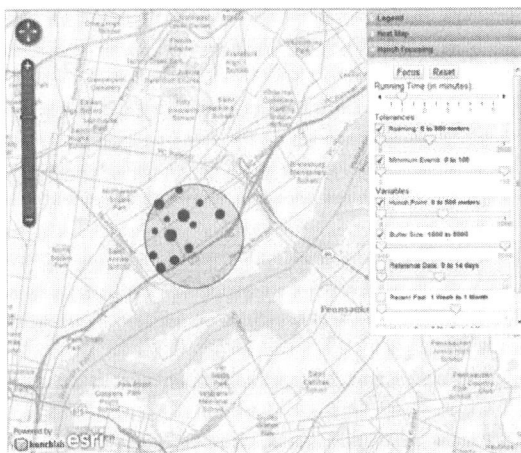

Figure 26-2: Theft from vehicle alert area within HunchLab before Hunch focusing

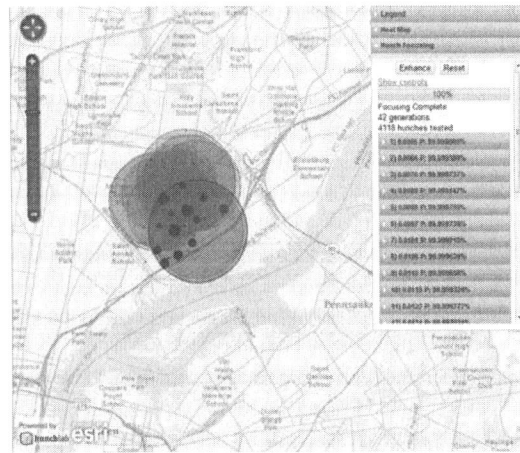

Figure 26-3: Theft from vehicle alert area within HunchLab after Hunch focusing

In the context of risk terrain modeling, it will be preferable to have only one model for a particular crime type within a law enforcement agency at any given time. As new crime incidents occur and their patterns change, a genetic algorithm would enable the automated exploration of many possible model variations. From a software perspective, applying a new, even slightly improved model is trivial. There are trade-offs, however. If such a change occurs too frequently, users may become frustrated with a system that appears to be changing the forecast on a frequent basis. Such frequent changes also reduce the ability of officers to internalize the discovered model and to incorporate it into their daily actions.

To combat this problem one approach is to adopt a "champion-challenger" methodology. After an initial champion model is adopted, the system can continue to evolve the model over successive generations as new incidents enter the database and then hold these challenger models in a staging area. Configuration options would then allow an agency to specify the criteria upon which a new challenger would overtake the currently employed champion model. The criteria might be as simple as a schedule, so that the model is fixed for a given time period. Alternatively, the criteria might be more complex and allow a new model to be adopted before the specified timeframe is expended if the challenger model is significantly better than the current champion. In addition, such a system could favor champion models that have a track record of utility instead of simply adopting a new variation that would only improve the model's usefulness slightly. Such an approach allows the analyst to apply new models in the manner that works best for their agency.

Genetic algorithms provide us with a means to discover useful risk terrain model parameters and weights derived from diverse and novel datasets. By testing large quantities of possible models iteratively, a system could present an analyst with distinct options scored according to various priorities. The computational power required to execute a model with sufficient speed to run thousands of permutations will necessitate significant improvements in geoprocessing performance. However, by reducing the labor cost of including new data sets that may or may not ultimately prove useful, such a system would also encourage the analyst to explore new ideas, evaluate and challenge convention rather than to simply spend time running a single model.

Providing Interactive Mobile Interfaces

RTM relies on informed but creative thinking about criminogenesis and the data sets that can serve as proxies for various criminogenic risk factors. With policing resources stretched thin, many departments have few crime analysts, let alone the resources to ensure that multiple analysts are familiar with RTM methodologies. This situation can represent a bottleneck for an organization—a problem especially concerning in an organization that needs to be responsive to dynamically changing conditions in its jurisdiction. Moving RTM to a server-based platform may make it possible to convert RTM from an offline task occurring solely within a crime analysis unit to a risk forecasting technique pervasive across the agency and used interactively in day-to-day decisions.

Transforming risk terrains into actionable intelligence for both strategic and tactical decision-making is the most critical step in the process. In addition to optimizing the process of selecting and operationalizing data and adjusting model parameters, a move to server-based geoprocessing enables the process of risk terrain modeling to be shared more meaningfully within a law enforcement organization. Server-based geoprocessing allows RTM methodologies to be implemented within a mobile application deployed on handheld tablet computing devices distributed to police officers at every level. The benefits of a dynamic server-based RTM knowledge-base are twofold: on the one hand, an organization can ensure that the most up-to-date risk terrains generated by expert crime analysts are distributed widely; conversely, the use of RTM by beat officers can ensure that the collective observations and front-line experience of officers throughout the organization are incorporated into the modeling process. Actively engaging officers with the risk terrain modeling methodology—rather than imposing recommendations in a top-down fashion—may have the added benefit of improving buy-in throughout the organization.

Currently, data terminals have generally been limited to ruggedized laptops mounted in police vehicles. However, recent improvements in hardware, software and networks are providing new ways to distribute this type of analytical capability to the field. Tablets and smart phones are two important new platforms that will be increasingly important for deployment of intelligent policing tools. We believe that tablet devices such as the Apple iPad will be particularly important for visual applications such as RTM. The use of tablets can disseminate knowledge throughout an organization in a far more timely and effective manner than distributing the outputs of a desktop-based model. Expert crime analysts within an organization would be able to create and maintain baseline risk terrain models founded on the most current data and the latest academic theory. The baseline risk terrain models for each crime type would have a default setting that remains unchanged. Stored on a server, each baseline model would be simultaneously available to all users, and could be accessed in the field on tablet devices. Officers would then be able to interact with dynamic risk terrains to view and customize the model by adding, subtracting or reprioritizing the risk factors to reflect current conditions. Thus, RTM could provide officers will the ability to not only identify and respond rapidly to changing risk levels, but also to explore the factors that put a neighborhood at risk, internalizing this knowledge and putting it into practice with police intervention where it is likely to be needed most.

Officers' interactions with the risk terrain models could also be captured and used to improve the baseline models, thus enabling officers to benefit not only from the expert knowledge of crime analysts, but also from the collective knowledge of their fellow officers. As officers customize the baseline risk terrain maps by changing input risk factors or altering weights, this knowledge will be captured and stored on the server for later analysis. In addition to redefining risk terrain models to reflect their observations and experience, officers could offer feedback on the baseline models through simple ratings systems, such as a thumbs-up or thumbs-down. All of this information about the use of the risk terrains by officers in the field would be made available to expert crime analysts, who could use it to tune the baseline models on an ongoing basis to ensure that shared models reflect current social, temporal and environmental conditions as well as the observations of officers in the field.

*U*sing tablets to both disseminate information and gather knowledge to improve risk terrain models through an iterative process embodies the best aspects of an intelligence-led policing process. For the expert crime analysts within a department, distributed, server-based modeling also enables the collection of better raw data, improved operationalization of risk factors, and more rigorous scenario testing. By accelerating risk terrain modeling through distributed geoprocessing and the use of GPUs, evolving the RTM models and parameters with automated computer algorithms, and publishing interactive models through mobile devices, server-based risk terrain modeling promises to provide a useful tool on the path to improving public safety.

Chapter 27::
How Risk Terrain Modeling Might Contribute to the Development of Optimal Early Warning Systems

By Michael Toomey and Leslie W. Kennedy | *Rutgers University*

Early warning systems have long existed for many types of threats and hazards, and in various different shapes and at different levels of sophistication. Gas canaries, for instance, were used in coalmines for many years in order to detect gas leaks, so as to give the miners some time in which to execute an evacuation procedure. Likewise, weather forecasts continue to provide people with some degree of early warning regarding inclement weather conditions, enabling them to make some level of preparations for future events. However, such early warning systems are often sub-optimal in several ways. Warnings may not be provided in adequate time to allow sufficient preparations to occur, or may not even occur until the threat in question has materialized. Gas canaries were only able to provide a warning that a gas leak had already occurred, rather than that one was imminent. Furthermore, warning systems often do not adequately highlight vulnerability to a given threat. For instance, weather reports which warned of Hurricane Katrina provided little clue that a humanitarian catastrophe was imminent. The differential abilities of people in New Orleans to deal with the disaster were certainly not considered in the response of the authorities[332].

The purpose of this chapter is to examine how early warning systems might be improved so as to take into account the likelihood of an impending humanitarian, financial, or environmental disaster. Specifically, it will ask "what are the requirements of optimal modern early warning systems? What successes have modern systems had in reaching this archetype?" Finally, it will also ask "how can Risk Terrain Modeling (RTM) be used to improve on current early warning systems?" We will argue that in order for early warning to be most effectively utilized, several concepts need to be implemented. Early warning systems themselves need to approach the hazards which they are designed to warn against from an integrated perspective, in order to provide accurate and effective warning. Furthermore, they must take into account the differential abilities of people to respond to the same hazard, i.e. they must be adapted to consider vulnerability to a particular threat, rather than simply warning about the imminence of that threat's occurrence. We argue that RTM allows for the presence of variables which could help provide more accurate and reliable warnings, and which would be crucial to indicating the differential vulnerabilities of people in a given area to a particular threat: "the advantage of RTM is that it provides a picture of a landscape in terms of factors that contribute to negative events...that are more enduring than just the characteristics of the people who frequent these places"[333]. We also state that RTM can be used to help adapt existing early warning systems to take more integrated approaches to risk and threat assessment. As such, we contend that RTM can provide a valuable addition to present early warning systems, and will prove to be extremely useful in the development of an optimal system.

Components of An Optimal Early Warning System

*A*n analysis of the literature available on the subject of risk balance and risk assessment clearly displays the importance of information regarding early warnings in adequately dealing with threats in the modern world. Early warning is a vital component in the risk assessment phase of risk management. As Kennedy et. al. point out, during this phase, it is vital to ensure that as much information as possible is gathered in order to ensure that in the subsequent decision-making phase, adequate and appropriate steps to mitigate the threat in question are being taken and the correct decisions are being made[334]. Likewise, in talking about warning systems that target violent conflicts, Davies and Gurr argue that the earlier a warning can be given regarding the imminence of the eruption of hostilities, the more likely it will be that effective preventive measures will be taken[335]. As such, early warning is crucial to ensure that accurate information is provided in a timely fashion.

By the same token, it is equally important that an effective warning system provides an absolute minimum of either 'false positive' results (where an alarm is raised, but the feared threat never emerges or materializes) or 'false negatives' (where an event occurs in the absence of any alarm being raised). Any warning system whose warnings cannot be trusted, or who fails to provide sufficient warning, is therefore doomed to obsolescence. On this note, however, there is a little bit more debate. While it is patently clear that any effective warning system should ideally have no 'false negative' results, for some there is more room for 'false positives'. Wyatt, for instance, claims that the reasons people give for seeking to eliminate incorrect warnings from any system is because of the unnecessary panic it would create: however, he points to the World War II air raid alarms which occasionally sounded without being followed by an attack as being evidence that people are willing to tolerate such false alarms if the system is otherwise reliable and provides adequate warning when a hazardous event is imminent[336]. With that being said, it must be remembered that although the occasional occurrence of false warnings would not necessarily result in disaster, continuous occurrences of this would dilute the significance and noteworthiness of the warning being provided.

On the basis of these fundamental requirements, there seems to be several necessities for the provision of adequate early warning. Of those, the most obvious one is the need for an integrated approach to threats and hazards. This is true of all types of warning system, from those designed to deal with financial and currency crises, to those that warn of impending food shortages, famines and droughts. Indeed, a major international conference hosted by the Government of Germany in 2006 in co-operation with the UN International Strategy for Disaster Reduction (UNISDR) advocated multi-hazard, integrated warning systems as being more economical, sustainable and efficient, and capable of providing more complex conceptualizations of the range of threats and risks that people face[337]. The National Drought Mitigation Center at the University of Nebraska-Lincoln also identified warning systems which adopted integrated, multi-disciplinary approaches to threats as being more desirable, as they allowed for a comprehensive assessment of conditions at ground-level, rather than those that focused purely on one field[338]. Specifically, they gave the example of traditional drought early warning systems paying too much attention to precipitation levels in order to predict drought severity, without looking at other vital sources of information such as soil moisture, ground water levels, and so on[339].

Similarly to this, great attention must be also paid to the range and types of data sources used. Effective systems need to draw their data from a vast range of sources. This is a requirement that seems to be universal to all types of warning systems: certainly, the approaches of a variety of systems (prospective or otherwise) would point to this. For instance, in their proposal for the development of a warning system designed to warn against impending financial crises, Goldstein et. al. state that any effective system would necessarily have to use as large a sample of previous crises as possible in order to find correlates to watch for, and would require data updates on a monthly rather than a yearly basis[340]. Bakker shows that regular monitoring of information derived from a variety of open sources has been identified as crucial to the development of a working conflict warning system[341], a point repeated by Davies and Gurr, who state that open sourced data from a variety of sources is necessary for functional Early Warning[342]. However, of equal importance are the types of data being collected. While a strong quantitative element based on accurate and reliable statistics is vital, practical human analysis[343], grassroots information and local knowledge[344], and a strong theoretical understanding of the causes of various disasters and/or conflicts[345] must all be included to ensure that data is relevant and will be able to help provide accurate warnings.

Additionally, the issue of resources is of great importance. As Kennedy et. al. note, ideal risk assessment processes are often disrupted because countries lack the resources to continually analyze threats and vulnerabilities[346]. Likewise, Bakker points out that governments are often preoccupied with current crises, and do not have the will or the resources necessary to deal with tomorrow's problems today[347]. Dorn adds to this, stating that financial and managerial considerations have previously constrained the United Nations in their attempts to develop effective systems[348]. In this sense, the immediate financial and economic predicament of a state that is faced with a particular risk might outweigh the potential benefits of implementing and maintaining advanced early warning systems, a point heightened by the fact that in many cases, the countries in most dire need of reliable early warning systems are those with the least abundance of resources. As such, in order to remain relevant to those countries that are most in need of them, warning systems should be relatively cheap and cost-efficient.

Finally, as we move forward into the 21st Century, early warning systems should be capable of taking into account the differential levels of risk that people face. In other words, warning systems should be able to warn not just about the likelihood of an event occurring, but also about what sort of effects an event might have on the region where it occurs. Traditionally, early warning systems have provided a uniform warning to all those that are likely to be affected by a particular threat: a smoke alarm might alert all members of a household that the house is on fire, but it will not specify which rooms are currently on fire, or which people are in most imminent danger of smoke inhalation. In the context of a house fire, it is not necessary to take into account these differential levels of risk, as there is going to be very little difference in the relative vulnerabilities of each person that is affected by the threat in question. However, the need to consider vulnerability becomes more prescient when one focuses on more macro-level disasters such as conflicts and wars, hurricanes, earthquakes, droughts and famines, and so on. In these instances, those who have more or less access to resources will be affected to a greater or lesser degree by the hazard in question[349]. The need for such predictive capabilities has been thrown sharply into focus by disasters such as Hurricane Katrina and the Haiti Earthquake disaster. In both cases, it is quite clear from the resulting catastrophes that, while the authorities may have had some foreshadowing that an event was to imminently transpire (admittedly, in the case of the Haiti Earthquake, given the difficulties of predicting earthquakes, the authorities would likely have had no more than a couple of minutes warning that an event was about to occur[350]), they were completely unprepared for, and unable to deal with, the humanitarian situation which was to emerge in the wake of the event. It is necessary that if early warning systems are to play a full role in the risk management process, they need to pay at least some attention to the differentiated risk levels different people face. This is to ensure that aid and resources are sent to areas that are most vulnerable and in need of help. This would then help mitigate the effects or likelihoods of humanitarian situations in the region in question.

Towards an Optimal Early Warning System: The Role of Risk Terrain Modeling

*I*n order for effective early warning systems to be able to provide reliable and timely warnings regarding the risk not only of a particular event occurring, but also about the possibility of a related humanitarian disaster, several criteria need to be satisfied. Early warning systems need to adopt integrated approaches to the threats which they are warning against: as such they need to look at a variety of causes and risks. In concert with this, information needs to be drawn from a wide variety of sources, in order to ensure that all known causal variables, based on a strong theoretical background, are incorporated into the system. Early warning systems also need to exert a low demand on resources, so as to make them more easily accessible. And finally, it should ideally include an analysis of the relative vulnerabilities of those people who are most likely to be affected by the event in question, so as to assist in effective risk-management processes and to ensure that aid is provided to those people and places in most urgent need of help. The FEWSNET system developed by the US Agency for International Development has come closest to meeting all these requirements; it should come as no surprise, then, that despite it not taking a fully integrated view of all risks associated with famine and food insecurity, it is viewed by many experts as being the most effective Early Warning System of its type in the world.

It is quite clear from world events that these requirements are still not being met, and that early warning, risk assessment, and risk management is not being approached in an integrated fashion. An obvious example here is the recent Japanese earthquake. In terms of providing an alert that an earthquake was imminent, the system worked almost flawlessly, undoubtedly saving lives[351]. Likewise, the steps taken to mitigate the damage done to buildings by an earthquake achieved their intended goals; even tall, high-rise buildings wavered, but failed to collapse (although some buildings were not fully prepared for an earthquake as powerful as the one that occurred)[352]. However, the threats associated with an earthquake were not approached in an integrated fashion, with consideration being given regarding vulnerability to all related risks. As a result, preparation for the subsequent tsunami which hit the country was relatively inadequate. For instance, in the case of the Fukushima Nuclear Power Plant, backup power generators failed when the plant was hit by the tsunami, as they had not been prepared to deal with such an event; additionally, cooling systems which relied upon the backup power were not adequately prepared for the generator's failure[353]. The failure of the authorities to prepare the plant for all eventualities indicates that an integrated approach to the risks and threats associated with earthquakes was not undertaken, while also highlighting the necessity of integrated approaches.

With this in mind, we must now consider how such procedures may be incorporated into existing early warning systems. From this perspective, we should look to the possible input of RTM, and how this might be able to consolidate the above factors in order to make existing early warning systems optimally effective, in a similar manner to the FEWSNET system. It must be noted that RTM is not, in itself, an Early Warning System, and as such not be viewed as a replacement for such Systems; rather, it is an instrument which can be used to enhance the capabilities of other Systems through a variety of means:

1) it can help solve certain resourcing issues, due to the lack of expensive specialist software/hardware required for it to function;

2) it can enable early warning systems to generate easily accessed and easily understood warnings through the use of GIS maps;

3) it can improve risk assessment capabilities by increasing flexibility and facilitating integrated threat analyses, and by allowing for the inclusion of various different correlates and sources of information;

4) most importantly, it can be easily re-tooled to explain not only what threats are likely to occur in a certain area, but also to elaborate on the differential vulnerabilities of people within the area being studied.

These improvements can be incorporated into a wide variety of warning systems, and are not necessarily specific to any single issue: we will now expand on these points.

1) Resourcing issues:

*I*n terms of resourcing issues, the usefulness of RTM comes partially from the added value it can provide for a relatively insignificant cost. RTM does not require specialized or expensive software or hardware: while specific GIS software packages can be used to generate risk terrains, free-to-access online tools such as Google maps may also be used[354]. In terms of hardware, all that is needed to generate these models is a computer with internet access. RTM might also potentially reduce certain costs related to the analysis of threats, as it only requires one person to load the data into the analysis package and thus generate the desired risk terrain maps.

2) Easily accessed and understood warnings:

$\mathcal{A}$s noted above, an issue that some early warning systems have had is that the warnings they provided were neither easily understood, nor easily accessed. As Wulf and Debiel argue, public accessibility is an important ingredient in an ideal Early Warning System[355]. RTM can help solve this issue through its use of GIS mapping systems. Risks are explained on a 'hotspot' map, which clearly enumerates where threats are more likely to occur within a geographic space. These maps can then be posted online (or elsewhere) in such a way as to make the warning as publically accessible as possible.

3) Improved flexibility and inclusion of varied information sources:

$\mathcal{R}$TM is a very flexible tool which can easily be used to provide risk assessment in a wide range of fields. Indeed, RTM has previously been used to predict the risk gang-based violence and criminality and shootings in American cities: the same processes that allow RTM to predict these incidents can thus be used for various different issues. However, the flexibility of RTM goes further than this. RTM can use as many correlates associated with a particular threat as have been identified through "…meta-analysis or other empirical methods, literature review, professional experience, and practitioner knowledge…"[356]. As such, it can be easily amalgamated into an existing early warning system. Indeed, due to its requirement of several different indicators in order to provide differentiated maps, RTM can encourage warning systems to adopt integrated, multi-threat approaches to the hazard they intend to warn against.

4) Vulnerability prediction:

$\mathcal{T}$he most significant addition RTM can provide to any early warning system is its capacity for highlighting risk levels and predicting the differential vulnerabilities experienced within population groups. It has already been used to provide a somewhat similar service, in predicting the risk levels of gun shooting incidents in Irvington, New Jersey[357]. In this case, RTM has been used to assist police units allocate resources, not just to areas with current high crimes levels, but also to areas which are most likely to become hotspots again in the future[358]. Maps that are subsequently produced give a clear idea of which areas are more likely to be vulnerable to the emergence of criminality in the future.

This focus on future threat mitigation could be of crucial benefit to early warning systems in different spheres. Similarly to what was noted earlier, the same processes that allow RTM to predict where crime hotspots are most likely to develop can also be used to predict where conflicts may emerge, or to say where post-event humanitarian disasters might happen. What would be required to do this would be a complex understanding of what causes these issues, based on a strong appreciation of the various theoretical explanations. This would then provide a varied set of correlates, whose occurrence would then be monitored throughout the territory in question. Such an approach would thenceforth allow for the most cost-effective risk management procedures: if we accept Davies and Gurr's argument, that early warning of conflicts can make its prevention more likely and the chances of extreme costs being incurred less likely[359], then the form of assistance RTM can provide (essentially pre-early warning services) would be extremely beneficial in ensuring early warning systems are optimally effective.

Again, using the example of the 2011 Japanese earthquake and tsunami disaster, the application of RTM to existing warning systems would most likely have been able to contribute significantly to the country's preparedness. RTM would have been able to give a detailed analysis of the vulnerability to earthquake-related risks (such as tsunamis) faced by the Japanese authorities, while also allowing for the possibility of it being tailored to specific locations (such as the vulnerability of the various nuclear power plants to tsunamis). Based on a combination of factors such as, e.g., economic profiles of the areas studied, relief, coastline, average elevation of land and property in a given region and so on, one would have been able to provide a useful picture of vulnerabilities in an area to earthquakes and related phenomena; this picture would not only have encouraged systemic thinking and integrated conceptualizations of all the risks associated with earthquakes, but would have allowed the Japanese authorities to understand at a glance where resources would need to be targeted in advance of any disaster. This information would then have allowed authorities to understand which risks were greatest (and where), which issues should have received priority treatment, where resources would be most effectively allocated, and so on. While RTM was not taken up in time to help prevent this particular calamity, its future implementation could help mitigate the effects of disasters in the future.

Conclusion

*B*ased on the events of recent months and years, it is clear that quite a bit of work is required to make various forms of early warning systems optimally effective. Even foremost systems, such as the FEWSNET warning system, do not approach the concept of risk in a completely unified manner and overlook certain areas (in the case of FEWSNET, this is the lack of focus on famine and food insecurity as being possible causes of conflict). Likewise, in countries where warning systems and action plans for specific risks are virtually at the highest possible standard (Japan, in this case), risks have been dealt with in a singular approach, with insufficient attention being paid to the interconnectivity of risk. From this perspective, RTM can be extremely useful in helping develop the capabilities of early warning systems and encourage integrated conceptualizations of risk. RTM can add great value to existing early warning systems, without requiring a major outlay of expense. It can provide warnings and threat analyses in a simple and clear manner. However, its biggest benefits are in its flexibility and its ability to integrate a wide variety of data sources and correlates, and its capacity to provide analyses of differential risk and vulnerability levels, and where risks are most likely to be raised to their highest levels. These benefits can allow decision-makers and authorities to generate accurate predictive maps of where given threats may cause the greatest damage to property and life, and can thus allow for optimal resource allocation and the application of preventive measures to mitigate the effects of any future event. This would be a major addition to various different early warning systems, and would go a long way towards the creation of an optimal system. It must be noted that while RTM can be a great addition to the risk-assessment phase of risk management, it is not sufficient on its own to prevent catastrophes; there needs to be political will among decision makers to allocate resources to vulnerable areas, and mitigation processes must be efficiently designed and executed in order to take advantage of the improved information. However, the complexity of the questions and issues these decision makers face can be greatly simplified by implementation of RTM into early warning systems, to create an optimally effective system.

Chapter 28::
Accommodating Different Approaches to Crime Analysis: Hypothesis Testing, Pattern Analysis, and Agent Based Modeling

By Leslie W. Kennedy | *Rutgers University*

We are confronting a world in which there are more data, more technology to analyze these data, more demand for explanations about how things connect, and increased interest in forecasting future events. In meeting these imperatives, we have seen the development of new partnerships across disciplines where researchers and technologists are attempting to create new solutions to data problems and produce analytical strategies that provide better tools for analysts, policy makers, and decision-makers. These partnerships are developing around opportunities that have been afforded by the major steps forward in digitizing and geo-referencing data. This has opened the way for initiatives that allow for a broader inquiry of the spatial and temporal characteristics of these data. In the area of crime analysis, for example, these developments have opened up the possibilities that patterns that appear in data can be studied in terms of real time risks or they can be viewed in terms of future challenges that may manifest themselves as threats to social order, the environment, or the economy.

In looking at the component parts of this emerging, and converging, world-view, researchers from many different disciplines have proposed new ways of addressing crime data and tying it to outcomes analysis. My intention here is to examine how this process has influenced approaches to public security and review the steps that have been taken to improve the work in this area, both conceptually and technically. In this inquiry, I will address the current debates in police science concerning the most useful research frameworks and data to apply to decision-making, particularly in light of the increased interest in the application of sophisticated computer modeling to social behavior. Modeling is certainly not new to behavioral science, as it has been around a long time in economics, demography, psychology, political science, and so on. However, modeling is only now making its way into the more general fields of social science that have been less accustomed to using highly sophisticated data applications in practical terms, such as crime analysis, partly because of past resistance from the user groups but also because of a previous lack of good data and sophisticated analytical tools. How police organizations and criminologists manage these new initiatives will provide an important basis for future action, both strategically and tactically, as they confront new challenges of constrained resources, newly emerging crime problems, and increased demands for innovation and accountability.

Competing Perspectives in Criminological Analysis

*I*n the ongoing advances that have been made in data collection techniques and the unexpected windfall of resources that came in the post-9/11 era expenditures on advanced computational software, many different groups with a variety of data skills have been attracted into the security field, in general, and crime analysis, in particular. With them, they have brought advanced data analysis and modeling skills. In addition, they have promoted the view that security can be looked at in the same way that other forms of human behavior can, divided into two identifiable components: (1) through models of programmed behavior and (2) through analysis of patterns that can be extracted from mining data. The social scientists already working in crime analysis have not fully embraced these newcomers partly, it would appear, due to differences in the understandings that they have of the underlying principles governing the behavior that they are studying. But differences also emerge because of their approach to analysis based on using existing information already collected by agencies. The ideas of data mining or agent based modeling could seem superfluous when there are already plenty of data sets around to analyze and established hypotheses to test derived from a fairly extensive research literature. So, the social scientists believe that they have a fairly complete understanding of what to look for in data and the data that they need is now available either from police departments or government agencies that collect, compile and disseminate this information.

This difference in perspective has led to an emerging conflict over the most effective way of conducting crime analysis and assisting police decision-making. Sparrow[360] has discussed this conflict in terms of the how social versus natural scientists are influencing the evolution of the field of police science. He suggests that the scientific approach to pattern identification and data mining is actually more compatible to the work of police and crime analysts than the social scientific approach, as it allows for a broad based assessment of problems and their remediation rather than working on pre-existing assumptions of how crime takes place. He suggests that police researchers need to adopt this scientific approach as it encourages them to be more open to emerging issues. He criticizes the new approaches offered in evidence based policing, drawn from social science, that suggest more rigorous evaluation of police programs, arguing that this "gold standard" of research is unrealistic in its application to policing. The evidence-based approach promotes the integration of evaluation into police management and is very programmatic while the focus on pattern analysis and data mining is more likely to promote an environment that encourages serendipitous findings. Although he does not intend to dismiss all social science research, Sparrow implies that rigorous evaluation of crime and police activities is impractical and out of the reach of most police agencies in their need for rapid response to new and emerging problems. Part of his criticism of the evidence based approach also focuses on a dichotomy offered by Weisburd and Neyroud[361] of the differences between social science approaches, which are reflective of social trends, and science based approaches, that tend to be more technologically based. Sparrow rejects this distinction, suggesting that the dichotomy instead is between the imperative for controlled assessment versus data based pattern analysis.

This critique provides an interesting take on modern police research but is somewhat off base. The argument for evidence-based approaches derives from an effort to improve research data and make results more compelling. It also comports closely to scientific methods (to a degree that some are uncomfortable with how unattainable this approach is in the real world). This approach is most relevant when agencies need to evaluate programs and determine the successes of interventions. But, while it may be a desired outcome of crime researchers to meet this high standard, the day-to-day interactions between criminologists and crime analysts (and by extension, police leaders) suggest a more nuanced approach to data. The tension between science and social science is accurately reflected by Weisburd and Neyroud in their characterization of the competing efforts made by vendors of data management software to sell highly sophisticated analytical programs to crime analysts who want to provide analytical support to police agencies using off-the-shelf technology for data acquisition and analysis. But this distinction in approach does not just influence the steps taken to get the attention of police leaders over which analytical technique to use. Instead, this divide appears in the research literature between groups that are advocating pattern analysis in pure exploratory and model building approaches versus those who advocate analysis strategies based on theory, past findings, and careful evaluation.

We can argue that, in basic terms, this divide between disciplinary perspective is not desirable nor is it inevitable for crime analysts or criminologists to choose one approach over the other. Instead, we can cast the differences in perspective between social scientists and technologists (or social scientist and natural scientists) as complementary and mutually supporting. This is particularly well demonstrated in the work that has evolved in the applications of Geographic Information Systems (GIS) to crime analysis. The different camps are not really operating in opposition to one another. Let us examine the bases upon which to assess this by looking at the points of convergence in data production, analysis, and applications.

Considering Risk and Uncertainty: Forecasting Crime Outcomes

We begin by considering these approaches to crime analysis in the context of risk, a measure by which we can study issues in public security. In both scientific and social scientific approaches, risk is a key factor and the measurement approach is usually based on the assessment of probable risk[362]. In the first instance, scientists are focused on the reduction of uncertainty in their analysis, using approaches that reduce variability and enhance control of conditions under which risk is increased. Social scientists are less concerned about uncertainty (as there is so much in the research that they are involved in) and more interested in establishing correlation through techniques that enhance the explanatory power of key variables in explaining risk. The social science approach to crime, which is more likely than the natural science approach to be based on field studies, is often criticized (both inside and outside of the disciplines) for being inexact and subject to a great deal of error. However, the data available and the ability to control the extraneous factors that influence outcomes often dictate the choice of analytical methods[363].

The lack of attention to uncertainty in social science has provided some impetus for some social scientists to investigate means of increasing the accuracy and robustness of their explanations[364] and has been an important basis upon which, despite the perception that they are worlds apart, they have begun to examine ways in which scientists and mathematicians can assist in this work. This is particularly true in the work that has developed around spatial and temporal analysis of crime, where spatial scientists have already been quite active in the development of tools and software for managing and analyzing data. Interestingly enough, this exploration of the applications of scientific methods to crime analysis has also fueled the efforts to bring into the field more rigorous evaluation techniques[365], a move that is criticized by Sparrow as being unproductive.

In light of these methods, social scientists have been developing means of improving their analysis strategies in studying the spatial and temporal characteristics of crime, particularly in the refinements that have taken place in the utilization of GIS. These advances have been partly a function of the sophisticated algorithms that have been developed to automate the process of analyzing social phenomenon using large scale data sets, in a way that is responsive to the social science approach to conceptually driven research. Developing these tools has been a way for mathematicians to articulate ideas, such as, pattern formation and behavioral concentration that can be tested through spatial analysis. The usefulness of these tools in the work on spatial influence of urban features on crime, for example, is now showing real benefit and has become a standard tool in the repertoire of crime analysts. Importantly, what these approaches take account of is the fact that all of these risks take place in a common geography, thus providing a digital anchoring point to which social, behavioral, and physical characteristics can be tied together through maps and spatial analysis.

At the same time, there has been an emerging literature around "crime and place" in criminology that examines the relative influence of factors in the environment on crime. This place-based approach has led to a series of hypothesis-driven questions that specify how such things as public housing or schools concentrate crime around them, that is, serve as crime generators or how certain locations that are conducive to illicit trade, like drug markets, attract violence. The tests that have been done using this approach have tended to rely on statistical assessment using simple chi-square or regression analysis and have demonstrated significant but not particularly strong effects. The findings of this research, although not compelling in terms of predictive power, have had an important impact on the ways in which police agencies are currently operating, incorporating this type of information more closely into decision-making. The intelligence based approach to law enforcement now has spatial analysis as a central component in its operation, extending from the day to day guidance provided by Compstat to special teams of analysts that program and implement strategic interventions[366].

As these approaches develop, we would argue that the interface between the pattern analysis and modeling approaches and the perspectives grounded in theory and research share common territory. An example of this is shown in research conducted on crime in Los Angeles by Short, et al[367]. They demonstrate how computational mathematics can be used to identify the development of crime patterns using a technique that models out predicted outcomes based on pre-set decision rules. Their approach allows them to account for the complexity of individual behavior over time and space producing spatial renditions of how this behavior is most likely to emerge. This is a tool that provides the basis for taking into account the interactions that occur between the different elements in the landscape. The discussion of genetic algorithms in an earlier chapter of this compendium by Manik-Perlman and Heffner is another example of this approach.

In the case of crime, this approach permits a calculation of the likelihood that offenders may act in a certain way depending on opportunities in a specific location and the deterrent effect of guardians. So, these analytical strategies are used to provide a background of behavior patterns that can be used to anticipate future actions. But, further, the Short et al work demonstrates how their models can be compared against real data produced by criminologists based on a hypotheses driven research model. While the study of crime using their models leads them to suggest that crime would displace under situations in which law enforcement suppression is applied, they openly question this finding given the extensive literature from field studies on the non-displacement of crime[368]. This led the authors not to reject their methodology but rather to point to a contradiction in the conditions under which their results would actually conform to the criminological research findings. They speculate that their findings that crime displaces happens because their models are based on homogeneous environments that promote displacement while the field studies are done in heterogeneous settings where displacement is discouraged. The approach that the authors undertake is not to dismiss the data or techniques of the other perspective but to consider their results in terms of a "ground truthing" that allows a confirmation or rejection of findings. This type of multi-method problem solving enriches our analytical approaches and benefits problem-solving.

Developing a Multi-method Approach to Crime Analysis

*I*n the social science approach to the study of crime risk, we have established the need to identify, through the research that has been done, the correlates of crime. Using this approach we are able to develop hypotheses about what factor is more likely to be present in an area that is conducive to certain types of crime. This is the intent of Part 2 of this compendium, identifying the known risks to provide a basis for including them in our analysis of the contexts in which the likelihood of crime increases. To examine these risks, we have developed a procedure (i.e., RTM) that allows us to consider these layers simultaneously. But, the model that we produce is not only a function of the risk correlates that we identify in the research literature. The model can also be used to identify newly emergent patterns in behavior that come from the interaction of the risk factors and from feedback that occurs when the model is used in enforcement and the results of this are included in a new risk map. In doing this analysis, risk must be assigned to continuous geographic surfaces for strategic and tactical responses to crime. While the crime event might occur at a finite place, risk is a continuous dynamic value that can increase or decrease in intensity and cluster or dissipate in different areas (i.e. even areas remote from a crime event) over time. Risk values, therefore, are tied to geography. Regarding crime, risk values are the measure of a geography's potential for a crime event to occur. Risk changes with geography. Public safety resources are also often deployed to certain geographies. Assessing risk, therefore, will allow for a more strategic allocation of resources and is a key element in understanding the nature of crime emergence and desistence.

The risk of a crime event occurring at a specific location is determined by many factors. Sometimes all of those factors must interact at the same place and time for the event to occur. For example, individual meteorological factors that are incorporated into weather forecasting do not necessarily produce rain, thunder storms or hurricanes by themselves. It is only when they intersect in space and time that they have the greatest potential to yield a particular outcome. Other times, only one or a few factors may be required to interact about the same geography and at certain times for a particular event to occur. Understanding the spatial-temporal interaction effects of certain factors is key to assessing and valuing risk. Risk assessment aids in crime prevention by addressing underlying causes. It is through the adaptation of a standardized measure of calculating the intersection of risk occurring throughout the landscape that we can develop a systematic way of forecasting criminal behavior.

The insights provided by pattern analysis are more likely to emerge from the exploration of the spatial patterns that emerge in our examination of crime types. This is particularly relevant as we test and retest our hypothesis-driven maps, creating new ones based on new data and responses to interventions. The RTM has flexibility in that it can include risk layers pre-defined by hypotheses or it can accommodate layers that have a spatial character that we might speculate relate to crimes but the research literature has not explicitly made this connection. RTM also provides the platform on which we can build agent based modeling approaches. These would involve the identification of risk factors as the basis upon which decision rules for offenders and victims can be based. In addition, the models can include information that would be useful for police in judging the risk of certain outcomes. These models could then be incorporated into a mapping exercise that demonstrates likely outcomes that can be altered through a ongoing shift in how risk is judged, either through an expert system or through feedback from forecasts based on known correlates of crime.

*I*ncorporating these approaches into an RTM provides us with a useful analytical tool for forecasting crime. But, in addition, it allows us to develop different levels of evaluation to determine the effectiveness of intervention. Below are three possible types of evaluation that could occur. These include, planned interventions, directed patrol, and altering decision management.

Planned Interventions

*W*hile most police activity is based on an ongoing pattern of response, increasingly police have adopted a strategy for planned interventions to deal with certain chronic problems. This might include violent crime reduction programs, drug market disruptions, burglary deterrence programs, and so on. Most of these programs are implemented in a way that conforms to the ongoing activities of the police departments; although, initiatives such as the special terrorist response teams, work outside of these normal practices. Important for these interventions is a sense of their effectiveness and this is where evaluations can be most useful. There are other examples of this type of evaluation, including the steps that can be taken to examine how CCTV can be implemented and targeted[369]. Now, the evaluation can be process based, where the actual implementation of the program is reviewed, or outcomes based, where clear objectives are set and then assessed. While evidence-based approaches would demand careful controls, evaluations that are less rigidly managed and where there is ex-post facto assessment of outcomes, can be useful in determining program effectiveness.

Directed Patrol

$\mathcal{M}$ost policing will continue to be response-based, just given the nature of the behavior that is to be controlled. But, this does not mean that there is complete uncertainty over where crime will occur. The ad-hoc pattern based approach can be useful in developing risk models based on factors that are not anticipated by past outcomes or past research. This means that data mining can be a useful way of updating and managing police response where directed patrol becomes more likely to occur and provides the ongoing preventive background of policing that complements planned interventions. Now, this form of directed patrol can come, as well, from hypotheses driven analysis. They are not mutually exclusive, which is exactly the point of using both approaches.

Risk Based Decision-Making

$\mathcal{P}$olice agencies are increasingly called upon to respond to a variety of pressures within the communities that they serve. When looked at in terms of risk, they need better information both about the hazards that occur in the community and the threats to their own organization in completing their work. As a consequence, law enforcement is looking to improve its overall intelligence process, integrating information more directly into decision-making. The role that RTM can play emerges from querying historical and real-time data to provide a picture of the crime patterns, the interventions of police, and the changing context of the community. This information can be important in managing the organization in ways that decisions about the conduct of crime suppression are realistic, tested against reality, and effective.

Conclusion

$\mathcal{I}$n sum, the role of the criminologist is changing to accommodate to the new technological and data realities. These changes can lead to a conflict in approaches or they can provide new opportunities for collaboration and the development of more robust tools for assessment and evaluation. The development of integrating frameworks, such as risk terrain modeling, offers not only a tool for managing data but also for consolidating different approaches to crime into an effective mechanism for decision-making. There really is no reason to isolate these different approaches from one another, rather they can be use as complementary and mutually supportive. Particularly when looking at changes in social and spatial environments over time, it is useful to have these different approaches to analyze different dimensions of the data.

References and Endnotes

References

Abbey, A. (2002). Alcohol-related sexual assault: A common problem among college students. *Journal of Studies on Alcohol, 14, 118-128.*

Abbott, A. (1997). Of time and space: The contemporary relevance of the Chicago. *Social Forces, 75,* 1149-1182.

Ahrens, M. (2009). *Vacant building fires.* Quincy, MA: National Fire Protection Association, Fire Analysis and Research Division.

American Prosecutors Research Institute (2004). *Unwelcome guests: A community prosecution approach to street-level drug dealing and prostitution.* Alexandria, VA: American Prosecutors Research Institute, National Center for Community Prosecution.

Andresen, M.A., & Malleson, N. (2011). Testing the stability of crime patterns: implications for theory and policy. *Journal of Research in Crime and Delinquency, 48*(1), 58-82.

Andrews, D. A. (1989). Re-arrest is predictable and can be influenced: Using risk assessments to reduce re-arrest. *Forum on Corrections Research, 1,* 11-18.

Arson Strike Force. (1980). *Predicting arson risk in New York City: A first report.* New York, NY: Arson Strike Force.

Azavea. (2006). Crime spike detector: Using advanced geostatistics to develop a crime early warning system.

Azavea. (2007-2011). Geographic crime analysis, early warning, and risk forcasting. *HunchLab.* Retrieved April 8, 2011, from http://www.azavea.com/hunchlab

Bakker, E. (n.d.). Early warning by NGOs in conflict areas. *Centre for International Conflict Analysis and Management.* Retrieved January 1, 2011, from http://cicam.ruhosting.nl/early-warning.pdf

Basta, L. A., Richmond, T. S., & Wiebe, D. J. (2010). Neighborhoods, daily activities, and measuring health risks experienced in urban environments. *Social Science and Medicine, 71,* 1943-1950.

Beauregard, E., Proulx, J., Rossmo, D. K., Leclerc, B. & Allaire, J. F. (2007). A script analysis of patterns in the hunting process of serial sex offenders. *Criminal Justice and Behavior, 34,* 1069-1084.

Benson, C. & Matthews, R. (1995). Street prostitution: Ten facts in search of a policy. *International Journal of Sociology of Law, 23,* 395-415.

Berk, R. (2009). *Asymmetric loss functions for forecasting in criminal justice settings.* Unpublished manuscript.

Bernasco, W. & Block, R. (2011). Robberies in Chicago: A block level analysis of the influence of crime generators, crime attractors, and offender anchor points. *Journal of Research in Crime and Delinquency, 48*(1), 33-57.

Bernasco, W. (2006). Co-offending and the choice of target areas in burglary. *Journal of Investigative Psychology and Offender Profiling, 3,* 139-155.

Bernasco, W. (2010). A Sentimental journey to crime: Effects of residential history of crime location choice, *Criminology, 48*(2), 389-416.

Block, R.L. & Block, C.R. (1995). Space, place & crime: Hot spot areas & hot places of liquor-related crime. In J. E. Eck & D. Weisburd (Eds.). *Crime and Place: Crime Prevention Studies* (Vol. 4) (pp. 145-184). Monsey, NY: Criminal Justice Press.

Blumstein, A., & Wallman, J. (Eds.). (2000). *The crime drop in America.* New York, NY: Cambridge University Press.

Bowers, K.J., & Johnson, S.D. (2005). Domestic burglary repeats and space-time clusters: The dimensions of risk. *European Journal of Criminology, 2*(1), 67-92.

Bowers, K.J., Johnson, S.D., & Pease, K. (2004). Prospective hot-spotting: The future of crime mapping?. *British Journal of Criminology, 44,* 641-658.

Braga, A.A. (2002). Gun violence among serious young offenders. *Problem-Oriented Guides for Police: Problem-Specific Guides Series.* Washington, DC: U.S. Department of Justice, Office of Community Oriented Policing Services.

Braga, A.A. (2003). Gun violence among serious young offenders. *Problem-Oriented Guides for Police: Problem-Specific Guides Series.* Washington, DC: U.S. Department of Justice, Office of Community Oriented Policing Services.

Brantingham, P. J. & Brantingham, P. L. (1995). Criminality of place: Crime generators and crime attractors. *European Journal on Criminal Policy and Research, 3,* 1-26.

Brantingham, P. J., & Brantingham, P. L. (1981). *Environmental Criminology.* Beverly Hills, CA: Sage.

Brantingham, P.J. & Brantingham, P.L. (1998). Environmental criminology: From theory to urban planning practice. *Studies on Crime and Crime Prevention, 7,* 31-60.

Brantingham, P.L., & Brantingham, P.J. (1991). Notes on the geometry of crime. In P.L. Brantingham, & P.J. Brantingham (Eds.), *Environmental Criminology* (pp. 27-54). Prospect Heights, IL: Waveland Press, Inc.

Brantingham, P.L., & Brantingham, P.J. (1993). Environment, routine, and situation: Toward a pattern theory of crime. In R.V. Clarke., & M. Felson (Eds.), *Routine Activity and Rational Choice* (pp. 259-294). New Brunswick, NJ: Transaction Publishers.

Brantingham, P.L., Brantingham, P.J., Vajihollahi, M., & Wuschke, K. (2009). Crime Analysis at multiple scales of aggregation: A topological approach. In D. Weisburd, W. Bernasco, & G.J.N. Bruinsma (Eds.), *Putting crime in its place: Units of analysis in geographic criminology* (pp. 81-107). New York, NY: Springer.

Brook, B. (2011). Fukushima Nuclear Accident- a simple and accurate explanation. *Brave New Climate.* Retrieved April 3, 2011, from http://bravenewclimate.com/2011/03/13/fukushima-simple-explanation/

Brown, R., & Thomas, N. (2003). Aging vehicles: Evidence of the effectiveness of new car security from the Home Office Car Theft Index. *Security Journal, 16*(3), 45-54.

Bureau of Justice Statistics. (n.d.). *Assault.* Retrieved February 26, 2011, from http://bjs.ojp.usdoj.gov/index.cfm?ty=tp&tid=316

Bureau of Justice Statistics. (n.d.). *Homicide.* Retrieved February 16, 2010, from http://bjs.ojp.usdoj.gov/index.cfm?ty=tp&tid=311

Burgess, E. W. (1928). Factors determining success or failure on parole. In A. A. Bruce, E. W. Burgess, & A. J. Harno (Eds.), *The workings of the indeterminate sentence law and the parole system in Illinois* (pp. 221-234). Springfield, IL: Illinois State Board of Parole.

Caplan, J. M, Kennedy, L.W., & Petrosian, G. (in press). Police-monitored CCTV cameras in Newark, NJ: A quasi-experimental test of crime deterrence. *Journal of Experimental Criminology.*

Caplan, J. M. & Kennedy, L. W. (2010). *Risk terrain modeling manual: Theoretical framework and technical steps of spatial risk assessment* [Electronic version]. Newark, NJ: Rutgers Center on Public Security.

Caplan, J. M. (2011, forthcoming). Mapping the spatial influence of crime correlates: A comparison of operationalization schemes and implications for crime analysis and CJ practice. *Cityscape.*

Caplan, J.M., Kennedy, L.W., & Miller, J. (2011). Risk terrain modeling: Brokering criminological theory and GIS methods for crime forecasting. *Justice Quarterly, 28*(2), 360-381.

Caplan, J.M., Moreto, W., & Kennedy, L.W. (2011). Forecasting global maritime piracy utilizing the risk terrain modeling (RTM) approach to spatial risk assessment. In L.W. Kennedy, & E. McGarrell (Eds.), *Crime and Terrorism Risk: Studies in Criminology and Criminal Justice.* New York, NY: Routledge.

Capowich, G.E. (2003). The conditioning effects of neighborhood ecology on burglary victimization. *Criminal Justice and Behavior, 30,* 39–61.

Catalano, S. M. (2004). Criminal victimization, 2003. *The key elements of problem-oriented policing.* Washington, DC: Bureau of Justice Statistics,

Center for Problem-Oriented Policing. Retrieved November 29, 2010, from www.popcenter.org/about/?p=elements

Chainey, S., Tompson, L., & Uhlig, S. (2008). The utility of hotspot mapping for predicting spatial patterns of crime. *Security Journal, 21,* 4-28.

Chajewski, M., & Mercado, C.C. (2009). An evaluation of sex offender residency restriction functioning in town, county, and city-wide jurisdictions. *Criminal Justice Policy Review, 20,* 44-61.

Clare, J., Fernandez, J., & Morgan, F. (2009). Formal evaluation of the impact of barriers and connectors on residential burglars' macro-level offending location choices. *The Australian and New Zealand Journal of Criminology, 42*(2), 139–158.

Clarke, R. & Eck, J. (2005). *Crime analysis for problem solvers in 60 small steps.* Washington, DC: U.S. Department of Justice, Office of Community Oriented Policing Services.

Clarke, R. V. & Felson, M. (1993). *Routine activity and rational choice (Vol. 5), advances in criminology theory.* New Brunswick, NJ: Transaction.

Clarke, R. V. & Goldstein, H. (2003). *Theft from cars in center-city parking facilities: A case study.* Washington, DC: U.S. Department of Justice, Office of Community Oriented Policing Services.

Clarke, R. V. (2002). *Shoplifting.* Washington, DC: U.S. Department of Justice, Office of Community Oriented Policing Services.

Clarke, R.V. (1999). *Hot Products: Understanding, anticipating and reducing demand for stolen goods.* Policing & Reducing Crime, Police Research Series Paper 112. London, UK: Home Office Policing and Reducing Crime Unit.

Clarke, R.V., Perkins, E., & Smith Jr., D.J. (2001). Explaining repeat residential burglaries: An analysis of property stolen. In G. Farrell, & K. Pease (Eds.), *Repeat Victimization* (pp. 119-132). Crime Prevention Studies (Vol.12).

Cobbina, J. E., Miller, J., & Brunson, R. K. (2008). Gender, neighborhood danger, and risk avoidance strategies among urban African American youth. *Criminology, 46*(3), 673-709. Retrieved October 3, 2010 from http://www.umsl.edu/~ccj/pdfs/Gender%20neighbrhood%20danger%20and%20risk%20avoidance.pdf

Cohen, L.E. & Felson, M. (1979). Social change and crime rate trends: A routine activity approach. *American Sociological Review, 44,* 588-608.

Cohen, L.E., & Cantor, D. (1981). Residential burglary in the United States: Life-style and demographic factors associated with the probability of victimization. *Journal of Research in Crime and Delinquency, 18*(1), 113-127.

Companion, M. (2008) 'The underutilization of street markets as a source of food security indicators in famine early warning systems: a case study of Ethiopia', *Disasters,* 32(3), 399-415

Copes, H. (1999). Routine activities and motor vehicle theft: A crime specific approach. *Journal of Crime and Justice, 22,* 125-145.

Couclelis, H. (1992). People manipulate objects (but cultivate fields): Beyond the raster-vector debate in GIS. In A. Frank, I. Campari, & U. Formentini (Eds.), *Theories and methods of spatio-temporal reasoning in geographic space: Lecture notes in computer science 639* (pp. 65-77). New York, NY: Springer-Verlag.

Davies, J.L., & Gurr, T.R. (1998). Preventive measures: An overview. In J.L. Davies, & T.R Gurr (Eds.), *Preventive measures: Building risk assessment and crisis early warning systems.* Lanham, MD: Rowman and Littlefield Publishers, Inc.

Dedel Johnson, K. (2005). School Vandalism. Washington, DC: Office of Community Oriented Policing Services, U.S. Department of Justice.

Dedel, K. (2005). *School Vandalism.* Washington, DC: U.S. Department of Justice, Office of Community Oriented Policing Services.

Dedel, K. (2007). *Drive-by shootings.* Washington, DC: U.S. Department of Justice, Office of Community Oriented Policing Services.

Dorn, A.W. (2000). Towards an effective UN Early Warning System: A review and recommendations. *WalterDorn.* Retreived January 28, 2011, from http://www.walterdorn.org/pubs/26

Duwe, G., Donnay, W., & Tewksbury, R. (2008). Does residential proximity matter? A geographic analysis of sex offense recidivism. *Criminal Justice and Behavior, 35,* 484-504.

Eck, J.E. (1995). A general model of the geography of illicit retail marketplaces. In J. E. Eck & D. Weisburd (Eds.). *Crime and Place: Crime Prevention Studies* (Vol. 4) (pp. 67-94). Monsey, NY: Criminal Justice Press.

Eck, J.E. (2001). Policing and crime event concentration. In R. Meier, L.W. Kennedy, & V. Sacco (Eds.), *The process and structure of crime: Criminal events and crime analysis* (pp. 249-276). New Brunswick, NJ: Transactions.

Eck, J.E., & Liu, L. (2008). Contrasting simulated and empirical experiments. *Journal of Experimental Criminology, 4*(3), 195-213.

Eck, J.E., Chainey, S., Cameron, J.G., Leitner, M., & Wilson, R. E. (2005). *Mapping Crime: Understanding hot spots.* Washington, DC: National Institute of Justice.

Eck, J.E., Clarke, R., & Guerette, R. (2007). Ricky facilities: crime concentration in homogeneous sets of establishments and facilities. *Crime Prevention Studies, 21,* 225-264.

Egenhofer, M. & Mark, D. (1995). Naïve geography. In A. Frank & W. Kuhn (Eds.), *Spatial information theory: A theoretical basis for GIS: Lecture notes in computer science 988* (pp. 1-15). International Conference COSIT '95, Semmering, Austria. New York, NY: Springer-Verlag.

Farrell, G., Phillips, C., & Pease, K. (1995). Like taking candy: Why does repeat victimization occur? *British Journal of Criminology, 35*(3), 384-399.

Fisher, B., Cullen, F., & Turner, M. (2000). *The sexual victimization of college women.* Washington, DC: U.S. Department of Justice, National Institute of Justice and Bureau of Justice Statistics.

Fleming, Z. (1999). The thrill of it all: Youthful offenders and auto theft. In P. Cormwell (Ed.), *Their own words: Criminals on crime* (pp. 71-79). Los Angeles, CA: Roxbury.

Fox, J. A., & Zawitz, M. W. (2004). *Homicide trends in the United States: 2002 update.* Washington, DC: U.S. Department of Justice, Bureau of Justice Statistics.

Frank, A. (1993). The use of geographical information systems: The user interface is the system. In D. Medyckyj-Scott & H. Hearnshaw (Eds.), *Human factors in geographic information systems* (pp. 3-14). London, UK: Belhaven Press.

Frank, A., & Mark, D. (1991). Language issues for GIS. In D. Maguire, M. Goodchild, & D. Rhind (Eds.), *Geographic Information Systems: Principles* (pp. 147-163). London, UK: Longman.

Freundschuh, S.M., & Egenhofer, M.J. (1997). Human conceptions of spaces: Implications for geographic information systems. *Transactions in GIS, 2*(4), 361-375.

Glensor, R. W., & Peak, K. J. (2004). *Crimes against tourists.* Washington, DC: U.S. Department of Justice, Office of Community Oriented Policing Services.

Glueck, S., & Glueck, E. (1950). *Unraveling juvenile delinquency.* New York, NY: Commonwealth.

Goldstein, M., Kaminsky, G.L., & Reinhart, C.M. (2000). *Assessing financial vulnerability: An early warning system for emerging markets.* Washington DC: Institute for International Economics.

Goldstein, P. J. (1985). The drugs/violence nexus: A tripartite conceptual framework. *Journal of Drug Issues, 39,* 143-174.

Gottfredson, S. D., & Moriarty, L. J. (2006). Statistical risk assessment: Old problems and new applications. *Crime and Delinquency, 52,* 178–200.

Government of Germany. (2006). Developing early warning systems: A checklist. In T. Kausch, M. Husain, & T. McDonald (Eds.), *EWC III: Third international conference on early warning -From concept to action* (pp. 3). Bonn, Germany. Retrieved April 3, 2011, from http://www.pacificdisaster.net/pdnadmin/data/original/ISDR_2006_Developing_early_warning.pdf

Greenfield,L. (1997). *Sex offenses and offenders.* Washington, DC: U.S. Department of Justice, Office of Justice Programs.

Groff, E. R. (2007a). Simulation for theory testing and experimentation: An example using routine activity theory and street robbery. *Journal of Quantitative Criminology, 23,* 75–103.

Groff, E. R. (2007b). 'Situating' simulation to model human spatio-temporal interactions: An example using crime events. *Transactions in GIS, 11*(4), 507–530.

Groff, E. R., & La Vigne, N. G. (2002). Forecasting the future of predictive crime mapping. *Crime Prevention Studies, 13,* 29–57.

Groff, E.R., & La Vigne, N.G. (2001). Mapping an opportunity surface of residential burglary. *Journal in Crime and Delinquency, 38,* 257 – 278.

Guerette, R.T., & Bowers, K.J. (2009). Assessing the extent of crime displacement and diffusion of benefits: A review of situational crime prevention evaluations. *Criminology, 47*(4), 1331-1368.

Hall, J. R. (2010). *Intentional fires.* Quincy, MA: National Fire Protection Association, Fire Analysis and Research Division.

Harocopos, A. & Hough, M. (2005). *Drug Dealing in Open-Air Markets.* Washington, DC: U.S. Department of Justice, Office of Community Oriented Policing Services.

Harrell, E. (2005). *Violence by gang members, 1993-2003.* Washington, DC: U.S. Department of Justice, Bureau of Justice Statistics.

Harries, K. (1999). *Mapping crime: Principle and practice.* Washington, DC: U.S. Department of Justice, Office of Justice Programs.

Heffner, J. (2010). HunchLab: Contagious crime and genetic algorithms. *Azavea Journal, 5*(5).

Henn, S. (2011). The effectiveness of Japan's earthquake early-warning system [Electronic version]. *American Public Media: Marketplace.* Retrieved April 3, 2011, from http://marketplace.publicradio.org/display/web/2011/03/11/pm-the-effectiveness-of-japans-earlywarning-earthquake-system/

Henry, L.M., & Bryan, B.A. (2000). *Visualizing the spatio-temporal patterns of motor vehicle theft in Adelaide, South Australia* [Lecture]. GISCA National Key Centre for Social Applications of GIS.

Hepburn, L. M., & Hemenway, D. (2004). Firearm availability and homicide: A review of the literature. *Aggression and Violent Behavior, 9*(4), 417-440. http://www.albany.edu/sourcebook

Humphrey, S., & Kahn, A. (2000). Fraternities, athletic teams and rape: Importance of identification with a risky group. *Journal of Interpersonal Violence, 15*(12), 1313–1322.

Jacobson, J. (1999). Policing drug hot-spots. *Police research series, paper 109.* London, UK: Home Office.

Johnson, S. D., Bowers, K. J., Birks, D., & K. Pease. (2008). Prospective mapping: The importance of the environmental backcloth. In D. Weisburd, W. Bernasco, & G. Bruinsma (Eds.), *Putting crime in its place: Units of analysis in geographic criminology.* New York, NY: Springer.

Johnson, S. D., Bowers, K. J., Gamman, L., Mamerow, L., & Warne, A. (2010). *Thefts of customers' personal property in cafés and bars.* Washington, DC: U.S. Department of Justice, Office of Community Oriented Policing Services.

Johnson, S.D. (2008). Repeat burglary victimization: A tale of two theories. *Journal of Experimental Criminology, 4,* 215-240.

Johnson, S.D., Birks, D.J., McLaughlin, L., Bowers, K. J., & Pease, K. (2007). Prospective crime mapping in operational context. *Home Office online report.* London, UK: Home Office.

Johnson, S.D., Sidebottom, A., & Thorpe, A. (2008). *Bicycle theft.* Washington, DC: U.S. Department of Justice, Office of Community Oriented Policing Services.

Kennedy, D.M., & Braga, A.A. (1998). Homicide in Minneapolis: Research for problem solving. *Homicide Studies, 2*(3), 263-290.

Kennedy, L.W., & Baron, S.W. (1993). Routine activities and a subculture of violence: A study of violence on the street. *Journal of Research in Crime and Delinquency, 30*(1), 88-112

Kennedy, L.W., & Caplan, J.M. (in press). Risk terrain modeling. In J.C. McGloin, M.L. Sullivan, & L.W. Kennedy (Eds.), *When crime appears: The case of emergence.* New York, NY: Routledge.

Kennedy, L.W., & Van Brunschot, E.G. (2009). *The risk in crime.* New York, NY: Roman and Littlefield.

Kennedy, L.W., Caplan, J.M., & Piza, E.L. (2010, online first). Risk clusters, hotspots, and spatial intelligence: Risk Terrain Modeling as an Algorithm for Police Resource Allocation Strategies. *Journal of Quantitative Criminology.*

Kennedy, L.W., Marteaache, N., & Gaziarifoglu, Y. (2010). *Global risk assessment: The search for a common methodology.* Newark, NJ: Rutgers Center on Public Security. Retrieved January 18, 2011, from http://www.rutgerscps.org/Publications.htm

Kilpatick, D.G., Resnick, H.S., Ruggiero, K.J., Conoscenti, L.M., & McCauley, J. (2007). *Drug facilitated, incapacitated and forcible rape: A national study.* Washington, DC: U.S. Department of Justice, National Institute of Justice.

Kinshott, G. (2001). *Vehicle related thefts: Practice messages from the British Crime Survey.* London, UK: Home Office.

Koss, M., & Cleveland III, H. (1996). Athletic participation, fraternity membership and date rape: The question remains - Self-selection or different causal processes? *Violence Against Women, 2*(2), 180-190.

Koss, M., & Gaines, J. (1993). The prediction of sexual aggression by alcohol use, athletic participation and fraternity affiliation. *Journal of Interpersonal Violence, 8*(1), 94-108.

LaPeter Anton, L. (2010, January 2). After a burglary, victim must buy back items from pawn shop. *St. Petersburg Times* [Electronic version]. Retrieved January 2, 2010, from http://www.tampabay.com/features/humaninterest/after-a-burglary-victim-must-buy-back-items-from-pawn-shop/1062282

Levenson, J.S. (2007). Residence restrictions and their impact on sex offender reintegration, rehabilitation, and recidivism. *Association for the Treatment of Sexual Abusers Forum, 18*(2).

Levinson, D. (2002). *Encyclopedia of crime and punishment* (Vol. 1). Thousand Oaks, CA: SAGE Publications, Inc.

Lewis, A. (1999). *The prevention and control of arson.* Borehamwood, UK: Fire Protection Association.

Lippman, M. (2009). *Contemporary criminal law: Concepts, cases, and controversies* (2nd ed.). Thousand Oaks, CA: SAGE Publications, Inc.

Loukaitou-Sideris, A. (1999). Hot spots of bus stop crime: The importance of environmental attributes. *Journal of American Planning Association, 65*(4), 395 - 411.

Madensen, T.D., & Eck, J.E. (2008). *Spectator violence in stadiums.* Washington, DC: U.S. Department of Justice, Office of Community Oriented Policing Services.

Maguire, K. (Ed.) (2007). *Sourcebook of criminal justice statistics.* [Electronic version]. Retrieved from http://www.albany.edu/sourcebook

Maguire, K. (Ed.) (2009). *Sourcebook of criminal justice statistics* [Electronic version]. Retrieved from

Malczewski, J., & Poetz, A. (2005). Residential burglaries and neighborhood socioeconomic context in London, Ontario: Global and local regression analysis. *The Professional Geographer, 57*(4), 516 – 529.

Mark, D. (1993). Human spatial cognition. In D. Medyckyj-Scott, & H. Hearnshaw (Eds.), *Human factors in geographical information systems* (pp. 51-60). London: Belhaven Press.

Mawby, R.I. (2001). *Burglary.* Portland, OR: Willan Publishing.

Mazerolle, L., Kadleck, C., & Roehl, J. (1998). Controlling drug and disorder problems: The role of place managers. *Criminology, 36*(2), 371-402.

McCord, E.S., & Ratcliffe, J.H. (2007). A micro-spatial analysis of the demographic and criminogenic environment of drug markets in Philadelphia. *Australian and New Zealand Journal of Criminology, 40*,(1), 43-63

McCue, C. (2007). *Data mining and predictive analysis: Intelligence gathering and crime analysis.* Burlington, MA: Butterworth-Heinemann.

McGloin, J., Sullivan, C., & Kennedy, L.W. (forthcoming). When crime appears: The role of emergence. New York, NY:Routledge.

McNamara, R.H. (Ed.). (2008). *Homelessness in America* (Vol. 1). Westport, CN: Praeger Perspectives.

Mears, D.P., Scott, M.L., & Bhati, A.S. (2007). Opportunity theory and agricultural crime victimization. *Rural Sociology, 72,* 151–184.

Miethe, T. & Meier, R. (1994). *Crime and its social context: Toward an integrated theory of offenders, victims, and situations.* Albany, NY:SUNY Press.

Miller, B.A., Downs, W.R., Gondoli, D.M., & Keil, A. (1987). The role of childhood sexual abuse in the development of alcoholism in women. *Violence and Victims, 2,* 157–172.

Millie, A. (2008). Vulnerability and risk: Some lessons from the UK Reducing Burglary Initiative. *Police Practice and Research, 9*(3), 183 – 198.

Monk, M.K., Heiononen, J.A., & Eck, J.E. (2010). *Street robbery.* Washington, DC: U.S. Department of Justice, Office of Community Oriented Policing Services.

Moreto, W. D. (2010). *Applying risk terrain modeling to urban residential burglary in Newark, NJ.* Newark, NJ: Rutgers Center on Public Security. Retrieved June 5, 2011, from http://www.rutgerscps.org/rtm/BurglaryRTM_CaseStudy_Brief.pdf

Moreto, W. D., Piza, E. L., & Caplan, J. M. (n.d.). *'A plague on both your houses?': Risks, repeats and reconsiderations of urban residential burglary.* Unpublished Manuscript.

National Drought Mitigation Center. (2000). Improving drought early warning systems in the context of drought preparedness and mitigation: Summary of breakout sessions. In D.A. Wilhite, M.V.K. Sivakumar, & D.A. Wood (Eds.), *Early warning systems for drought preparedness and drought management: Proceedings of an expert group meeting held September 5-7, 2000, in Lisbon, Portugal* (pp. 200). Lisbon, Portugal: Author. Retrieved from http://www.drought.unl.edu/MONITOR/EWS/ch15_summary.pdf

National Highway Traffic Safety Administration. (2008). Final theft data; Motor vehicle theft prevention standard. *Federal Register, 73*(199), 60633-60638.

National Institute of Justice. (1997). *A study of homicide in eight U.S. cities: An NIJ intramural research project.* Washington, DC: US Department of Justice, Office of Justice Programs, National Institute of Justice.

National Insurance Crime Bureau. (2005-09). *Hot wheels.* Des Plaines, IL: The Bureau.

Office of National Drug Control Policy. (2000). *Drug-related crime fact sheet.* Washington, DC: Office of National Drug Control Policy.

Papachristos, A.V., Braga, A.A., & Hureau, D. (2011). *Six-degree of violent victimization: Social networks and the risk of gunshot injury.* Retrieved February 26, 2011, from Social Science Research Network website, http://papers.ssrn.com/sol3/papers.cfm?abstract_id=1772772

Plouffe, N., & Sampson, R. (2004). Auto theft and theft from autos in parking lots in Chula Vista, CA. In M.G. Maxfield & R.V. Clarke (Eds.), *Understanding and preventing car theft: Crime Prevention Studies* (Vol. 17). Monsey, NY: Criminal Justice Press.

Portland Police Bureau and Campbell Resources Inc. (1991). *Crime Prevention in overnight lodging: A guide to preventing drug activity, prostitution and other illegal behavior in hotels and motels.* Portland, OR: City of Portland.

Poyner, B. & Webb, B. (2006). *Crime Free Housing in the 21st Century.* London, UK: UCL Jill Dando Institute of Crime Science.

Quetelet, M. (1842). A treatise on man. Edinburg, UK: Chambers.

Raines, G.L., Sawatzky, D.L., & Bonham-Carter, G.F. (2010, Spring). Incorporating expert knowledge: New fuzzy logic tools in ArcGIS 10. *ArcUser.* Redlands, CA: ESRI.

Rand, M.R. (2008). *Criminal victimization, 2007.* Washington, DC: U.S. Department of Justice, Bureau of Justice Statistics.

Ratcliffe, J. H. & Rengert, G. F. (2008). Near repeat patterns in Philadelphia shootings. *Security Journal, 21*(1-2), 58-76.

Ratcliffe, J. H., & McCullagh, M.J. (1998). Identifying repeat victimization with GIS. *British Journal of Criminology, 38*(4), 651-662.

Ratcliffe, J.H. (2009, August). *Near repeat calculator (version 1.3).* Philadelphia, PA: Temple University.

Ratcliffe, J.H., & McCullagh, M.J. (2001). Chasing ghosts? Police perception of high crime areas. *British Journal of Criminology, 41,* 330-341.

Ratliff, E. (2011). Taming the wild. *National Geographic, March.*

Regini, L.A. (1998). Combating gangs. *FBI Law Enforcement Bulletin, 67*(2), 5-12.

Rengert, G. (1996). Auto theft in central Philadelphia. In R. Homel (Ed.), *Policing for prevention: Reducing crime, public intoxication and injury: Crime prevention studies* (Vol. 7). Monsey, NY: Criminal Justice Press.

Rengert, G., & Wasilchick, J. (1985). *Suburban burglary: A time and a place for everything.* Springfield, IL: Charles C Thomas

Rengert, G., Radcliffe, J., & Chakravorty, S. (2005). *Policing illegal drug markets: Geographic approaches to crime reduction.* Monsey, NY: Criminal Justice Press.

Renzetti, C.M., & Edleson, J.L. (Eds.). (2008). *Encyclopedia of interpersonal violence* (Vol. 1). Thousand Oaks, CA: SAGE Publications, Inc.

Rice, K.J., & Smith, W.R. (2002). Sociological models of automotive theft: Integrating routine activity and social disorganization approaches. *Journal of Research in Crime and Delinquency, 39*(3), 304-336.

Roncek, D.W., & Maier, P.A. (1991). Bars, blocks, and crime revisited: Linking the theory of routine activities to the empiricism of "hot spots". *Criminology, 29(4),* 725-753.

Roth, J. (1994). *Firearms and violence.* Washington, DC: National Institute of Justice.

Rubin, J. (2010). Stopping crime before it starts. *LA Times,* August 21. Retrieved December 5, 2010, from http://articles.latimes.com/2010/aug/21/local/la-me-predictcrime-20100427-1

Salzano, E., Agreda, A.G., Di Carluccio, A., & Fabbrocino, G. (2009). Risk assessment and early warning systems for industrial facilities in seismic zones. *Reliability Engineering & System Safety,* 94(10), 1577-1584.

Sampson, R.J. & Raudenbush, S. (1999). Systematic social observation of public spaces: A new look at disorder in urban neighbourhoods. *American Journal of Sociology, 105,* 603-651.

Sampson, R.J. (2002). *Acquaintance rape of college students.* Washington, DC: U.S. Department of Justice, Office of Community Oriented Policing Services.

Sampson, R.J. (2004). *Theft of and from autos in parking facilities in Chula Vista California: A final report to the U.S. Department of Justice.* Washington, DC: U.S. Department of Justice, Office of Community Oriented Policing Services on the Field Applications of the Problem-Oriented Guides for Police Project.

Sampson, R.J., & Groves, W.B. (1989). Community structure and crime: Testing social disorganization theory. *American Journal of Sociology, 94,* 774-802.

Schmerler, K. (2005). *Disorder at budget motels: Problem specific guide No. 30.* Washington, DC: U.S. Department of Justice, Office of Community Oriented Policing Services.

Scott, M.S. (2001). *Disorderly youth in public places.* Washington, DC: U.S. Department of Justice, Office of Community Oriented Policing Services.

Scott, M.S., & Dedel, K. (2006a). *Assault in and around bars* (2nd ed.). Washington, DC: U.S. Department of Justice, Office of Community Oriented Policing Services.

Scott, M.S., & Dedel, K. (2006b). *Street prostitution.* Washington, DC: Office of Community Oriented Policing Services, U.S. Department of Justice.

Shaw, C., & McKay, H. (1969). *Juvenile delinquency and urban areas.* Chicago, IL: University of Chicago Press.

Sherman, L.W. (1995). Hotspots of crime and criminal careers of places. In J.E. Eck, & D. Weisburd (Eds.), *Crime and place: Crime prevention studies* (Vol. 4) (pp. 35-52). Monsey, NY: Criminal Justice Press.

Sherman, L.W., Gartin, P.R., & Buerger, M.E. (1989). Hot spots of predatory crime: Routine activities and the criminology of place. *Criminology, 27,* 27-55.

Sherman, L.W., Shaw, J.W., & Rogan, D.P. (1995). *The Kansas City gun experiment.* Washington, DC: U.S. Department of Justice, Office of Justice Programs, National Institute of Justice.

Shoham, S., Knepper, P. & Kett, M. (Eds.). (2010). *International handbook of criminology.* Boca Raton. FL: CRC Press.

Short, M.B., Brantingham, P.J., Bertozzic, A.L. & Tita, G.E. (2010). Dissipation and displacement of hotspots in reaction-diffusion models of crime. *Proceedings of the National Academy of Sciences,* 107(9), 3961–3965.

Short, M.B., D'Orsogna, M.R., Brantingham, P.J., & Tita, G. (2009). Measuring and modeling repeat and near-repeat burglary effects. *Journal of Quantitative Criminology,* 25, 325-339.

SIFY News. (2011). Japan's earthquake-proof buildings helped limit damage. *SIFY.com.* Retrieved April 3, 2011, from http://www.sify.com/news/japan-s-earthquake-proof-buildings-helped-limit-damage-news-national-ldmoozfecef.html

Smith, M.J., & Clarke, R.V. (2000). Crime and public transport. In R. Clarke (Ed.), *Crime and Justice: A Review of Research* (pp. 169-234). Chicago, IL: The University of Chicago Press.

Smith, W.R., Frazee, S.G., & Davison, E.L. (2000). Furthering the integration of routine activity and social disorganization theories: Small units of analysis and the study of street robbery as a diffusion process. *Criminology,* 38, 489-523.

Sparrow, M.K. (2011). *Governing science.* Boston, MA: Harvard Kennedy School.

Spelman, W. (1995). Criminal careers of public places. In J. E. Eck & D. Weisburd (Eds.), *Crime and place: Crime prevention studies* (Vol. 4) (pp. 115-144). Monsey, NY: Criminal Justice Press.

Stucky, T.D., & Ottensan, J.R. (2009). Land use and violent crime. *Criminology, 47,* 1223-64.

Sutton, M. (2010). *Stolen goods market.* Washington, DC: Office of Community Oriented Policing Services, U.S. Department of Justice.

Sutton, M., Schneider, J., & Hetherington, S. (2001). Tackling theft with the market reduction approach. *Home Office Crime Reduction research series paper 8.* London, UK: Home Office Policing and Reducing Crime Unit.

Taylor, R.B. (1997). Social order and disorder of street-blocks and neighborhood: Ecology, microecology and the systemic model of social disorganization. *Journal of Research in Crime and Delinquency, 24,* 113-155.

Taylor, R.B., & Harrell, A.V. (1996). *Physical environment and crime.* Washington, DC: National Institute of Justice.

Tennenbaum, A.N., & Fink, E.L. (1994). Temporal regularities in homicide: Cycles, seasons, and autoregression. *Journal of Quantitative Criminology, 10*(4), 317-342.

Testa, M., Livingston, J.A., Tamsen, C., & Frone, M.R. (2003). *The role of women's substance use in vulnerability to forcible and incapacitated rape.* Buffalo, NY: Research Institute on Addictions.

Tewksbury, R., & Mustaine, E.E. (2008). Where registered sex offenders live: Community characteristics and proximity to possible victims. *Victims & Offenders, 3,* 86-98.

Tilley, N., Smith, J., Finer, S., Erol, R., Charles, C., & Dobby, J. (2004). *Problem solving street crime: Practical lessons from the street crime initiative.* London, UK: Home Office Research, Development and Statistics Directorate.

Tomlin, C. (1994). Map algebra: One perspective. *Landscape and Urban Planning, 30,* 3-12.

Townsley, M., Homel, R., & Chaseling, J. (2000). Repeat burglary victimisation: Spatial and temporal patterns. *The Australian and New Zealand Journal of Criminology, 33*(1), 37-63.

Truman, J.L., & Rand, M.R. (2010). *Criminal victimization, 2009.* Washington, DC: U.S. Department of Justice, Bureau of Justice Statistics

Tseloni, A., Osborn, D.R., Trickett, A., & Pease, K. (2002). Modeling property crime using the British Crime Survey: What have we learnt?. *British Journal of Criminology, 42,* 109-128.

Tseloni, A., Wittebrood, K.,Farrell, G., & Pease, K. (2004). Burglary victimization in England and Wales, the United States and the Netherlands: A cross-national comparative test of routine activities and lifestyle theories. *British Journal of Criminology, 44,* 66-91.

U.S. Department of Housing and Urban Development. (1999). *In the crossfire: The impact of gun violence on public housing communities.* Washington, DC: U.S. Government Printing Office.

U.S. Department of Justice, Federal Bureau of Investigation. (2008). *Crime in the United States 2007.* Washington, DC: U.S. Government Printing Office.

U.S. Department of Justice, Federal Bureau of Investigation. (2010). *Crime in the United States 2009.* Washington, DC: U.S. Government Printing Office.

U.S. Department of Justice, National Gang Intelligence Center. (2009). *National gang threat assessment.* Washington, DC: U.S. Government Printing Office.

United States Fire Administration. (1997). *Arson in the United States.* Washington, DC: Federal Emergency Management Agency, United States Fire Administration.

United States Fire Administration. (2001). *Arson in the United States* (Vol. 1(8)). Washington, DC: Federal Emergency Management Agency, United States Fire Administration.

United States Fire Administration. (2009). *Intentionally set outdoor fires* (Vol. 9 (6)). Washington, DC: Federal Emergency Management Agency, United States Fire Administration.

Van Brunschot, E.G., & Kennedy, L.W. (2008). *Risk balance & security.* Los Angeles, CA: Sage Publications.

Walby, S. & Allen, J. (2004) *Domestic violence, sexual assault and stalking: Findings from the British Crime Survey.* Home Office Research Study 276. London: Home Office. Retrieved March 15, 2010 from http://rds.homeoffice.gov.uk/rds/pdfs04/hors276.pdf.

Walker, S., Spohn, C., & DeLeone, M. (2007). *The color of justice: Race, ethnicity, and crime in America.* Belmont, CA: Thompson Higher Education.

Walsh, J.A., & Taylor, R.B. (2007). Community structural predictors of spatially aggregated motor vehicle theft rates: Do they replicate?. *Journal of Criminal Justice, 35,* 297-311.

Wechsler, H., Lee, J.E., Kuo, M., & Lee, H. (2000). College binge drinking in the 1990s: A continuing problem: Results of the Harvard School of Public Health 1999 College Alcohol Study [Electronic version]. *Journal of American College. Health, 48,* 199-210. Retrieved October 5, 2010, from http://www.hsph.harvard.edu/cas/Documents/cont_problem/rpt2000.pdf.

Weisburd, D. (2008). Place-based policing. *Ideas in Policing Series.* Washington, DC: Police Foundation.

Weisburd, D., & Neyroud, P. (2011). Police science: Towards a new paradigm. Boston, MA: Harvard Kennedy School.

Weisburd, D., & Piquero, A. (2008). How well do criminologists explain crime? In M. Tonry (Ed.), *Crime and justice: An annual review of research* (Vol. 37). Chicago, IL: University of Chicago Press.

Weisburd, D., Bushway, S., Lum, C., & Yang, S. (2004). Crime trajectories at places: A longitudinal study of street segments in the city of Seattle. *Criminology, 42*(2), 283-322.

Weisburd, D., Mastrofski, S., McNally, A., Greenspan, R., & Willis, J. (2003). Reforming to preserve: Compstat and strategic problem solving in American policing. *Criminology and Public Policy, 2*(3), 421-456).

Weisburd, D., Mastrofski, S., McNally, A.M., & Greenspan, R. (2001). *Compstat and organizational change: Findings from a national survey.* Washington, DC: The Police Foundation.

Weisel, D.L. (2002). *Graffiti.* Washington, DC: Office of Community Oriented Policing Services, U.S. Department of Justice.

Weisel, D.L., Smith, W.R., Garson, G.D., Pavlichev, A., & Wartell, J. (2006). *Motor vehicle theft: Crime and spatial analysis in a non-urban region.* Washington, DC: U.S. Department of Justice.

Winchester, S.W.C., & Jackson, H. (1982). Residential burglary: The limits of prevention. *Home Office Research Study 74.* London, UK: HMSO.

Wright, R.T., & Decker, S.H. (1994). *Burglars on the job: Streetlife and residential break-ins.* Boston, MA: Northeastern University Press.

Wright, R.T., & Decker, S.H. (1997). *Armed robbers in action: Stickups and street culture.* Boston: Northeastern University Press.

Wulf, H., & Debiel, T. (2009). Conflict early warning and response mechanisms: Tools for enhancing the effectiveness of regional organisation? A comparative study of the AU, ECOWAS, IGAD, ASEAN/ARF and PIF. *Regional and Global Axes of Conflict Working Paper*, No.49

Wyatt, P.J. (2002). Early warning and remediation: Minimizing the threat of bioterrorism. *Wyatt-Lorenz LLC.* Retrieved January 27, 2011, from http://www.wyatt-lorenz.com/bioterrorism_wyatt.htm

Xu, J., Kennedy, L.W., & Caplan, J.M. (2010a). *Searching for conditional locational interdependence (CLI) of crime concentration: Extending risk terrain modeling of gun shootings in an urban environment.* [Unpublished manuscript]. Retrieved from rutgerscps.org/publications/CLI_Brief.pdf

Xu, J., Kennedy, L.W., & Caplan, J.M. (2010b). *Crime generators for shootings in urban areas: A test using conditional locational interdependence as an extension of risk terrain modeling.* Newark, NJ: Rutgers Center on Public Security.

Yeater, E. A., & O'Donohue, W. (1999). Sexual assault prevention programs: Current issues, future directions, and the potential efficacy of interventions with women. *Clinical Psychology Review, 19,* 739–771. Retrieved October 7, 2010 from http://www.popcenter.org/problems/rape/PDFs/yeater.pdf.

Zanin, N., Shane, J., & Clarke, R. (2004). Reducing drug dealing in private apartment complexes in Newark, New Jersey. Washington, DC: U.S. Department of Justice, Office of Community Oriented Policing Services on the Field Applications of the Problem-Oriented Guides for Police Project.

Zawacki, T., Abbey, A., Buck, P. O., McAuslan, P., & Clinton-Sherrod, A. M. (2003). Perpetrators of alcohol-involved sexual assaults: How do they differ from other sexual assault perpetrators and nonperpetrators? *Aggressive Behavior, 29*, 366-380. Retrieved October 6, 2010 from http://www.swc.osu.edu/posts/documents/perpetrators-of-alcohol-involved-sexual-assaults-article-2003.pdf.

Zgoba, K.M., Levenson, J., & McKee, T. (2009). Examining the impact of sex offender residence restrictions on housing availability. *Criminal Justice Policy Review, 20*, 91-110.

Endnotes

[1] Kennedy & Van Brunschot, 2009

[2] Data were provided by the NJ State Police through the Regional Operations Intelligence Center and the many datasets they maintain, validate and update regularly to support internal crime analysis and police investigations.

[3] Loukaitou-Sideris, 1999

[4] Xu, Kennedy & Caplan, 2010a, 2010b

[5] The random number ensured that every cell had an equal chance of being sorted above or below the 10% cut point. For example, if 11 out of 100 cells had a risk value of four, and they were sorted in descending order, the top 10% of cells to be designated as "high risk" would all have values of four. But, the 11% cell would be excluded due to a rather arbitrary standard sorting algorithm.

[6] Taylor & Harrell, 1996; Taylor, 1997

[7] Groff & LaVigne, 2001, 2002

[8] Johnson, Birks, McLaughlin, Bowers, & Pease, 2007

[9] e.g., Tilley, Smith, Finer, Erol, Charles, & Dobby, 2005; Wright & Decker, 1997

[10] Smith, Frazee, & Davison, 2000

[11] Kennedy & Van Brunschot, 2009: p4

[12] Brantingham & Brantingham, 1995

[13] Weisburd, 2008; Weisburd, Mastrofski, McNally, & Greenspan, 2001; Rubin, 2010

[14] Raines, Sawatzky, & Bonham-Carter, 2010; Tomlin, 1994

[15] Clarke & Felson, 1993

[16] Weisburd, 2008

[17] Brantingham & Brantingham, 1981

[18] Brantingham & Brantingham, 1995

[19] e.g., Sherman, Gartin, & Buerger, 1989; Harries, 1999; Eck, Chainey, Cameron, Leitner, & Wilson, 2005

[20] Weisburd, 2008

[21] Abbott, 1997: p1152

[22] Freundschuh & Egenhofer, 1997

[23] Kennedy and Van Brunschot, 2009, p. 4

[24] Andrews, 1989; Burgess, 1928; Glueck & Glueck, 1950; Gottfredson & Moriarty, 2006

[25] Couclelis, 1992; Frank & Mark, 1991

[26] Couclelis, 1992

[27] Couclelis, 1992, p. 66

[28] Freundschuh & Egenhofer, 1997

[29] Freundschuh & Egenhofer 1997

[30] Egenhofer & Mark, 1995

[31] Frank, 1993; Mark 1993; Freundschuh & Egenhofer, 1997

[32] Brantingham & Brantingham, 1981

[33] Caplan, Kennedy, & Miller, 2011

[34] Moreto, Piza and Caplan, n.d.; Moreto, 2010

[35] Freundschuh & Egenhofer, 1997

[36] e.g., Caplan et al., 2011; Kennedy et al., 2010; Brantingham & Brantingham, 1995; Block & Block, 1995; Spelman, 1995; Clarke & Eck, 2005; Eck, Clarke, & Guerette, 2007

[37] Clarke & Felson, 1993

[38] It is realized that these results are arguably due to identifying a larger catchment area to which shootings are aggregated. Compared to feature points themselves, this is true. However, the coverage area of places with density values above +1 standard deviations is 0.806 square miles, and the coverage area of places within one block of a criminogenic feature is 0.725 square miles; this is about one quarter of 1% of Irvington's total area. So, more shootings occurred in a smaller area that was deemed affected by nearby criminogenic features in a conceptually meaningful way.

[39] e.g., Tilley, Smith, Finer, Erol, Charles, & Dobby, 2004; Wright & Decker, 1997; Smith, Frazee, & Davison, 2000

[40] United States Fire Administration, 2001

[41] Maguire, 2009

[42] Lewis, 1999

[43] United States Fire Administration, 2009

[44] United States Fire Administration, 2001

[45] Ahrens, 2009

[46] Arson Strike Force, 1980

[47] Lewis, 1999

[48] Lewis, 1999

[49] Johnson, 2005

[50] Lewis, 1999

[51] United States Fire Administration, 1997

[52] Hall, 2010

[53] United States Fire Administration, 2001

[54] United States Fire Administration, 2001

[55] United States Fire Administration, 2001

[56] United States Fire Administration, 2001

[57] Dedel Johnson, 2005

[58] Penetration is defined as "vaginal intercourse, cunnilingus, fellatio or anal intercourse between persons or the insertion of a hand, finger or other object into the anus or vagina by either the actor or upon the actor's instruction". See http://www.state.nj.us/njsp/divorg/operations/vsu.html for complete definition and see http://www.nj-statute-info.com/getStatute.php?statute_id=1563 for statute

[59] "In most of the sexual assaults involving non-strangers, the crime occurs in the suspect or victim's own home, and many of them involve the use of drugs and alcohol by both victim and suspect" (See Archambault, J. (n.d.) from http://webcache.googleusercontent.com/search?q=cache:HRLhoxsq_0sJ:www.mysati.com/Downloads/Handout_DSA.doc+In+most+of+the+sexual+assaults+involving+non-strangers,+the+crime+occurs+in+the+suspect+or+victim%27s+own+home,+and+many+of+them+involve+the+use+of+drugs+and+alcohol+by+both+victim+and+suspect&cd=1&hl=en&ct=clnk&gl=us&client=firefox-a).

[60] Pedophiles choose prepubescent children whereas hebephiles choose pubescent but not yet 18.

[61] Acrhambault, J. (n.d.) from http://webcache.googleusercontent.com/search?q=cache:HRLhoxsq_0sJ:www.mysati.com/Downloads/Handout_DSA.doc+In+most+of+the+sexual+assaults+involving+non-strangers,+the+crime+occurs+in+the+suspect+or+victim%27s+own+home,+and+many+of+them+involve+the+use+of+drugs+and+alcohol+by+both+victim+and+suspect&cd=1&hl=en&ct=clnk&gl=us&client=firefox-a

[62] Zawacki, et al., 2003

[63] Yeater & O'Donahue, 1999

[64] Wechsler, Lee, Kuo, & Lee, 2000

[65] It is important to note that only 18% met legal definitions of rape/attempted rape, or sexual assault. (see Zawacki, et al., 2003)

[66] See Duwe, Donnay, & Tewksbury, 2008

[67] Zgoba, Levenson, & McKee, 2009

[68] Chajewski, & Mercado, 2009

[69] Beauregard, et. al., 2007

[70] Walby & Allen, 2004

[71] Zawacki, et al. 2003

[72] Levenson, 2007

[73] Tewksbury & Mustaine, 2008

[74] Cobbina, Miller, & Brunson, 2008

[75] Bureau of Justice Statistics, n.d.

[76] Scott, & Dedel, 2006a

[77] Madensen, & Eck, 2008

[78] U.S. Department of Justice, National Gang Intelligence Center, 2009

[79] Office of National Drug Control Policy, 2000

[80] Rand, 2008

[81] Maguire, 2007

[82] Truman & Rand, 2010

[83] Truman & Rand, 2010

[84] U.S. Department of Justice, Federal Bureau of Investigation, 2010

[85] Rand, 2008

[86] Bureau of Justice Statistics, n.d.

[87] Bureau of Justice Statistics, n.d.

[88] Scott & Dedel, 2006a

[89] Maguire, 2007

[90] Madensen & Eck, 2008

[91] Catalano, 2004

[92] Renzetti & Edleson, 2008

[93] Levinson, 2002

[94] Catalano, 2004

[95] Scott & Dedel, 2006a

[96] Renzetti & Edleson, 2008

[97] U.S. Department of Justice, Federal Bureau of Investigation, 2009

[98] Goldstein, 1985

[99] Copes, 1999

[100] Brown & Thomas, 2003

[101] National Insurance Crime Bureau, 2005-2009

[102] National Highway Traffic Safety Administration, 2008

[103] Rice & Smith, 2002; Weisel, Smith, Garson, Pavlichev, & Wartell, 2006

[104] Roncek & Maier, 1991

[105] Roncek & Maier, 1991

[106] Fleming, 1999

[107] Plouffe & Sampson, 2004

[108] Poyner & Webb, 2006

[109] Henry & Bryan, 2000

[110] Miethe & Meier, 1994; Rengert, 1996; Weisel et al. (2006)

[111] Walsh & Taylor, 2007

[112] Walsh & Taylor, 2007; Miethe & Meier, 1994

[113] Miethe & Meier, 1994; Weisel et al., 2006; Rice & Smith, 2002

[114] Kinshott, 2001

[115] Mawby, 2001; U.S. Department of Justice, Federal Bureau of Investigation, 2010

[116] Wright & Decker, 1994; Winchester & Jackson, 1982
[117] Mawby, 2001
[118] Capowich, 2003; Ratcliffe & McCullagh, 1998; Sampson & Groves, 1989
[119] Millie, 2008
[120] Bernasco, 2010; Bernasco, 2006; Brantingham & Brantingham, 1991
[121] It is vital to assess factors related to social disorganization in a specific city as such factors will vary and may or may not apply. See Sampson and Groves (1989) for the seminal article on social disorganization theory.
[122] Evans (1992) as cited by Mawby (2001, p.23); Clarke, 1999
[123] Sutton, Schneider, & Hetherington, 2001; LaPeter, 2010. *St. Petersburg Times (January 2nd)*, 2010, retrieved online: http://www.tampabay.com/features/humaninterest/after-a-burglary-victim-must-buy-back-items-from-pawn-shop/1062282
[124] Clare, Fernandez, & Morgan, 2009; Brantingham & Brantingham, 1991
[125] Tseloni, Osborn, Trickett, & Pease, 2002; Wright & Decker, 1994; Cohen & Cantor, 1981
[126] Tseloni, Wittebrood, Farrell, & Pease, 2004
[127] Cohen & Felson, 1979: pp. 588 – 604.
[128] Rengert & Wasilchick, 1985; Capowich, 2003; Rengert & Wasilchick, 1985
[129] Brantingham, Brantingham, Vajihollahi, & Wuschke, 2009
[130] Bowers, Johnson, & Pease, 2004; Clarke, Perkins, & Smith, 2001; Townsley, Homel, & Chaseling,, 2000; Ratcliffe & McCullagh, 1998
[131] Malczewski & Poetz, 2005
[132] Harocopos & Hough, 2005
[133] Benson & Matthews, 1995
[134] Wright & Decker, 1997
[135] Scott & Dedel, 2006b
[136] Eck, 1995; Harocopos & Hough, 2005
[137] Harocopos & Hough, 2005
[138] Braga, 2002
[139] Harocopos & Hough, 2005
[140] Eck, 1995; Jacobson, 1999
[141] Harocopos & Hough, 2005
[142] Eck, 1995
[143] Harocopos & Hough, 2005
[144] U.S. Department of Justice, Federal Bureau of Investigation, 2010
[145] U.S. Department of Justice, Federal Bureau of Investigation, 2010
[146] Smith & Clarke, 2000
[147] Glensor & Peak, 2004
[148] Johnson, Bowers, Gamman, Mamerow, & Warne, 2010
[149] Clarke, 2002
[150] U.S. Department of Justice, Federal Bureau of Investigation, 2010
[151] Sampson, 2004
[152] Clarke & Goldstein, 2003
[153] Johnson, Sidebottom, & Thorpe, 2008
[154] Maguire, 2007
[155] Maguire, 2007
[156] Clarke, 2002
[157] Sutton, 2010
[158] Sutton, 2010
[159] Truman & Rand, 2010
[160] Glensor & Peak, 2004
[161] Smith & Clarke, 2000
[162] Johnson, Sidebottom, & Thorpe, 2008
[163] Clarke, 2002
[164] Lippman, 2009
[165] Scott, 2001
[166] Scott, 2001
[167] Harocopos & Hough, 2005
[168] Regini, 1998
[169] Weisel, 2002
[170] Lippman, 2009
[171] McNamara, 2008
[172] Harocopos & Hough, 2005
[173] Walker, Spohn, & DeLeone, 2007
[174] Scott, 2001
[175] Bureau of Justice Statistics, n.d.
[176] Harrell, 2005
[177] Braga, 2003
[178] Kennedy & Braga, 1998
[179] Dedel, 2007
[180] U.S. Department of Justice, Federal Bureau of Investigation, 2010
[181] Hepburn & Hemenway, 2004
[182] Office of National Drug Control Policy, 2000

[183] Office of National Drug Control Policy, 2000
[184] U.S. Department of Justice, Federal Bureau of Investigation, 2010
[185] National Institute of Justice, 1997
[186] U.S. Department of Justice, Federal Bureau of Investigation, 2010
[187] U.S. Department of Justice, Federal Bureau of Investigation, 2010
[188] U.S. Department of Justice, Federal Bureau of Investigation, 2010
[189] Fox & Zawitz, 2004
[190] Sherman, Shaw, & Rogan, 1995
[191] Dedel, 2007
[192] Tennenbaum & Fink, 1994
[193] Benson & Matthews, 1995
[194] Scott & Dedel, 2006b
[195] Schmerler, 2005
[196] Scott & Dedel, 2006b
[197] Scott & Dedel, 2006b
[198] Portland Police Bureau and Campbell Resources Inc., 1991; Scott & Dedel, 2006b
[199] Scott & Dedel, 2006b
[200] American Prosecutors Research Institute, 2004; Scott & Dedel, 2006b
[201] Scott & Dedel, 2006b
[202] Scott & Dedel, 2006b
[203] Testa, Livingston, Tamsen, & Frone, 2003
[204] Sampson, 2002
[205] Abbey, 2002
[206] Sampson, 2002
[207] Miller, Downs, Gondoli, & Keil, 1987
[208] Koss & Cleveland, 1996
[209] Humphrey & Kahn, 2000
[210] Koss & Gaines, 1993
[211] Sampson, 2002
[212] Fisher, Cullen, & Turner, 2000
[213] Greenfield, 1997
[214] Kilpatick, Resnick, Ruggiero, Conoscenti, McCauley, 2007
[215] Kennedy & Baron, 1993
[216] Kennedy & Baron, 1993, p.40 in Street Crime edited by Mike Maguire, Wright & Decker, 1997, p.62
[217] Wright & Decker, 1997, p.62
[218] Wright & Decker, 1997, pp.63-65
[219] Wright & Decker, 1997, pp.69-70; Tilley, Smith, Finer, Erol, Charles, & Dobby, 2004, p.68
[220] Scott & Dedel, 2006b, p. 11; Tilley, Smith, Finer, Erol, Charles, & Dobby, 2004, p.68
[221] Wright & Decker, 1997, p. 72
[222] Tilley, Smith, Finer, Erol, Charles, & Dobby, 2004; p.59
[223] Tilley, Smith, Finer, Erol, Charles, & Dobby, 2004, p.38; Wright & Decker, 1997, pp.76-87
[224] Tilley, Smith, Finer, Erol, Charles, & Dobby, 2004; p.3
[225] Tilley, Smith, Finer, Erol, Charles, & Dobby, 2004; p.29, p.53
[226] Wright & Decker, 1997, pp.81
[227] Tilley, Smith, Finer, Erol, Charles, & Dobby, 2004; p.29, p.76
[228] Tilley, Smith, Finer, Erol, Charles, & Dobby, 2004; p.29
[229] Shoham, Knepper, & Kett, 2010; p.620.
[230] Monk, Heiononen, & Eck, 2010, p.5
[231] Shoham, Knepper, & Kett, 2010; p.633
[232] Wright & Decker, 1997, pp.79
[233] Monk, Heiononen, & Eck, 2010, pp.4-18
[234] Shoham, Knepper, & Kett, 2010; p.634
[235] Monk, Heiononen, & Eck, 2010, pp.16-18
[236] Shooting. (2011). In Cambridge Dictionary. Retrieved from http://dictionary.cambridge.org/dictionary/british/shooting
[237] U. S. Department of Justice, National Gang Intelligence Center, 2009
[238] U.S. Department of Housing and Urban Development, 1999
[239] U. S. Department of Justice, National Gang Intelligence Center, 2009
[240] Dedel, 2007
[241] Roth, 1994
[242] Blumstein & Wallman, 2000
[243] Braga, 2003
[244] Papachristos, Braga, & Hureau, 2011
[245] Braga, 2003
[246] Sherman, Shaw, & Rogan, 1995
[247] Dedel, 2007
[248] Kennedy & Baron, 1993; Scott & Dedel, 2006b; Tilley, Smith, Finer, Erol, Charles, & Dobby, 2005; Wright & Decker, 1997
[249] Block & Block, 1995; McCord & Ratcliffe, 2007; Roncek & Maier, 1991; Stucky & Ottensman, 2009; Tilley, Smith, Finer, Erol, Charles, & Dobby, 2005; Wright & Decker, 1997
[250] We would like to specifically thank Eric Piza - GIS specialist at Newark P.D. for providing the data on risky facilities and robberies

[251] Kennedy, Caplan, & Piza, 2010
[252] Kennedy, Caplan, & Piza, 2010
[253] Spelman, 1995
[254] Weisburd, Bushway, Lum, & Yang, 2004; Weisburd, 2008
[255] Spelman, 1995
[256] Bernasco & Block, 2010
[257] Caplan & Kennedy, 2010
[258] see Groff and LaVigne 2001, 2002
[259] Brantingham and Brantingham 1993
[260] Ratcliffe and McCullagh 2001
[261] Many thanks to Eric Piza of the Newark Police Department for providing the data on at-risk complexes and burglaries.
[262] Zanin, Shane, Clarke, 2004; For a more in-depth description of how at-risk complexes were geocoded, see Kennedy, Caplan, and Piza (2010).
[263] Mawby, 2001; Wright & Decker, 1994
[264] Values were based on weighted values for specific variables, for example, one block (500 feet) from a guardian infrastructure was operationalized as -2 (lowest risk value); while, two blocks (1000 feet) was -1 (low risk).
[265] A Moran's I value of 0 indicates independence or no spatial autocorrelation among geographical units/cells. Using GeoDa (a freestanding software application) and ArcMap's Spatial Statistics Tools, Moran's I value was calculated to be 0.05, respectively, for both software applications.
[266] See www.riskterrainmodeling.com
[267] Scott & Dedel, 2006a
[268] Office of National Drug Control Policy, 2000
[269] Sherman, Gartin, & Buerger, 1989
[270] Sherman, 1995
[271] Caplan, Kennedy, Miller, 2011; see also Risk Terrain Intro Brief.pdf
[272] Brantingham & Brantingham, 1995
[273] U.S. Census Bureau
[274] U.S. Department of Justice, Federal Bureau of Investigation, 2009
[275] Caplan, Kennedy, & Miller, 2011
[276] Personal communication, Jonas Baughman, May 20, 2010 [Kansas City, Missouri Police Department].
[277] Caplan, Kennedy, and Miller, 2010
[278] Kennedy & Van Brunschot, 2009
[279] DRAGNET is a custom-made database used for tracking and responding to narcotics-related activity reported to the KCPD by both police officers and citizens.
[280] A Knock & Talk is an investigative technique when investigators respond to a location and talk to occupants in hopes of gaining useful information about a crime and/or consent to search that location to locate contraband or wanted subjects when a warrant has not yet been obtained.
[281] The KCPD's CSTAR Unit is an analytical unit responsible for GIS mapping, crime analysis, and CompStat-related functions.
[282] According to the NJ State Police Crime Reports, the violent crime rate in 2006—before the task force, was 22.4 per 1,000, with a murder count of 21. In 2009, the violent crime rate was 18.2 per 1,000, with a murder count of 17. Total numbers of violent crimes in 2006 were 1,321; in 2009 were 1024.
[283] Groff 2007; Basta, Richmond, & Wiebe, 2010
[284] Bowers & Johnson, 2005
[285] Short, 2009; Johnson, 2008; Ratcliffe & Rengert, 2008
[286] Although, see the research by Sampson and Raudenbusch (1999) that emphasizes the importance of social efficacy in combating crime
[287] Brantingham & Brantingham, 1998; Groff, 2007; Miethe & Meier, 1994; Caplan, Kennedy & Miller, 2011
[288] Brantingham & Brantingham, 1995
[289] Weisburd & Neyrud, 2011
[290] Eck, 2001; Mears, Scott, & Bahti, 2007
[291] Eck, 1995
[292] Block & Block, 1995
[293] Eck, 1995; Ritter, 2006
[294] Mazerolle, Kadleck, & Roehl, 2004; Eck, 1995
[295] Farrell, Phillips & Pease, 1995
[296] Ratcliffe & Rengert, 2008
[297] Bowers & Johnson, 2005
[298] Johnson, 2008
[299] Kennedy & Van Brunschot, 2009
[300] Berk, 2009; Chainey, Tompson, & Uhlig, 2008; Caplan, Kennedy & Miller, 2010
[301] According to the NJ State Police Uniform Crime Reports, the violent crime rate in 2006—before the task force, was 22.4 per 1,000, with a murder count of 21. In 2009, the violent crime rate was 18.2 per 1,000, with a murder count of 17. Total numbers of violent crimes in 2006 were 1,321; in 2009 were 1024.
[302] Brantingham & Brantingham, 1981
[303] Brantingham & Brantingham, 1981
[304] www.rutgerscps.org/rtm/KCPD_RTMinAction_InsightsBrief_1.pdf
[305] Incidents that follow instigator violent crime events, as identified by the "Other functions" tool of the Near Repeat Calculator.
[306] Center for Problem-Oriented Policing, 2010
[307] Quetelet, 1842
[308] Brantingham & Brantingham, 1981
[309] Shaw & McKay, 1969
[310] Brantingham & Brantingham, 1981
[311] Kennedy & Van Brunschot, 2009
[312] Andresen & Malleson, 2010
[313] Guerette & Bowers, 2009
[314] see Short, Brantingham, & Tita, 2010

[315] Farrell, Phillips, & Pease, 1995
[316] Farrell, Phillips, & Pease, 1995: 386
[317] Farrell, Phillips, & Pease, 1995: 386
[318] see Guerette & Bowers, 2009
[319] Weisburd, 2008
[320] Johnson, Birks, McLaughlin, Bowers, & Pease, 2007; Johnson, Bowers, Birks, & Pease, 2008
[321] Caplan & Kennedy, 2010: p118
[322] Caplan & Kennedy, 2010: p16
[323] This material is partly based upon work supported by the National Science Foundation under Award Numbers: IIP-0750507 and IIP-0945742. Any opinions, findings, and conclusions or recommendations expressed in this publication are those of the authors and do not necessarily reflect the views of the National Science Foundation.
[324] Caplan & Kennedy, 2010: p109
[325] Caplan & Kennedy, 2010: p48
[326] grant number 2006-33610-16777
[327] award number IIP-0945742
[328] McCue, 2007
[329] Ratliff, 2011
[330] Heffner, 2010
[331] Azavea, 2006
[332] Van Brunschot & Kennedy, 2008
[333] Caplan & Kennedy, 2010: p25
[334] Kennedy, Marteaache, Gaziarifoglu, 2010
[335] Davies & Gurr, 1998
[336] Wyatt, 2002
[337] Government of Germany (2006) 'Developing Early Warning Systems: A Checklist', in Kausch, T., Husain, M., McDonald, T. (eds.) *EWC III: Third International Conference on Early Warning; From concept to action*, Bonn, Germany, 27-29 Mar., available at: http://www.ewc3.org/upload/downloads/checklist.final_pdf.pdf (accessed on 4/3/2011) p3
[338] National Drought Mitigation Center, 2000: p200
[339] National Drought Mitigation Center, 2000: p202
[340] Goldstein, Kaminsky, Reinhart, 2000
[341] Bakker, n.d.
[342] Davies & Gurr, 1998: p5
[343] Dorn, 2000
[344] Companion, 2008
[345] Wulf & Debiel, 2009: p2-3
[346] Kennedy, Marteaache, & Gaziarifoglu, 2010: p4-5
[347] Bakker, n.d.: p5-6
[348] Dorn, 2000
[349] Van Brunschot & Kennedy, 2008: p48
[350] Salzano, Agreda, Di Carluccio, & Fabbrocino, 2009
[351] Henn, 2011
[352] SIFY News, 2011
[353] Brook, 2011
[354] Caplan & Kennedy, 2010: p23
[355] Wulf & Debiel, 2009: p30
[356] Caplan & Kennedy, 2010: p23
[357] Caplan & Kennedy, 2010
[358] Caplan & Kennedy, 2010: p37
[359] Davies & Gurr, 1998: p2-3
[360] Sparrow, 2011
[361] Weisburd & Neyroud, 2011
[362] Kennedy & Van Brunschot, 2010
[363] see Weisburd & Piquero, 2008
[364] see new work on emergence, Eck & Liu, 2006 ; McGloin, Sullivan, & Kennedy, forthcoming
[365] see Sherman, Gartin, & Buerger, 1989
[366] Ratcliffe, 2009
[367] Short, D'Orsogna, Brantingham, & Tita, 2010
[368] for a summary of these studies, see Guerette & Bowers, 2009
[369] see Caplan, Kennedy, & Petrosian, 2011

Proof

Made in the USA
Charleston, SC
21 July 2011